Effective Business Communication

by Dr. Jill Schiefelbein
Founder, The Dynamic Communicator®

Effective Business Communication For Dummies®

Table of Contents

CHAPTER 6: **Leveraging the Communication Power of Asking Questions**

CHAPTER 7: **Holding Productive and Meaningful Conversations**

CHAPTER 11: **Calm, Cool, and Confident: Making and Delivering Presentations**

PART 4: PERSUADING AND DRIVING RESULTS

CHAPTER 12: **Knowing the People You're Trying to Persuade**

Introduction

Communication is not a one-size-fits-all field. No two messages, situations, or audiences are the same. In today's fast-paced and diverse business environment, communication challenges are more prevalent than ever. From the nuances of cross-cultural interactions and the intricacies of digital communication to the art of crafting persuasive messages and handling conflict with grace, the hurdles can seem endless.

One of the most significant challenges is the sheer volume of communication channels. With emails, instant messaging, social media, video calls, and face-to-face meetings all playing a role in your daily interactions, it's easy to feel overwhelmed — not to mention the burgeoning fields of generative AI and synthetic media! Each medium has its own set of rules and nuances, and mastering them requires skill *and* adaptability. The rise of remote work has added another layer of complexity, making it crucial to convey your message clearly and effectively across countries, borders, platforms, and time zones.

Another challenge is understanding and navigating cultural differences in a globalized business environment. What might be considered polite and straightforward in one culture can be perceived as vague or even rude in another. This cultural diversity enriches the business landscape but also requires a high level of cultural sensitivity and communication savvy. Misunderstandings can lead to conflicts, missed opportunities, damaged relationships, and inefficiencies.

But don't worry — in this book I provide the information and guidance you need to meet these challenges with confidence and become a more effective and confident communicator.

About This Book

Welcome to *Effective Business Communication For Dummies*, your guide to navigating the science and art of communication in the professional world. I'm thrilled to have you here! As a professor and communication strategy consultant for companies all over the world, I know the transformative power that effective communication can bring to your career and personal life. This book is designed to be your go-to resource for developing the skills you need to communicate with clarity, confidence, and impact, whether you're just starting out or looking to refine your existing abilities.

Effective Business Communication For Dummies includes practical tips, real-world examples, and actionable strategies. From crafting persuasive messages and delivering compelling presentations to navigating the complexities of digital communication and cross-cultural interactions, this book covers it all. Everyone has the potential to become a dynamic communicator, and my goal is to make the journey as straightforward and enjoyable as possible.

But this book is more than just a business communication training manual. It's a companion on your journey to becoming a savvy communicator. Think of it as a friendly mentor, guiding you through the nuances of business communication with a focus on practical application and personal growth. Whether you're looking to boost your career, enhance your professional relationships, or simply become a better communicator, *Effective Business Communication For Dummies* is here to support you every step of the way!

Foolish Assumptions

As you'll soon discover when you start reading this book, I discourage people from making assumptions in any business interaction. In that context, I think most assumptions are foolish. However, I'm guilty of making the following foolish assumptions about you, and I wrote this book accordingly:

>> **You're working in a business setting or are charting your own entrepreneurial path.** Whether you're an entry-level employee or the CEO of a global tech company, if you're interacting with people in a business setting, you're engaged in business communication.

>> **You're eager to improve your business communication knowledge and skills.** Your level of competence and abilities doesn't matter. You may be struggling, or you may be highly effective and wanting to become even better. What's important is your willingness to learn.

>> **You're not in the market for an academic book on the underlying theories behind various business communication topics.** What you want is practical, real-world advice on how to communicate effectively in a wide range of business scenarios. (I do touch on some key theories and frameworks to provide context that can improve your understanding and the reasons behind certain strategies and best practices.)

Icons Used in This Book

Throughout this book, icons in the margins highlight important points that I call out for special attention. Here are the icons I use and what they mean.

EXAMPLE

Although I've included plenty of examples throughout this book, this Example icon flags the longer, more extensive real-world examples. The purpose of these examples is to show how key communication concepts, strategies, and techniques play out in actual business scenarios.

REMEMBER

I'd love for you to remember everything you read in this book, but if you can't quite do that, remember the important points I've flagged with this icon.

TIP

I've gathered these tidbits of information and insight from my many years of education, training, and experience — distilled to save you time and effort.

WARNING

"Pump the brakes!" Before you take another step, read these warnings. I provide this cautionary content to help you avoid the common pitfalls that are otherwise likely to trip you up, leading to misunderstandings, unproductive conflicts, and damaged business relationships.

Beyond the Book

Business communication is a broad topic that encompasses everything from communication fundamentals to public speaking, persuasion, interviewing and feedback conversations, digital communication, intercultural communication, and the legal and ethical aspects of business communication. In *Effective Business Communication For Dummies*, I cover the fundamentals of business communication in the context of these topics. However, even if you manage to master everything there is to know about business communication, you can always discover something new, especially after putting your learning into practice. This book is no substitute for real-world experience and lifelong learning. I encourage you to continue developing your mastery of business communication beyond this book. Here are some tips:

>> **Flex your interpersonal muscles.** Put yourself out there. Interact with people as much as possible, especially if you work remotely. Don't allow yourself to become isolated or communicate exclusively via text and email. Seek opportunities to interact with people in person or at least via videoconferencing in real-time.

>> **Interact in as wide a range of business situations as possible.** These include public speaking, business negotiations, customer service, team meetings, project management, marketing and public relations, crisis situations, and others. The broader your experience, the more effective you'll be in any situation. Plus, interacting in ways that aren't normally part of your day-to-day work can give you additional perspectives that can add value to your professional acumen.

>> **Embrace (or at least become versed in) the latest communication technologies and channels.** Digital communication is growing and evolves quickly. In the past, all you needed was experience with email, word processing, and maybe presentation software. Now, you need to be skilled in social media, generative artificial intelligence (AI) such as ChatGPT, synthetic media and digital likeness (created by companies like Render, Colossyan, ElevenLabs, and Synthesia), videoconferencing platforms, and more — there's no telling what tomorrow will bring. These tools can make you a more effective and efficient communicator.

>> **Continue to build your knowledge through books, articles, videos, and other relevant content from reputable sources.** Explore other sources for information and guidance on how to communicate more effectively. Some books to consider are *Public Speaking For Dummies,* by Malcolm Kushner, *Persuasion & Influence For Dummies,* by Elizabeth Kuhnke, and *Business Writing For Dummies,* by Natalie Canavor (all published by Wiley). If you have a specific question, ask ChatGPT or type it into your favorite search engine. Check out business communication videos on YouTube (including some beauties from way back in 2012 that you can find under my name).

In addition to the material in the print book or e-book you're reading right now, this product comes with some access-from-anywhere goodies on the web. Check out the free Cheat Sheet at `www.dummies.com` for tips and techniques on how to communicate more effectively and efficiently. When you get to the site, simply type **Effective Business Communication For Dummies cheat sheet** in the search bar to find it.

You can follow me online, at `www.thedynamiccommunicator.com`, where you can find additional content and join my mailing list to receive practical communicative use cases for AI. You can also find me on all my social channels — including Instagram, Facebook, and LinkedIn — by using my handle: @dynamicjill.

Where to Go from Here

As with all *For Dummies* guides, you can read this book from cover to cover or skip around to the topics you find most interesting or applicable to the business communication challenge you're facing. If you choose to skip around, use the table of contents at the front of the book or the extensive index at the back of the book as your guide.

Browse the part titles and chapter titles, or simply flip through the book to find a topic that catches your eye. Feel free to explore the pages and dip into whatever topics seem most relevant to you at the moment. You don't need to read the book from cover to cover, though you may find yourself compelled to do so because each tool, strategy, and technique adds up to a complete and comprehensive business communication toolkit.

1

Business Communication Fundamentals

Recognize the high cost of ineffective, inefficient business communication in time, money, resources, and lost opportunities.

Develop a foundational understanding of business communication by exploring definitions, communication models, and the essential elements that contribute to effective communication.

Get up to speed on the basics of nonverbal communication — using body language, vocal variations, space, silence, and everything else that's not words — to clarify and reinforce your message.

Differentiate between communication channels (media), such as in person, videoconferencing, on-demand video, text, and email.

Appreciate the importance of choosing the right communication channel to meet your goal and identify the pros and cons of each channel type.

Choose the most effective and efficient channel — with the help of some guidance from media richness theory (MRT) and media synchronicity theory (MST).

Chapter **1**

Talking about Communication in the Workplace

Whenever you're approaching a broad and complex topic such as business communication, you're wise to wade in slowly and develop a general understanding before taking a deeper dive into the details. This chapter eases you into the topic and provides a framework for understanding.

Here, you develop an appreciation of the importance of effective business communication and how it differs from personal communication. You evaluate your knowledge and skills and become familiar with the fundamentals of effective business communication. And, you get a small taste of the skills needed to start applying those techniques to specific situations you're likely to encounter in the workplace.

Understanding the Importance of Effective Business Communication

Business doesn't exist without communication. It's communication with yourself and others that leads to new ideas and innovations. It's communication that drives the formation of new businesses and secures the funding needed for its growth. It's communication that draws customers and drives sales. It's communication that enables businesses to function. And it's communication that empowers employees to be their best, collaborating with each other and helping their organizations flourish.

Clearly, effective communication is essential for businesses to thrive, but it's also important for you to be successful in the workplace and to further your career. In this section, I highlight the benefits you'll reap by becoming a more effective communicator — and the potential costs you'll pay if you don't.

Appreciating the benefits of effective communication

Regardless of how long you've been in the workforce — 30 seconds or 30 years — you can discover something that makes you a more effective communicator. If you're younger, you may benefit from a focus on the fundamentals. If you're older, you may discover that what you've been doing all those years could be even more effective as you become familiar with technologies that improve your ability to reach more people and communicate more efficiently. Wherever you are on the continuum, being a savvy and skilled communicator enables you to do the following:

>> Convey information, ideas, and instructions clearly and efficiently.

>> Improve your ability to make decisions, solve problems, and collaborate with others inside and outside your organization.

>> Accelerate your career advancement and/or business growth.

>> Negotiate effectively to get more of what you want.

>> Empower others through your leadership skills.

>> Engage your team members to build a more cohesive team.

>> Embody confidence, charisma, and professionalism.

>> Expand relationships and build new ones.

Skilled communicators draw people and opportunities to themselves because people know that they're dealing with someone who's easy to work with and gets things done.

Counting the costs of ineffective communication

Ineffective business communication can be costly to both organizations and individuals. Consider these costs:

» Inefficiencies — time wasted on clarifying instructions, fixing mistakes, and redoing work

» Missed opportunities due to an inability to communicate ideas clearly, persuade others, or communicate your skills and value to coworkers and supervisors

» Damaged relationships leading to tension and conflict with colleagues, which can create a negative work environment

» Frustration and stress that result from an inability to understand or be understood

» Lost sales or customers

» Loss of job security (in extreme cases)

Distinguishing Business Communication from Personal Communication

In many ways, personal and business communication are similar: Both require you to listen and understand others and tailor your messaging to your audience. The skills you develop by reading this book and practicing will improve your ability to communicate both in the workplace and with family members, friends, and others. After all, people are people. However, business communication has some nuances that are important to consider.

Business communication and personal communication differ in purpose, tone, and structure. In business communication, the emphasis is on efficiency, professionalism, and clarity for the purpose of achieving specific goals or objectives, such as completing a project, negotiating a deal, or serving customers. It typically follows specific protocols and formats, such as emails, reports, presentations, and meetings.

The language used tends to be more precise and technical, aiming to convey clear, concise, and unambiguous messages. In many cases, you may even be required to communicate with an audience you know little to nothing about — talk about a challenge!

Personal communication, on the other hand, prioritizes empathy, emotional support, and social bonding, focusing more on personal connection and less on meeting specific, goal-oriented objectives. It tends to be informal and centers around building and maintaining trust, sharing feelings, and interacting in social settings. It's more spontaneous and less structured, encompassing conversations, text messages, social media interactions, and casual emails. The tone is often more relaxed, and the language more conversational, allowing for emotional expression and personal connection.

These two types of communication are not mutually exclusive. You can have business communication within personal relationships and vice versa. But the main difference is the goal of the communication — and that goal will drive your communicative choices, including tone, channel, form, and more — all of which are covered throughout this book.

Conducting a Self-Assessment

So you think you're a good communicator. . . .

You're not alone. Drawing from my more than 20 years of studying, teaching, and training others in business communication, I can tell you that the majority of people consider themselves to be effective communicators. However, if that were the case, I wouldn't have a business! I believe that most people intend to be good communicators, but most are good communicators in the way they want to be communicated with. Being a good communicator in a way that adapts to the needs, styles, and preferences of others is a much bigger challenge. Many people take their communication abilities for granted, assuming that their audience will always understand their messages as intended. However, this assumption often proves false.

To gain a more objective assessment of your communication skills, answer the following questions:

>> When I explain complex ideas, do people understand me the first time?

>> When I delegate or give instructions, do I get the outcomes I expected?

>> Do people usually understand my email messages and texts without having to ask follow-up questions?

>> Do I pay close attention when others are talking to me, ask questions to clarify what they're saying, and summarize what they said back to them to verify that I understood correctly?

>> Am I mindful of my body language (posture, gestures, facial expressions) and that of others, and is my body language consistent with what I'm saying?

>> Do I adjust my communication style to different audiences and situations, carefully considering their needs and interests?

>> Am I comfortable communicating via different channels, such as email, text, phone, in person, and videoconferencing?

>> Am I persuasive?

>> When I'm negotiating, do I strive to achieve mutually beneficial outcomes, and am I successful in those attempts?

>> Do I provide constructive feedback? (If you point out mistakes or areas for improvement without offering suggestions to address them, answer no to this question.)

>> Do my team members enjoy working with me?

>> Do I engage productively in conflicts? (If you avoid conflict or you become overly emotional, the answer to this question is no.)

If you answered no to any of these questions or you frequently feel frustrated, let down, or disappointed when you interact with others at work (a sure sign that you're not being understood or you're struggling to understand others), you have room to improve your business communication knowledge and skills, and this book can help.

Sharpening Fundamental Communication Skills

Effective business communication begins with fundamental skills — skills required regardless of the situation. These are the skills I focus on in the early chapters in this book, and they include the following:

>> Understanding the components of communication, including the communicators involved, the message, channels, feedback, context, and noise and the impact that each of these factors has on communication, as discussed in Chapter 2.

- » The ability to communicate verbally (using words) and nonverbally (using body language, graphics, and other visuals) — as explained in Chapter 3.

- » The ability to choose the most effective communication channel (in person, email, text, videoconferencing, or another mode of communication) for any given situation — something you find out how to do in Chapter 4.

- » Proficiency in *active listening* — the practice of paying close attention to what's being communicated verbally and nonverbally, asking questions to clarify your understanding, and summarizing what you heard back to your communication partner(s) to check for mutual understanding. I cover active listening in Chapter 5.

- » A talent for asking questions to obtain the information and understanding you need and to lead conversations in the desired direction, which is a skill you develop in Chapter 6.

- » The ability to engage in productive two-way conversations through reciprocity, self-disclosure, and give-and-take, which is the topic of Chapter 7.

- » The ability to make slight changes in how you express yourself that lead to major changes in how receptive people are to what you have to say. In Chapter 8, I share some subtle ways you can change your message or how you deliver it to communicate more effectively.

- » The importance of setting the stage for your communication and what you need to understand about how people make decisions and use willpower, which impact your ability to be effective, as I explain in Chapter 9.

Communication encompasses more than just words, messages, talking, speaking, or writing. When people claim to have great communication skills, they often refer to one or more of these abilities. Job advertisements and recruiters frequently seek candidates with "excellent written and verbal communication skills." However, being able to write a grammatically correct proposal or deliver a presentation without filler words doesn't necessarily equate to having good communication skills.

REMEMBER

As I define it, successful, dynamic communication is ultimately measured by the actions and results it generates, not merely by the message produced.

Avoiding Common Mistakes

Effective business communication is crucial for organizational success, but several common mistakes can hinder this process. In fact, these foibles can be quite costly, to your professional reputation and to the organization and others in it.

Here are some of the more common mistakes — remedies for which I present throughout the book:

>> **Not listening well:** Some people seem to think that communication is all about getting people to understand *them*. It's actually more about understanding *others* first. Listening enables you to evaluate your audience and their message so that you can more effectively tailor your message to their needs and interests.

>> **Using inappropriate language or tone:** No, I'm not talking about curse words (though that's part of it). I'm talking about using vague language, words and phrases, or a tone that may be interpreted as more confrontational than you had intended, or speaking or writing in a tone that's not the best fit for the situation (for example, too formal or informal for the context).

>> **Lack of empathy or cultural awareness:** Everyone's unique, and even the same person can behave differently depending on the circumstances. Not paying attention in the moment to a communication partner's perspective and feelings can lead to messages that seem harsh or insensitive. Likewise, failing to recognize and respect cultural differences can lead to miscommunication and even discrimination. Savvy communicators are sensitive to differences and are able to adapt their message and delivery to individuals and situations on the fly.

>> **Letting bias drive communication:** Bias is a distortion in rational thinking that leads a person to unfairly favor one thing, person, or group over another. Bias can result in poor decision-making, ineffective communication, and unfair treatment.

>> **Overloading the audience:** Providing too much information (TMI) at one time can overwhelm your communication partner(s). Breaking down information into manageable parts can make information more accessible and understandable. And, by overload, I also mean not overloading someone's inbox or blowing up their DMs.

>> **Misusing communication channels and tools:** Choosing the right channel and tool for the message is crucial. For example, email and text messages are helpful for passing along information or giving specific instructions or feedback, but when you need to discuss complex or sensitive issues or ideas or work out scheduling conflicts, a face-to-face meeting or a phone conversation is much more effective and efficient.

>> **Lacking in the feedback department:** Effective feedback is clear, specific, actionable, and ongoing. Merely criticizing what's wrong or failing to provide feedback prevents individuals, teams, and organizations from achieving their full potential. Providing no feedback or vague feedback that can't be implemented can lead to serious mistakes that undermine success.

YOU'RE NEVER NOT COMMUNICATING

I wish I could own the axiom "One cannot not communicate," but it's not my original idea. So, where did it come from, and why is it widely debated in introductory communication classes around the world? This concept comes from one of the five foundational axioms of communication proposed by Watzlawick, Beavin, and Jackson in their 1967 work *Pragmatics of Human Communication* (W. W. Norton & Company).

When I taught business communication at Arizona State University, I introduced this axiom to my students on the first day of class, sparking often heated debates. By the end of our discussions, students would explore every conceivable way to avoid communicating, ultimately recognizing that not communicating is, indeed, a form of communication. It's essential to understand that choosing not to communicate still conveys a message, and so does inconsistent communication.

>> **Not realizing that you're always communicating:** If you've ever been *ghosted* (suddenly cut off from all communication with someone), you know that silence can speak volumes, and it's easy to misinterpret. When you go silent, people often feel the need to assume what you're thinking, and, as I often point out, assumptions can be quite dangerous in the context of communication.

Communicating Effectively in Specific Contexts

Communication fundamentals can only take you so far. They're like learning to catch, throw, and bat in baseball or punt, kick, pass, block, and tackle in football. Communication fundamentals provide you with the skills you need, but then you need to know how to apply those skills in specific situations, just as you need to be able to use athletic skills effectively in competition.

In the later part of this book, I provide guidance on how to use your communication skills to accomplish common objectives, such as these:

>> Promote yourself without coming across as bragging and get others to sing your praises so that you don't have to toot your own horn too much (see Chapter 10).

>> Deliver persuasive presentations and become more persuasive overall. Presentations and persuasion play major roles in business communication, so I devote several chapters to these topics (see Chapters 11–13).

>> Negotiate effectively in the workplace with respect to salary, workload, resources, and opportunities for advancement. In Chapter 14, you find out how to negotiate in ways that create value so that you're not having to compromise (make trade-offs) to get what you want.

>> Deliver and receive feedback more effectively, which can come in handy for formal performance evaluations and more casual feedback interactions (see Chapter 15). By combining this guidance with what I discuss in Chapter 12 about communication direction, you can become skilled at giving and receiving feedback whether you're interacting with a supervisor or a subordinate.

>> Resolve conflict constructively. As you discover in Chapter 16, *conflict* is not a dirty word. It often serves as the trigger for growth and innovation. In fact, if you routinely avoid conflict, you are likely missing out on great opportunities.

>> Communicate effectively in a crisis. When crisis strikes, you need to shift to damage-control mode and get out ahead of any bad press. In Chapter 17, I explain how to prepare for and communicate effectively when everything's falling apart.

>> Get hired and recruit top talent. Whether you're making your first or next career move or trying to attract and persuade talented individuals to join your organization, you can use the guidance I provide in Chapter 18.

>> Collaborate productively. A great deal of business communication occurs in a team setting. In Chapter 19, I cover the various stages of team development to give you a better understanding of the group dynamics you're likely to encounter, provide guidance on team building, and explain steps to protect your team and make it more successful.

>> Communicate in global audiences. As our businesses span physical and geographical spaces, we have to be more aware of the cultural differences that make a difference and adapt our communication styles accordingly. I cover this in Chapter 20.

If you can communicate effectively in these common business scenarios, you're well on your way to becoming a respected and successful business leader in whatever role you choose to serve.

Putting Theory into Practice and Making It Yours

One of the biggest and most common mistakes I see people making in business communication is trying to fit their message delivery into a theoretical, idealized box. Sure, you can use certain communication frameworks and guidelines to become a better communicator. (And, of course, that's part of what this book is all about!) But theory is different from practice; theory *informs* practice. Okay, that probably sounds a bit too academic. Let me rephrase. . . .

When I teach anything related to communication, whether it's sales skills, the neuroscience of decision-making, how to humanize automation, how to demystify artificial intelligence to help your business, how to personalize communication at scale — in all these areas, the foundation remains constant. I like to view this foundation as my communication skeleton. It consists of all the scientifically researched and proven theoretical constructs of how humans communicate, behave, and interact and how they use various channels of communication. The skeleton remains consistent. However, in practice, the muscles around my skeleton flex in different ways in each and every context.

For example, I know the fundamentals of delivering an effective and persuasive business presentation. I can employ Monroe's motivated sequence (read more in Chapter 13) to structure an effective presentation. That's the skeleton. However, before I craft a presentation for a specific client and deliver it, I need to tone my muscles. I have to understand my client and their industry, their needs, their desires, their shortcomings, and their successes. I need to understand what makes them unique and what makes their customers special. I prepare in this way so that my muscles will flex in the best possible way to serve this specific audience.

However, people often try to fit their communication inside a box. They think that the challenges of business communication can be managed with a one-size-fits-all solution that stipulates specific rules that need to be followed to ensure the desired outcome. For example, some people think that when you're delivering a presentation, you must maintain a straight-back perfect posture behind a podium. They've been taught that speaking too fast or too slow is detrimental to their success and that showing too much enthusiasm can ruin a presentation. Sure, in some situations, certain rules may apply, but certainly not in all.

I was told early on by many professors — mind you, I had already won competitions and been selected to speak in front of crowds of thousands — that I would never be successful as a speaker because my presentation style didn't fit the textbook definition. Well, having reached audiences that number in the millions, and having run a successful speaking business for over a decade, I've proven those professors (who probably have never gotten paid to give a speech outside of a classroom) wrong. When you can understand the proverbial skeleton, you can decide how and when to flex your muscles, discovering a style that's uniquely yours and adaptable in any situation.

Though you get a lot of skeleton content in this book, I encourage you to make it your own by fitting it to your communication style, your personality, and the needs and interests of your communication partners. Remember that business communication doesn't have a secret formula for success; it's more like a dance that requires the partners to adapt to one another — and it takes two to tango.

TEACHING AN OLD DOG NEW TRICKS

It's never too late to learn. In fact, writing this book was a learning experience.

For well over two decades, I have cautioned audiences to avoid the common mistake of trying to fit their business communication into someone else's box. But that's exactly what I had to do to produce this book. In my excitement over being associated with an internationally recognized brand (the *For Dummies* brand), I didn't realize that I'd have to fit my unique, distinct, commercially successful communication style into someone else's stylized box. It proved far more difficult than I had anticipated as the author of multiple books and hundreds of articles.

Even I needed a refresher on communication skills and sought outside expertise and perspective to create what you're now reading. I suppose it is possible to teach an old dog new tricks!

Chapter **2**

Brushing Up on Business Communication Fundamentals

E ven without formal training, you've managed to communicate from the day you were born (and maybe even before then) to get what you wanted. All you had to do was express your distress or discomfort and you'd send caregivers scrambling to feed you, hold you, or change your diaper. Since that time, you've had plenty of formal training and education to sharpen your skills — classes in reading, writing, and speech. In short, you know how to communicate, so why would you need guidance on business communication fundamentals?

The reason is simple: A conceptual understanding of the fundamentals ensures that your communication is as effective and efficient as possible, and that you are both understanding others and being understood without having to exhaust everyone involved with frequent repetition and clarification. An understanding of what communication encompasses and the various components that enable it can make you a more effective and efficient communicator.

In this chapter, I provide you with several definitions of *communication* to work with, several standard models, and a list of key components so that you have a clear understanding of everything required for communication to occur. I even provide guidance on how to conduct a communication audit so that you're well-equipped to analyze your daily conversations and identify areas for improvement.

Checking Out Definitions of *Communication*

Given that communication focuses on exchanging information and establishing mutual understanding, you'd think it would have one clear definition that everyone agrees on. That's not the case. There are multiple definitions, and they're not mutually exclusive.

REMEMBER

Celebrate the fact that most words have multiple meanings. That's what makes language so rich. In fact, knowing the various definitions of *communication* that I present in the following sections gives you a broader understanding of what communication is all about.

Dictionary definitions

Merriam-Webster's Collegiate Dictionary contains five definitions related to human-to human *communication*:

- An act or instance of transmitting
- Information communicated
- A process by which information is exchanged between individuals through a common system of symbols, signs, or behaviors
- A system for communicating (like telephone or Wi-Fi)
- A technique for expressing ideas effectively (as in speech)

A textbook definition

Back in the 1960s, communication researchers Katz and Kahn defined communication as "the exchange of information and the transmission of meaning." They claimed that for communication to take place, someone had to send information to someone else who needed to receive *and* understand it.

Not bad for a definition from the '60s, but I and many of my colleagues would quibble with it. I say communication happens whenever information is transferred, but that *successful* communication occurs only when the recipient understands the meaning of that information. To fully grasp the distinction, think back to an incident in which you heard what someone told you but didn't fully understand their intended meaning. The speaker transferred information to you, so communication occurred, but the communication was unsuccessful because you and the speaker didn't reach a mutual understanding.

A practical definition for business applications

To ensure that your communication is effective, I encourage you to embrace an outcome-based definition of communication. I define *communication* as "an exchange of information that drives action." Action can range from increasing a person's understanding to persuading them to do something. Here are a few examples:

>> A customer buys a product based on your sales presentation.

>> You receive a promotion based on a performance conversation with your direct supervisor.

>> Your supervisor understands why you're upset about having your time-off request denied based on a brief conversation you had.

Communication isn't merely about the message; it's about the impact the message has on the recipient — what it causes the recipient to think, feel, or do.

REMEMBER

Communication is effective in a business environment when it initiates action or change. In the process of communicating, understanding can evolve. Communication is a foundation of relationship-building and is multidirectional. For example, as you attempt to persuade someone else to accept your viewpoint, you may also find yourself persuaded to think differently based on theirs.

Exploring Communication Models

A *communication model* is a simplified representation of the exchange of information and meaning. Numerous scholars and researchers in the communication field have proposed various communication models over the years. These models can be broken down into three categories — linear, interactive, and transactional — all three of which I cover in the following sections.

Sorry (not sorry) for donning my professorial hat as I take you on a deep dive into communication models. Understanding these models and the components of communication they highlight is important, especially in a business environment, because it enables you to identify key factors that contribute to effective communication.

Linear models

The earliest and simplest communication models are linear. According to these models, communication flows in one direction and involves only four elements:

» **Sender:** The person who sends the message

» **Message:** The information being conveyed

» **Channel:** The mechanism used to transmit the message, such as phone, radio, or television

» **Receiver:** The person who receives the message

Shannon and Weaver, engineers at Bell Telephone Labs, came up with one of the more popular linear communication models that has been adapted for the study of human communication, as shown in Figure 2-1.

FIGURE 2-1:
The Shannon-Weaver model of communication.

Interactional models

As researchers studied communication more and tested the elements of the linear model, they realized that communication doesn't flow in just one direction. In fact, communication can be a *dialogue*, involving two people who share messages back and forth. The models that emerged from this line of thinking were categorized as *interactional* models.

According to interactional models, communication involves messages sent back and forth between sender and receiver during the course of a conversation, and sometimes over different communication channels, creating a communication history. (See Figure 2-2.)

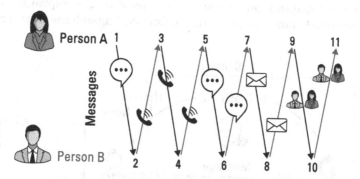

FIGURE 2-2:
An interactional
model of
communication.

"ONE CANNOT NOT COMMUNICATE"

Watzlawick, Bavelas, and Jackson, who outlined their interactional model in their 1967 book *Pragmatics of Human Communication* (W.W. Norton & Company), blew the minds of readers by claiming that "one cannot not communicate" — that people communicate as soon as they begin to interact with one another, whether intending to or not. In other words, everything you say and everything you don't say in word, posture, gesture, facial expression, and absence thereof sends a message. Consider, for example, an email you haven't responded to yet. That silence, your lack of response, communicates a message.

So, the question to ask yourself at all times is are you communicating what you intend to be communicating? If you ghost someone, for example, what message are you sending? What meaning and emotion are you trying to convey or evoke?

In a business context, what does a lack of intentional communication say to others? If you're a manager who fails to respond to your team members in a timely fashion, how are they likely to interpret your lack of communication? When you're not sending a message, you're leaving the meaning of that unsent message wide open for interpretation — and misinterpretation.

Transactional models

Transactional models of communication describe communication as an ongoing process in which participants exchange information and develop understanding within a context (see Figure 2-3). Instead of being labeled as senders and receivers, participants are *communicators*, and both are responsible for exchanging information and influence, often communicating with one another simultaneously.

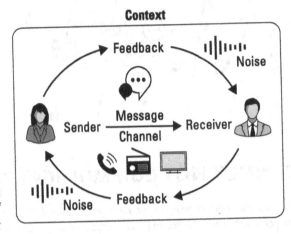

Wait a minute! You can send and receive at the same time? Yep, you sure can. Think about it. When you convey a message and someone is listening to you, that person is simultaneously conversing with you nonverbally (as I explain in greater detail in Chapter 3). If they furrow their brow to convey confusion, you may alter your communication on the spot to clarify.

REMEMBER

Transactional models are the most complex and precise. Though the linear and interactional models simply have one or more messages being exchanged between sender and receiver over one or more channels, transactional models account for additional elements, including feedback, context, and noise, as described in the next section.

Recognizing the Elements of Communication and Why They Matter

When people are communicating with one another, they tend to focus on the message. People often assume that if their message is clear, their communication will be effective. Unfortunately, communication is more complicated than that. Multiple elements contribute to determining communication success:

>> **Communicators (sender and receiver):** In linear and interactional communication models, the sender encodes the information in a form that can be understood (for example, language, images, video), and the receiver gets the information from the sender and decodes (interprets) it. In transactional models, all participants send, receive, code, and decode messages simultaneously. Each communicator's knowledge, personality, communication skills, and other qualities impact communication success.

>> **Message:** The message is the information, meaning, or feeling that the sender constructs to convey information or meaning to, or evoke a response from, the receiver. It must be clear to both sender and recipient to convey the intended meaning or evoke the desired response.

>> **Channel:** The channel is the medium used to convey the message. It may be face-to-face communication, videoconference, email, text, video, another medium, or a combination of media. The channel has a significant impact on the information exchanged and the speed and synchronicity of transmission. See Chapter 4 for more about choosing communication channels.

>> **Feedback:** Communication isn't just linear; it includes a feedback loop that describes the circular and synchronous nature of communication. The feedback loop's effectiveness and efficiency affect the ability of the communicators to exchange information, collaborate, and achieve mutual understanding.

>> **Context:** The situation or setting can impact the message and how it's conveyed and interpreted. Communication doesn't occur in a vacuum. Physical, psychological, social, cultural, and relational contexts all influence how communicators exchange information and understand one another.

REMEMBER

The less two people have in common, the greater the communication challenge. Imagine two people speaking different languages, being raised in vastly different cultures, or even working in totally different industries and trying to establish a shared understanding of a complex topic that one of them is familiar with and one is not.

>> **Noise:** Noise is anything that blocks or impairs sending, receiving, or understanding. For example, external (environmental) noise can prevent people from hearing one another, and internal noise (for example, being distracted by a problem unrelated to the current conversation) can prevent people from processing the information they're hearing. Proceed to the next section to find out more about noise and how to reduce or eliminate it.

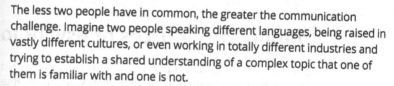

REMEMBER

All these elements are interrelated. For example, context impacts how communicators present and interpret information; the choice of channel (for example, email versus face-to-face) affects the feedback loop; what one communicator thinks about the others influences the message and can be a source of noise. All elements must work in concert to ensure effective, efficient communication.

Identifying and Addressing Sources of Noise

Noise is anything that detracts from the transmission, meaning, reception, or understanding of a message. It's not only a physical sound that makes hearing difficult. In this section, I present four common sources of noise — all of which can impair communication success — and provide guidance on how to reduce noise from each source.

TIP

Be more mindful of noise. The greater your awareness of different sources of noise interfering with your communication, the more likely you are to notice and address it before it has a chance to impair your message.

Quieting physical noise

Physical noise is anything in the environment that can interfere with communication. It could be a sound, such as sirens from emergency vehicles, or even something that can be seen, smelled, tasted, or felt (for example, a room being uncomfortably hot, cold, or crowded).

TIP

Whenever you're in a meeting, regardless of whether you're leading it, take note of any sources of physical noise and do your best to address them. For example, if you feel uncomfortably warm, you may ask whether anyone else is feeling the same way. If they are, you can request that the thermostat be adjusted or request to hold the meeting somewhere else.

Calming the sources of psychological noise

Psychological noise consists of thoughts and emotions that interfere with the mental processing of information. In other words, it's all in your head (or the heads of the people you're trying to communicate with). If you're the one who's distracted, you can do something about it immediately by focusing on the message you're delivering or receiving and blocking out everything else. If shifting your focus isn't possible, consider taking a time-out and dealing with whatever's distracting you and then returning to the conversation or meeting later. Most people would rather you excuse yourself than engage in the conversation in a distracted state of mind.

If other participants are distracted internally, you face a more daunting challenge because you can't read minds. If you're communicating face-to-face or via videoconference, you may be able to sense distraction by observing nonverbal cues.

You can then confront the person, courteously, for example, by asking if everyone is on the same page and able to engage. Take time to refocus the meeting/conversation and bring everyone back to the current discussion.

If you know that someone may have trouble focusing, for whatever reason — and assuming the conversation can wait — you can always say something like this: "I know you have a lot on your plate right now. Is this a good time to discuss project updates, or would it be easier to focus on the conversation more if we spoke tomorrow?" If the conversation can't wait, try saying something like this: "I know you have a lot on your plate right now. I need for you to switch gears for ten minutes so that we can iron out the project updates that I'll communicate to the team tomorrow."

Alleviating semantic noise

Semantic noise comes into play when communicators speak different languages, dialects, or interpret words, phrases, or information differently. It can also result from the use of acronyms that not everyone is familiar with and from grammatical errors that alter the intended meaning (or how others perceive the person who made the errors).

Have you ever been in a meeting in which someone is trying to use big words to try to impress people, but they're pronouncing the words incorrectly or using them in the wrong context? Yep, that's also an example of semantic noise. Big words may be sexy (at least from this author's perspective) but only when used correctly in appropriate situations. Most often, in business meetings, the simplest, clearest word is best.

To reduce semantic noise, define key terms, spell out acronyms at first usage, and check in regularly during the conversation or meeting to ensure that everyone is on the same page. Here's an example of defining a key term: "When I mention the leadership team today, I'm referring to those in the organization who are at a VP level or above." You can check to make sure everyone is on the same page by saying something like, "Before we move on to the next topic, I want to summarize where we are. . . ." (Bonus points for letting someone else provide the summary so that you can truly check for understanding.)

Mitigating hierarchical noise

Hierarchical noise may occur when people at different levels in an organization communicate with one another — in other words, when one person has more power than the others. For example, you may interpret a message differently depending on who sends it. If your supervisor tells you, "This needs to be done today," you may interpret it as an order or command. Whereas if one of your teammates presents it to you, you may interpret it as a statement or opening to a conversation.

TIP

Here are a few ways to reduce hierarchical noise in your organization (assuming you're in a position that empowers you to do so):

>> **Build a collaborative culture.** Organizations that have a strict hierarchical culture are more prone to hierarchical noise. Other corporate cultures are less structured and more focused on collaboration and results than on status and power. Check out *Company Culture For Dummies,* by Mike Ganino (and published by Wiley), for more about various corporate cultures.

>> **Streamline communication channels.** Encourage direct communication among everyone in the organization rather than require that communications be filtered through hierarchical layers.

>> **Encourage open, honest communication.** Reward, rather than penalize, members of your organization for speaking their minds, pitching ideas, and revealing opportunities for improvement.

Reducing noise in virtual environments

With the increased frequency of virtual meetings and digital communication channels, reducing noise in these environments has become increasingly important. When you're sending a message in person, noise is more obvious, making it more likely to be addressed. In a virtual environment, you may have nothing to clue you in on the fact that noise is interfering with the transmission, reception, or processing of information.

Here are a few tips for reducing noise in virtual environments:

>> **Prepare your audience:** When sending digital media to one or more people to process, let them know what they're getting and your expectations. For example, if you're sending a three-minute video, tell the recipient(s) how long it is and what you want them to do after viewing it, like this: "I need everyone to take three minutes, uninterrupted, to focus on this video and respond with your answers to the questions posed at the end. Please make sure to set aside the appropriate length of time to complete this task by noon tomorrow."

>> **Avoid technical glitches:** Provide detailed instructions on the software/ platform you're using to host the virtual meeting/presentation, including how to access the software, how to sign in, and how to navigate to the meeting. Encourage participants to sign in early and let you know if they anticipate

encountering any issues that may prevent them from participating (for example, they won't be near their computer, they don't have the software, or they've had problems using the software in the past).

TIP

Consider offering participants the option of connecting with you outside the meeting to work out any possible technical glitches prior to the scheduled meeting. A brief dry run can ensure that when the time comes, everyone can sign in and participate.

>> **Specify any environmental guidelines:** When scheduling a meeting in a virtual environment, establish guidelines for the meeting ahead of time so that people know how to prepare. For example, "Our meeting tomorrow requires everyone to be fully focused for 30 minutes so that we can discuss our expansion plans. I know many of you work from public places, but we have confidential matters to discuss, so please be sure to call in from a private, secure environment."

>> **Lay out the rules for questions and conversations:** For virtual meetings, clarify how you'll handle questions and side conversations; for example, you may say something like this: "For today's presentation, I ask that everyone remain on Mute and keep their cameras turned on. If you have questions for the speaker, enter them into the chat and we'll address them at the end. We want to make sure our presenter today can share their content clearly and with no unnecessary interruptions."

Paying Special Attention to History and Environment

One of the most challenging aspects of understanding communication is that it's about more than just the people in the room and the topic under consideration. Numerous factors influence how information is communicated and processed, as explained earlier, in the section "Recognizing the Elements of Communication and Why They Matter." In this section, I take a deeper dive into two key elements that contribute to the context in which communication commonly occurs: communication history and environment.

Communication history

Communication history consists of all the interactions, messages, impressions, perceptions, and bits of information that participants have shared among one another over time. It extends beyond the current topic of discussion to the history of their relationships with one another. For example, if one participant in a discussion has a reputation of exaggerating the facts or using rhetorical tricks to persuade others, any information or opinion they put forth is likely to be challenged or rejected outright.

Take, for example, a colleague that you've gotten along well with for more than a year. Then one day, their communication style seems terse, overly direct, and borderline rude. This isn't the history you have with the person, so you're able to take a breath and recognize that it's outside the norm. Later that day, you find out that they had a family medical emergency and were overly stressed — the communication style had nothing to do with you and everything to do with their situation. On the other hand, if you have no communication history with someone and make a poor first impression, it takes significantly more work to get back on a positive track.

Communication history can even exist when you've never even shared a single word with a person! As you read the following professions, I want you to notice what immediately comes to mind: university professor, used-car salesperson, financial advisor, kindergarten teacher. What immediately came to mind is the stereotype that you have for that role, which can be based on your personal experience, depictions in media, and other societal factors. That stereotype can influence — rightly or wrongly — your communication history with someone before you've even had your first conversation!

Is it fair? Not necessarily. Is it real? Sure is. This is why you're well advised not to burn bridges (ruin relationships, connections, or opportunities) over the course of your career. If you burn even one proverbial bridge, word spreads, chipping away at your reputation and impairing your ability to form positive relationships.

WARNING

Be very careful about everything you put out into the universe — all your personal and professional interactions, your blog posts, everything you share on social media platforms, and so on. Anything that can be shared in any way — digitally, on paper, by word-of-mouth — can become part of your communication history with others, including potential future employers. Pay attention to the information that's out there about you and make sure it aligns with the impression you want to make.

Environment

Environment can have a significant impact on not only the content of the information being communicated but also how the audience perceives and interprets it. For example, you wouldn't talk about the same topics in a meeting at work that you would talk about at the company picnic. One setting is professional, and the other is less formal. Asking about a raise or promotion at the company picnic, for instance, would probably compromise your chances of getting either.

In any situation involving communication (and that's every situation when you're in the presence of others), consider the environment. Here are some questions that can help you guide your evaluation:

>> Is this an appropriate environment to discuss the topic/issue?

>> Is everyone comfortable? For example, make sure the room has sufficient space and isn't too hot, cold, or stuffy.

>> Can the topic be covered in the allotted time? If a meeting is rushed, it can impact the ability to successfully convey the information or message.

>> Is the environment free of noise and other physical distractions? (See the earlier section "Quieting physical noise" for details.)

REMEMBER

In the workplace, meetings and conversations increasingly take place via virtual channels. These venues have environmental considerations as well, including whether all participants have the technology required to fully participate, whether audio or video is turned on or off, whether participants can interact via chat, and so on. Pay attention to variables in virtual environments as well.

Conducting a Communication Audit

A *communication audit* is a systematic process used to evaluate how effectively and efficiently information and meaning are being exchanged. You can conduct an audit before, during, or after a communication session or a project to identify and address areas for improvement.

To conduct a simple communication audit, evaluate the conversation or presentation based on the effectiveness of each of its components:

>> **Sender(s) and receiver(s):** Did the sender and receiver speak the same language and share a body of knowledge and understanding that enabled them to communicate effectively and efficiently? If not, what could they have done to improve their mutual understanding? See Chapter 12 for guidance on how to evaluate an audience.

>> **Message:** Was the message clear and concise? Did it resonate with the receiver? Could the message be modified in any way to make it more effective? For example, maybe the presenter could have used more visual elements or examples.

>> **Channel:** Was the communication channel used the best choice for this message, audience, and situation? For example, if the message was communicated via email, would a phone conversation or a brief videoconference have been more effective and efficient? See Chapter 4 for guidance on how to choose the right channel.

>> **Feedback:** Was the feedback sufficient to reveal any lack of information or potential misunderstanding of the message? If feedback was insufficient, how could it have been improved? For example, some channels, such as face-to-face and videoconferencing, are more conducive to feedback than others, such as email or texting. In some cases, simply encouraging an audience to ask questions can improve feedback.

>> **Context:** Did anything about the context in which the conversation occurred impact the exchange of information or the ability to achieve a mutual understanding? Context can be anything from the space in which the conversation took place to the psychological state of one or more parties to social or cultural differences or even the relationship between the sender(s) and receiver(s). What impact, if any, did any of these contextual elements have on the conversation and how could these elements have been addressed to improve the outcome?

>> **Noise:** Did noise impact the ability of the parties to communicate? Remember that noise is more than a physical sound. It can be psychological (such as a mental distraction), hierarchical (due to differences in position or status), or semantic (due to differences in languages or how people express themselves). If noise did impact the ability of the parties to communicate, how could that noise have been addressed to improve the exchange of information or ideas?

EXAMPLE

Suppose you just finished a presentation to your manager in which you asked for a more flexible work schedule — you want to switch from five days in the office to three days in the office and two remote. You worked incredibly hard preparing your arguments. Your data was impeccable; your logic, solid; your delivery, flawless. You even made a killer proposal with appealing visual charts! Yet you didn't get the result you wanted.

What happened? Well, go through the different elements I discuss in this chapter and try to figure it out.

You were the sender, and your manager was the receiver. You had your presentation laid out and went in with guns blazing. Your manager listened but didn't say much. Maybe you could have benefited by encouraging more *feedback*.

What else could have gotten in the way?

The *environment* was comfortable. You went to your manager's office and sat together at a table. So that's probably not it.

Could *noise* have played a role? Not that you're aware of, but your manager could've been feeling pressure from a supervisor to keep all employees onsite — a form of *hierarchical noise* and an outside factor that could have impacted how your request was received and processed. You didn't ask what the manager's reservations were after you received the verdict, so this factor is unknown.

How about *communication history?* This may have been the most significant factor. By going in without first asking about your manager's history with people on the team working from home or their personal experiences working from home, you missed a key data point — or multiple data points. This is likely where the communication went wrong. Next time, you'll know to gather more information ahead of time — and perhaps have more of a dialogue than a presentation.

When communication fails, don't be ashamed (it happens to all of us). Learn from your mistakes and the mistakes of others and use that insight to improve.

Chapter **3**

Communicating without Words: Nonverbal Communication

"**M**ore than Words" is the title of a popular song by Extreme, but it's also a useful definition of *nonverbal communication* — it's everything other than words that you use to communicate. It includes facial expressions, gestures, volume and tone of voice, posture, eye contact, appearance, physical proximity, and even touch. According to at least one estimate (from back in 1960, when people actually *talked* to one another), nonverbal communication accounts for approximately 93 percent of the meaning exchanged during an in-person interaction. (See the nearby sidebar "I Can't Believe It's 93 Percent!" for details about that estimate.)

Most researchers these days consider 93 percent to be the upper extreme. Today's estimates commonly specify a range of about 60 to 90 percent, but that's still a significant portion of communication that occurs nonverbally. In other words, to communicate most effectively, you're wise to pay attention to not only the words you say but also how you say them vocally and with your body language.

I CAN'T BELIEVE IT'S 93 PERCENT!

In the 1960s, psychologist Albert Mehrabian conducted a study that put him in textbooks for decades to come. (I mean, heck, he made it into this book, too.) He studied how more than 100 college students derived meaning from messages in face-to-face interactions.

He concluded that only 7 percent of meaning comes from words. Of the other 93 percent, different vocal dimensions (volume, tone, and so on) accounted for 38 percent, and body language (posture, gestures, facial expressions, and so on) accounted for the remaining 55 percent. (Wait! What? So, why do we spend so much time crafting messages?)

Unfortunately, people who quote the 93 percent stat often omit the fact that Mehrabian's study focused narrowly on situations in which a person's nonverbal communication contradicted the verbal message being conveyed. For example, if you say you're happy with a frown on your face, most people will conclude that you're unhappy. So that 93 percent statistic isn't accurate for all or even most situations.

What *is* important is that nonverbal communication contributes significantly to the messages people convey and how those messages are interpreted.

In this chapter, I present the various types of nonverbal communication and provide guidance on how to use them to your advantage.

Using Your Body to Communicate

A significant component of nonverbal communication is *body language* — the use of physical movements, expressions, and mannerisms to communicate without words, often instinctively or subconsciously instead of consciously. Body language includes gestures, facial expressions, and eye contact. In this section, I cover each category of body language and provide guidance on how to use your body to communicate more effectively.

Two topics I don't cover in any depth in this section are appearance and posture. I avoid these topics intentionally because the variations are too great among genders, industries, and specific contexts. The only specific advice I offer relevant to appearance is to *dress for the situation you're in*. Whether you want to admit it or not, people often form their initial judgments of others, at least in part, on appearance.

If you're not sure what to wear, ask someone you trust who's familiar with the environment, situation, or event. You don't want your communication to be derailed from the very start simply because you were unaware of any customs or norms for a meeting.

Using gestures to express yourself or emphasize what you're saying

Gestures are physical movements that express or help express thoughts or emotions or emphasize a spoken message. Common gestures include waving hello or goodbye, shrugging your shoulders to indicate uncertainty, nodding your head in agreement, covering your mouth to indicate shock, pointing to indicate direction, fidgeting to express nervousness, and many more.

Gesturing with your head

You're probably already familiar with the following common head gestures:

>> Nodding your head up and down to indicate agreement or answer "yes"

>> Pivoting your head from side to side to show disagreement or answer "no"

>> Tilting your head slightly to the side to indicate that you're thinking or confused

>> Bowing your head to show reverence or to communicate respect or submission

Head gestures include many subtle nuances. For example, the speed at which you nod your head makes a difference. A slow nod shows that you're listening and generally in agreement, whereas a fast nod may express agreement and indicate that you're eager to find out more. The distance you move your head while nodding can also carry a subtle meaning; for example, a big nod may indicate total agreement.

Rarely do gestures have universal meaning, and their meaning often varies in context and when combined with other gestures. For example, in many Asian cultures, nodding the head may indicate that the person heard your statement, not necessarily that they agree. A slow tilt of the head to the side could be a sign that a listener heard what you said and is thinking about it, but if that tilt is accompanied by a furrowed brow, it could be a sign that the listener is confused. A tilt with a smirk may indicate that the person disagrees with what you said.

NONVERBAL COMMUNICATION IN THE ANIMAL KINGDOM

I'm writing this chapter as I sit outside of the Bwindi Impenetrable National Forest in Uganda, where I spent two days trekking through the jungle to observe a family of mountain gorillas. Before starting the trek, our group was briefed multiple times about how to communicate with the gorillas — especially the silverback (the alpha) — in the event that we made eye contact.

Our guide demonstrated and explained the meaning of a few essential nonverbal utterances (grunts in a specific pitch and duration) and showed us how to communicate respect and submission to the silverback. If the alpha made eye contact with any of us, we were to avert our eyes downward immediately and slightly bow our head. If he started coming toward us, we were to remain still because any gesture could be interpreted as a sign of challenge.

These nonverbal gestures communicate the same meaning in most human cultures. Of course, that fact shouldn't be a surprise; we humans share over 98 percent of our DNA with the gorilla!

Gesturing with your hands

Hand gestures are an important component of business communication. You can use them to convey meaning, establish rapport, and clarify the meaning and tone of what you're saying. Here are two common hand gestures used in business situations and their meaning:

REMEMBER

>> **Handshake:** This universal gesture of greeting, agreement, or farewell signifies trust, respect, and professionalism.

Just like the beds in "Goldilocks and the Three Bears," your handshake should be not too hard or too soft but *just* right. And keep it short — typically 2 to 5 seconds in duration. Most experts (including this one) recommend a firm handshake, as it signals confidence. A handshake that's too firm can come across as aggressive, and one that's too soft can signal insincerity or weakness. Also important, in the United States and many Western cultures, is to maintain eye contact while shaking hands.

>> **Pointing:** Point with your index finger to call attention to something or indicate direction, but avoid pointing at people, because it can make them feel as though they're being blamed or are the object of unwanted attention.

TIP

A more subtle way to single out someone is to point by gesturing with your entire hand, palm up, as if you're introducing the person.

REMEMBER

Be sure your gestures are consistent with any spoken message. If your gestures contradict what you're saying, people will question your credibility. For example, if you're saying that you're confident about the company's future prospects but you're fidgeting with a pen while saying it, audience members won't believe you completely. In fact, they'll give more credence to your gestures. After all, actions speak louder than words.

WHAT YOU SEE IS MORE POWERFUL THAN WHAT YOU HEAR

The message you see is more powerful than the message you hear. If you don't believe that, try playing a few rounds of Simon Says — the classic children's game. The person leading the game, the person chosen to be Simon, tells all the other players what to do. As long as the leader starts the command with "Simon says," everyone else must do what they're told. However, if Simon issues a command without first saying, "Simon says," and a player follows that command, that player is out of the game.

To complicate the game, Simon acts out every command, regardless of whether that command is preceded by the phrase "Simon says." So one round may go something like this:

Simon says, touch your head.

Simon says, touch your shoulders.

Simon says, jump up and down.

Stop! (Simon stops jumping.)

Anyone who stops jumping is out of the game because Simon didn't say, "*Simon says* stop!"

This game is challenging for two reasons. First, it gets players in the habit of following orders so that when one of those orders is a little different (not preceded by "Simon says"), it breaks the natural flow. Second, all eyes are on the person playing Simon, and when Simon says, "Stop!" and stops jumping, the players see Simon stop before they have time to realize that Simon didn't say, "Simon says." People see 20–100 times faster than they hear; players tend to follow what they see faster than they can process what they hear.

The same is true when you're interacting with others in any environment or situation. People see and interpret your gestures faster than they hear and process your words, so be sure that your words and gestures align.

Making faces: Facial expression

Your face can express the entire spectrum of human emotions, from joy and love to sadness and hate and everything in between — curiosity, fear, disgust, surprise, boredom, interest, and more. While not exhaustive, Table 3-1 gives you a sampling of the many expressions that our faces can communicate and the possible meanings of each.

REMEMBER

You can communicate with posture alone, head gestures alone, hand gestures alone, facial expressions alone, or words alone, but combining two or more reinforces and amplifies the message — assuming, of course, that all the signals you're sending are consistent. If the messages you're sending verbally and nonverbally conflict, they'll cause confusion and dilute the meaning and understanding you're intending to convey.

TABLE 3-1

Expressions and Their Meanings

Facial Expression	Possible Meaning
Biting lips	Nervousness, anticipation, or flirtation
Blank stare	Detachment, boredom, or shock
Frown	Sadness, displeasure, or frustration
Furrowed brow	Anger, determination, or deep thought
Grimace	Pain, discomfort, or disgust
Narrowing eyes	Suspicion, anger, or concentration
Pursed lips	Disapproval, uncertainty, or thoughtfulness
Raised eyebrows	Surprise, interest, confusion, or disbelief
Raised eyebrows with a half-smile	Skepticism, amusement, or mild disbelief
Rolling eyes (often accompanied by a sigh)	Annoyance, exasperation, or dismissal
Smile	Happiness, friendliness, or amusement
Tightened jaw or clenched teeth	Anger, tension, or frustration
Wide open eyes	Astonishment, fear, or excitement
Wrinkled nose	Disgust, scrutiny, or judgment

Maintaining eye contact (without staring)

Maintaining eye contact is essential for effective face-to-face communication in business in North American cultures because it

>> Establishes trust and builds rapport

>> Conveys credibility and confidence

>> Shows that you're paying attention

>> Facilitates connection and understanding

>> Demonstrates leadership

>> Enhances negotiation

WARNING

Don't get into a staring contest. Let your eyes wander a little during the conversation. Try to notice everything about the person, including any body language they're using. Feel free to glance down at your notes occasionally (but not at your phone because looking at your phone during a conversation communicates that you're not fully present in the moment).

Keeping a Comfortable and Effective Distance

If you've ever been accosted by a close talker, you already know a little about proxemics and the impact it can have on communication. *Proxemics* is the study of cultural, behavioral, and sociological aspects of spatial distances between people. Standing too close can seem threatening, especially when accompanied by a harsh tone, command, or critique. Standing too far away may communicate fear or a lack of interest. Leaning in a little from a comfortable distance can indicate interest or attention. Leaning back with arms crossed may signal disagreement, boredom, or contempt.

Effective communicators are mindful of their proximity to the people they're conversing with, and they try to maintain a comfortable, effective distance. In this section, I introduce you to the four proxemic zones and provide guidance on how to arrange your workspace to make it more conducive to open communication.

Exploring the four proxemic zones

Edward T. Hall, the founder of proxemics, identified four proxemic zones that describe the distances people feel are appropriate between them based on their relationship to one another and the environment or situation they're in.

In this section, I describe the four proxemics zones to be aware of so that you can remain at a comfortable distance at all times while using space to your communicative advantage.

The intimate zone

In professional environments, you generally want to steer clear of the *intimate zone*, which ranges from the point at which you're physically touching someone to about 18 inches apart. In the business world, people very rarely breach this zone, and when they do, they risk becoming the target of disciplinary action and perhaps even a lawsuit. Rare exceptions to this rule apply to shaking hands or sitting close to someone in a meeting or at a conference when you're both facing the same direction.

Reserve the intimate zone for family members, close friends, and *really* close friends outside the work environment. Even when people shake hands, they tend to keep their bodies outside the intimate zone, extending their arms and hands as if to safely and respectfully bridge the distance.

REMEMBER

Keep in mind that proxemic zones vary among cultures. Latin cultures, for example, tend to be more comfortable being closer than many in the United States. See Chapter 20 for more about communicating across cultures.

Personal space

Personal space, with a range of 1–4 feet, is typically the best distance to default to if you already have a relationship with someone—such as a coworker or a boss. Typically, the closer your relationship (not meaning intimate, but more along the lines of longevity, strength, and so on), the less personal space someone needs to feel comfortable.

TIP

To project confidence and power, fill an appropriate amount of space whenever you enter a room or sit at a table. In business, taking up space is often a sign of power and confidence. Of course, you don't want to be elbowing people and shoving others out of the way or invading their personal space, but don't shrink into yourself or try to wedge yourself into a tight spot — doing so projects weakness and a lack of confidence. If you don't have enough space, politely ask people to move over so that you have the space you need.

The social zone

The *social zone* is the distance people feel comfortable around strangers before they start getting to know them. Most researchers estimate that this zone ranges from about 4 to 12 feet.

TIP

If you find yourself in the social zone with someone you're attempting to build a relationship with, don't rush it! Slowly move closer and gauge the reaction of the other person. If they step closer, great! If they step back or appear to be nervous, they're not ready. Respect each person's personal space, realizing that each person's comfort zone can be different and can change as the situation evolves.

If you've ever been on a crowded plane, bus, or train, you've probably noticed that many people don't converse with one another. Some may even appear anxious or stare down at their feet or the feet of their fellow passengers. One of the reasons for their discomfort is that they're forced into sharing their intimate zones with complete strangers. If you sit next to someone, they may even be reluctant to strike up a conversation. Respect their space, and if you need to converse with them, take a gradual approach.

Public distance

Public distance is that space that's comfortable amid total strangers outside the confines of any social or business setting. It's typically over 12 feet. Imagine how you'd feel if you were walking down a street and someone walking toward you on the opposite side suddenly decided to cross over to your side. You'd probably feel a little uncomfortable or maybe even threatened because now the person was on track to enter your personal space.

Obviously, in some settings, public space is much closer; for example, when you're sitting in a bar or restaurant or traveling on a plane, bus, or train or walking on a crowded sidewalk. In a business setting, public space typically applies only to the people on stage in a crowded room who may be a considerable distance from their audience.

Arranging your workspace or workplace for the culture you want to nurture

When you're arranging your office or an entire workplace, put some thought into the message you want to convey and the culture you want to foster. For example, if you're trying to build a collaborative culture in which everyone communicates freely with one another, create an open floor plan with collaborative workspaces, modular or moveable furniture, and whiteboards. Make sure leadership offices are accessible; for example, establish an open-door policy. If you're in a position of authority, come out from behind your desk and sit in a chair at their level when people come to you for advice or a performance review.

In contrast, if you're trying to create a strong hierarchical work environment, give everyone on the leadership team a big, fancy office and assign everyone else cramped cubicles or a shared workspace. Use barriers between management and staff, like walls and large desks, as constant reminders of your differences in status and power. Of course, I'm not recommending this approach. I'm just pointing out that you need to be conscious of the message you're sending to others when you arrange space. Be intentional when making choices. Don't think exclusively about your comfort and privacy. Consider how your choices will impact the ways people interact with one another. See the nearby sidebar "Tuning in to the world around you" for some real-world examples.

TUNING IN TO THE WORLD AROUND YOU

You can discover a great deal about how to arrange space by observing how others arrange their space.

Think about being called into the principal's office at school or (if you never experienced that because you weren't as . . . overachieving as I was growing up) think of entering your boss's office and finding them sitting behind their desk. That desk is a nonverbal communicator of power. It's there to tell people who's in charge and who's not. Chances are good that the person on the other side of the desk is also seated in a bigger chair that makes them significantly taller than you. That's another nonverbal communicator of power. Physical barriers like these hinder the free exchange of information.

Similar barriers are used in traditional classroom settings. The teacher is at the front of the room, often seated behind a desk or standing behind a podium while students are seated behind their own mini-desks facing the front of the room. The teacher is sending the clear message "I'm in charge and you're not." Many classrooms, at all levels of education, are changing to more open seating arrangements and roundtable discussions to accommodate a more open and collaborative learning experience. When teacher and students are seated together, education becomes more dynamic, with students taking on a more active role in the process.

Many doctors are rearranging their offices to encourage patients to communicate more openly. Rooms now include chairs, along with the traditional examination table. Before your physical exam, you sit in a chair, often at the same level as the doctor, to discuss why you're there. Studies show that this form of communication results in patients sharing more information with their doctors. This conversational, consultative approach encourages patients to play a more active role in their own health, partnering with the doctor to optimize the treatment outcome.

Getting in touch with haptics

Haptics is the study of the sense of touch, and it doesn't (and shouldn't) have much to do with business communication because, except for the occasional handshake or pat on the back, people don't regularly communicate by touch in a business setting. In fact, touching can make people you interact with feel uncomfortable and sometimes even threatened.

Case in point: At the G8 Summit in Saint Petersburg, Russia, President George W. Bush approached German Chancellor Angela Merkel from behind while she was seated and squeezed her shoulders, which she immediately shrugged off as she grimaced in response. This "unsolicited massage" as many in the media dubbed it, was captured on video and shared through media outlets around the world. This form of touch was inappropriate for a formal meeting such as the G8 summit, and it was clearly in violation of Merkel's personal space. Many even argued that it was sexist — that it would not have been done if a male were sitting in that same chair (based on the fact that Bush didn't provide unsolicited massages to anyone else in the room). The only good of it comes from the fact that it serves as a perfect example of what *not* to do in a professional setting.

Using Your Voice to Enhance Your Message

The words you say matter, but how you say those words matters as well, and sometimes even more so. How you pronounce words, how carefully you enunciate, how loud and fast you talk, the tone of your voice, and other aspects of how you deliver your lines can all impact the meaning of what you say and your audience's perception of you.

In this section, I provide guidance on how to speak more effectively and avoid mistakes that can detract from your meaning and the impression you're trying to make.

Paying attention to enunciation and pronunciation

A music teacher I had in elementary school told me that the most successful lip-syncers (yes, I was being given advice on lip-syncing, because I was *that* bad in the choir) committed to it by opening their mouth wide and silently enunciating every syllable of each word in the lyric. She was onto something, as I'd later learn in my public speaking career. The more you open your mouth to enunciate each syllable, the more clearly you project your voice and the easier it is for people to understand you. (Not to mention that it facilitates lip-reading for those who have a hearing impairment.)

Whenever you're speaking, focus on both pronunciation and enunciation:

>> *Pronunciation* is the act of speaking words in a way that is accepted or generally understood. For example, if you have a southern drawl, say "oil" instead of "awl." If you have a New England accent, work on saying "park your car" instead of "pahk yuh kah."

>> *Enunciation* is the act of pronouncing each syllable of a word clearly and distinctly. When you fail to enunciate, words become garbled or run together. The most successful communicators enunciate each syllable in each word, even when speaking quickly.

Mispronunciation and poor enunciation can harm your credibility, erode confidence, and result in misunderstandings. (With a last name like Schiefelbein, I'm no stranger to mispronunciation.)

Practice recording yourself speak and then listen to the recording to determine how well you're pronouncing and enunciating words. You may also try practicing with a speech-to-text app. If the app is having trouble figuring out the words you're saying, focus on being more intentional in your pronunciation and enunciation and try slowing down a bit.

Using paralanguage to enhance what you say

Paralanguage is the rate, volume, and pitch of your voice. It applies to all the vocal variations that aren't actual words but that impact the meaning of the words. In this section, I explain how to use these vocal variations to your advantage in your business communications.

In our remote and global workplaces, virtual meetings are ripe for practicing your nonverbal communication skills. While I prefer that anyone I'm meeting with has their camera on so that I can have more nonverbal cues to help understand their message, sometimes it's not possible in certain environments. If you're off camera for any reason, you'll really need to make sure that your paralanguage is on point!

Rate

Rate is the speed at which you speak — the number of words per minute. The average English speaker in North America speaks from 110 to 150 words per minute. Venturing too far out of this range, either way, sends a message. To be a more effective speaker, adjust your rate of speech to your purpose:

>> Slower to create a more intentional, dramatic delivery

>> Faster to convey a sense of excitement or energy

Volume

Volume is the loudness of your voice — it can range from a soft whisper to being so loud that people feel as though you're yelling at them. Always speak loudly enough that everyone can hear what you're saying without having to strain so that they don't miss any words. If you're speaking to a large audience, be loud enough so your voice reaches the back row. Beyond that, you can vary your volume for dramatic effect. Here are a few options:

>> Use variations in volume, rate, and tone to keep people from falling asleep. Speaking in a monotone voice makes people drowsy; it's like white noise.

> » When delivering a speech, consider using variations in volume to emphasize important points.

> » If you're building suspense, start by lowering your voice and then raise it to deliver the dramatic conclusion.

> » Speak softly (but loudly enough for everyone to hear) to convey a sense of intimacy or act as though you're letting the audience in on a secret.

WARNING

When nervous, people tend to speak too quickly. Be conscious of any tendency to speak so fast that your words run together. Practice relaxation techniques, such as controlled breathing, to modulate your speed.

Pitch

Pitch is the highness or lowness of your voice — the deepness or steepness. High-pitched voices often come off as squeaky, whereas lower-pitched voices come off as muffled or thundering. As with rate and volume, try to match the pitch of your voice to your message and the emotion you want to convey:

> » To stress a point or elicit excitement, raise the pitch of your voice.

> » To present a more serious point or set a more somber tone, lower your pitch.

> » Vary your pitch to hold your audience's attention and enhance the meaning and emotional content of your message.

THE PARALANGUAGE ROLLER COASTER

Over a decade ago (yes, I'm aging myself), I released a YouTube video called *Paralanguage Rollercoaster* (and, yes, if you Google it, you'll still find it *and* find 2012 me with some stellar shirt cuffs). The whole idea behind the video was to illustrate how variations in voice create interest and help capture and hold the attention of an audience during a speech.

Think about a roller coaster ride. If you were going one speed on a flat track the entire time, you'd be bored. Nobody would be waiting in line to experience that ride. What makes a roller coaster so much fun is the different sensations you experience! The slow, steady ascent. The fast-and-furious drop. The twists! The turns! The variation in the ride brings excitement and keeps you interested.

Similarly, a dynamic speaker uses variations in their paralanguage. They vary their rate, tone, volume, and pitch based on the message they're trying to convey. This strategy keeps the attention of the audience and helps to emphasize key points. It allows you to bring your listeners along on a vocal journey, helping them experience firsthand the emotions you're sharing by changing your voice accordingly.

Next time you're giving a speech, think about how you'll create these roller coaster moments for your audience using your voice.

Avoiding the use of filler words

Filler words are meaningless utterances that speakers often add to fill any pauses and try to make what they're saying appear to flow more smoothly. Here's an example: "Um, do you want to, uh, go to the, um, theater to, like, see a show, um, with me? We'll have a great time, you know?"

Filler words are rarely included in print like that. Even transcription services edit out the filler words, so people often are unaware that they have a problem. However, if you record yourself in casual conversations and in speeches and listen to the recordings, you can usually determine whether you have a problem. Used too frequently, filler words can erode your credibility, position you in an unconfident light, and impact your communicative success.

When I was in high school and early into my college years, I fell into the bad habit of seasoning my language with the word *like*. It got so bad, apparently, that my whole family, at a dinner, teamed up against me. Every time I said the word *like* during dinner, someone would slap their hand on the table. It was perhaps a bit harsh, but it truly drove the point home. Needless to say, I restrict my use of that word as much as possible now. And, if you find yourself struggling with a filler word— whether it's *like* or *um* or *uh* or *so* or some other utterance — you can have friends help you with this problem by calling you out on your filler word usage.

Conveying Meaning and Emotion Through Silence

"Silence Is Golden" is a song by Frankie Valli & The Four Seasons. It was also a phrase splashed across theater screens in the 1990s and 2000s to encourage theatergoers to be quiet during the movie. I love his phrase because it expresses how I feel about silence in business communication. As a means of nonverbal communication, silence is one of the most impressive tools at your disposal. When used strategically, silence is powerful. Here are a few ways to use silence to your advantage in a business setting:

» Pause before introducing the most poignant points of your message, including your take-home message — this pregnant pause, or slightly extended pause, is a powerful tool in drama and comedy alike. Successful stand-up comedians are masters of pausing purposefully before and after delivering a punch line to get the biggest laugh.

» Pause to listen and observe the audience's reaction. You can't talk and listen at the same time with total concentration. Pausing after you deliver a key point enables you to observe whether it has had the desired impact. (See Chapter 5 for more about listening.)

» Go silent or take a break during a negotiation to strengthen your position. For example, if, after you deliver what you believe is a fair offer, your negotiating partner counters your offer, waiting to respond sends a strong message that you're not interested in their counteroffer.

IN THIS CHAPTER

» **Exploring the landscape of communication channels**

» **Gauging different channels by how rich they are**

» **Choosing a channel based on your communication goal**

» **Optimizing your use of communication media**

Chapter **4**

Special Delivery: Picking the Right Way to Communicate

The other day, I was trying to make lunch plans with a colleague. After exchanging numerous text messages over the course of about 10 minutes, we were no closer to deciding on a date, time, and location than when we started. I eventually became so frustrated that I stopped texting and called my friend to talk it over. Within 60 seconds, 20 of which we spent exchanging the usual pleasantries, we had agreed upon a date, time, and location. The moral of this story is that the way people communicate can have a tremendous impact on communication efficiency and effectiveness. Texting is useful, but in situations that require collaboration, it's not usually the most effective communication channel.

A *communication channel* (or *medium*) is the means by which two or more people exchange information or establish a mutual understanding. Communication channels include face-to-face, text, email, phone, videoconferencing, and others. You can think of them as being like TV channels: You choose a TV channel depending on what you want to watch — news, comedy, sports, true crime, mystery, whatever. Each channel has its pros and cons, strengths and weaknesses, and suitability to your situation. Likewise, in business, you choose a communication channel based on the options you have available, the situation, and the desired goal or outcome. In some cases, a brief email message will do the trick. In other cases, you may be better off meeting with team members in a conference room or via videoconference.

In this chapter, I present the advantages and disadvantages of different communication channels and provide guidance for choosing the most efficient and effective channel for any given situation or communication goal.

Exploring Communication Channels

In business, you have a plethora of communication channels to choose from, with new channels continually emerging. Here's a relatively comprehensive list categorized by type (*synchronous* refers to real-time interaction; read more about synchronous and asynchronous communication in "Comparing Channels by How Rich They Are," later in this chapter):

>> Face-to-face (which is, by nature, synchronous)

>> Synchronous video (for example, a Zoom meeting)

>> Asynchronous video (on-demand content, such as a YouTube video)

>> Synthetic media videos (such as digital likeness and avatars)

>> Audio-narrated presentations (audio and slides)

>> Audio-only (such as an audiobook)

>> Synchronous text (live chat)

>> Text with or without static visuals (email, documents, and so on)

>> AI-generated text (unedited)

Choosing a communication channel in a business setting is an important step in sending a message. Choosing the right channel can increase receptivity, understanding, and impact. Choosing the wrong channel can cause your message to be misunderstood or misinterpreted.

Throughout this chapter, I offer more specific guidance on how to select a channel based on how rich it is and on the communication task or purpose.

Comparing Channels by How Rich They Are

Communication channels vary in how rich they are, such as the variety and volume of information they can convey and the degree of interaction they facilitate. For example, face-to-face communication is richer than written communication because written is relatively static and consists exclusively of words, whereas face-to-face allows two or more people to communicate back and forth in real time both verbally and nonverbally.

The notion that some communication media are richer than others is the guiding principle behind *media richness theory* — a framework for understanding how people choose communication media based on the richness of the media and the nature or purpose of the message. Richard Daft and Robert Lengel developed the theory in the 1980s in an attempt to explain how information changes via communication and how it could be conveyed more effectively. They determined that richer communication channels (or media) are more effective than others at reducing possible misinterpretations.

Media richness, as it pertains to choosing a channel for communication in a business context, is a measure of the following three criteria:

» **Number of social cues:** The more social cues a channel supports — visual, auditory, tactile, and so on — the richer it is. For example, face-to-face communication conveys information and meaning through the use of words, body language, gestures, facial expressions, touch, and tone of voice, whereas written communication is limited to words and, to a much lesser degree, tone.

» **Amount and immediacy of feedback:** High-richness channels, such as face-to-face, phone, and videoconferencing, support real-time interactions among participants; they can ask and answer questions to clarify what's being discussed or what they're being instructed to do. Low-richness channels, such as email and documents, don't facilitate interaction. Immediacy of feedback is determined by whether the channel is synchronous or asynchronous:

  • *Synchronous* is two-way, real-time communication, allowing for immediate interaction. Synchronous channels include face-to-face, phone, and videoconferencing.

  • *Asynchronous* is one-way or time-delayed interaction. Asynchronous channels include written, print media, on-demand video, and broadcasting (radio and TV for example).

Synchronicity increases the richness of a communication channel by allowing for immediate feedback.

>> **Degree of personalization:** Personalization involves customizing the message to the audience's needs. For example, if you're marketing a medication to doctors, your message will be significantly different from what you use to market the same medication to patients. The richer the communication channel, the greater the opportunity you have to personalize your messaging.

The higher a channel scores in each of these categories, the richer it is and the greater its communication potential. Based on these criteria, communication media can be ranked on a scale from low to high richness. Low-richness media are generally static and text based, such as email and text messages, letters, and formal documents. High-richness media include face-to-face conversations and videoconferences, which allow for immediate feedback, nonverbal cues, and a more personal exchange of information.

According to media richness theory, the greater the complexity of the message, the richer the channel needs to be (see Figure 4-1). Low-richness media is suitable for simple and routine communication, whereas high-richness media is required when the information is complex, feedback is needed, a sensitive subject is being discussed, or a nuanced understanding needs to be reached — when the information is open to multiple interpretations.

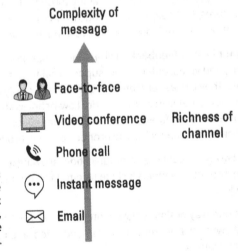

FIGURE 4-1:
The more complex the message, the richer the channel must be.

Media richness theory plays out in day-to-day examples in the workplace and in our personal lives. Say I'm going to meet a colleague for lunch and we need to decide when to meet and where to go. If I were simply telling my colleague, "Meet me at In-N-Out Burger on 16th Street tomorrow at noon," a text message would be sufficient. But if I were going to exchange more information back and forth to decide when and where to meet for lunch, switching to a richer medium (a phone call, for example) would be more efficient.

REMEMBER

Just because a channel is rich doesn't mean it's the best channel to use in a specific situation or that it will be effective. Like any other tool, a communication channel is efficient and effective only if used properly and in the right circumstances.

REMOTE OR IN-PERSON? THAT IS THE QUESTION

I've seen a lot of companies struggle with getting "back to work as normal" in the post-pandemic world. Understandably, employees who could perform just as well, if not better, working remotely aren't always eager to return to the confines of an office, a rigid schedule, and long commutes. To compound the problem, corporate leadership may struggle to justify the need for employees to work onsite when they're just as productive working remotely. Of course, some jobs require a physical presence, but many can be performed just as well remotely.

Whether you're trying to convince your supervisor to allow you to work remotely or you're a supervisor trying to explain to your team why their physical presence is needed, align your tasks and goals with the level of communication richness needed to accomplish those tasks and goals. If you can perform the same tasks and achieve the same goals as effectively and efficiently via low-richness communication channels, such as email and text messaging, then working remotely (entirely or mostly) can be a sensible arrangement. However, if your business outcomes would benefit from deeper personal relationships or frequent interactions and close collaboration, then being present physically may be best. Of course, hybrid arrangements may also be an option — for example, coming into the office one or two days a week and working remotely the other three or four.

What's most important is that you analyze your work situation objectively and your own ability (or your team's ability) to be productive when working remotely. Be honest, fair, and open-minded, whether you're a supervisor or a subordinate.

Considering Your Purpose: Conveyance or Convergence?

Your choice of communication channel depends a great deal on the nature or purpose of the communication task or the goal you're trying to accomplish. When considering the nature or purpose of a communication task or goal, you can look to *media synchronicity theory* (or *MST*) for guidance — it evaluates media based on their ability to support *synchronicity*, "the shared pattern of coordinated behavior among individuals as they work together." MST as expanded on by Alan Dennis, Robert Fuller, and Joseph Valacich suggests that communication involves two primary processes:

>> **Conveyance:** The ability of a communication medium to transmit information accurately and efficiently. Media that are high in conveyance include email and text messaging. For conveyance purposes, low-synchronicity media results in higher efficiency.

>> **Convergence:** The ability of a communication medium to facilitate mutual understanding and coordinate action among group members. Media that are high in convergence are face-to-face meetings and videoconferencing. For convergence purposes, high-synchronicity media are needed to ensure that everyone's on the same page.

To drive home the distinction between conveyance and convergence, think of the last time you sat through a meeting about something that could have been handled with a simple email message. You're sitting in a pointless meeting, twiddling your thumbs, anxious about the pile of work you have sitting on your desk — not very efficient. Why? Because whoever called the meeting used a high *convergence* medium for a high *conveyance* purpose.

REMEMBER

If your task or purpose requires conveyance (think of this as simply transmitting information), choose a communication channel with low synchronicity. If your task or purpose requires convergence (tasks that require coordination and collaboration), choose a communication channel with high synchronicity (see Figure 4-2).

To gauge a channel's level of synchronicity, consider how it stacks up in respect to the following five media capabilities:

>> **Symbol set:** The range and variety of symbols or cues available in a communication medium. Symbol sets include text, images, emojis, body language, variations in volume and tone (when someone's speaking), and more.

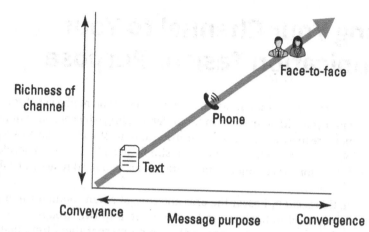

FIGURE 4-2:
Choose a channel based on the degree of conveyance or convergence required.

Richness of channel

Conveyance   Message purpose   Convergence

>> **Parallelism:** The ability to engage in multiple communication activities simultaneously. Videoconferencing, for example, is high in parallelism because it enables participants to speak to one another, see each other, and share documents and screens all at the same time.

>> **Transmission velocity:** The speed at which information can be transmitted and exchanged. Any medium that supports real-time communications, such as face-to-face, phone, or instant messaging, is high in transmission velocity. Communication media that have feedback delays built in, such as documents and videos, are low velocity.

>> **Rehearsability:** The ability of a medium to allow users to review and edit the content before transmitting it. Text-based communication is high in rehearsability, whereas face-to-face communication is low.

>> **Reprocessability:** The ability of a medium to be revisited and reviewed. For example, email is high in reprocessability, whereas a face-to-face conversation is low (unless the conversation is recorded or transcribed).

REMEMBER

Conveyance and convergence aren't mutually exclusive, and neither is better than the other. In fact, as Dennis, Fuller, and Valacich are careful to explain in "Media, Tasks, and Communication Processes: A Theory of Media Synchronicity" (*MIS Quarterly*, September 2008), "The successful completion of most tasks involving more than one individual requires both conveyance and convergence processes, thus communication performance will be improved when individuals use a variety of media to perform a task, rather than just one medium." In other words, when you're communicating or collaborating with others, you may need to employ multiple communication channels (email, instant messaging, in-person meetings, phone calls, and others) to complete the task or achieve your goal.

Matching Your Channel to Your Communication Task or Purpose

Knowing a little about media richness theory and media synchronicity theory provides you with a foundation for understanding why certain communication channels are more effective or more efficient than others in a given situation. However, when you're in the trenches, you simply need to be able to decide which channel is best for the communication task or goal you need to accomplish.

In this section, I cover the pros and cons of seven communication channels commonly used in business and divide them into two groups — synchronous (live) and asynchronous (on demand) — and I present them from highest to lowest in richness. And, as with any choice you make in communication, knowing your audience and their preferences is essential. I cover this extensively in Chapter 12.

Sizing up synchronous communication channels

Synchronous communication channels are those that provide the opportunity for participants to communicate with one another in real time. They include face-to-face, videoconferencing, phone conversation, and synchronous chat.

Face-to-face

Face-to-face is the crème de la crème of communication channels. It has everything you could ever want in a communication channel — the full spectrum of social cues, the ability to give and receive immediate feedback, and the opportunity to personalize the message on the fly. So, if face-to-face is the ultimate communication channel, why not use it all the time? Two reasons:

>> **It's not always an option.** Until humans manage to master the art of teleportation, they don't always have the convenience of interacting face-to-face.

>> **It's not always the most efficient.** For example, if you need to tell a team member to change the text size in the quarterly report from 10 point to 12 point, scheduling a meeting or even walking across the hall to the person's cubicle to deliver the message isn't the most efficient approach. Because your instruction has little chance of being misunderstood, you can deliver it most efficiently via email or instant message.

A synchronous (live, in real time) communication channel is likely to be the best choice when you need to do one or more of the following:

>> Persuade an individual or a group, deliver bad or sensitive news, or share personal information.

>> Quickly exchange ideas with others.

>> Get immediate feedback from participants.

>> Plan a course of action and schedule and delegate tasks.

When your task or purpose is to convey information or instructions that have little chance of being misunderstood, a rich, synchronous communication channel may not be the best match. Email or text is likely to be more efficient and get the job done just as well.

Videoconferencing

Videoconferencing is the next best thing to teleportation and second only to face-to-face on the richness scale. It allows for synchronous communication via audio and video and enables you to converse one on one or meet with dozens, hundreds, or even thousands of people at the same time. Videoconferencing offers several additional advantages, including the following:

>> A convenient and affordable solution for meeting "face to face" when you can't get everyone in the same room. As a bonus, it can be used to reduce travel expenses and your organization's carbon footprint.

>> The ability to share a file or screen with multiple people and allow them to provide feedback and markup at the same time.

>> The ability to collect information via meeting chat while a presentation is ongoing — creating more opportunities for feedback.

>> The option to have the meeting recorded and transcribed or even translated.

However, videoconferencing has some drawbacks, such as these:

>> Technology/connectivity issues can interfere with the ability to connect and communicate.

>> Limited screen space and differences in screen sizes can limit the effectiveness of visuals and make social cues less visible and more difficult to interpret.

>> Participants can turn off their cameras or mics at any time during the conference, eliminating social cues important for communication.

>> When a controlled environment isn't present, opportunities for noise are increased. (See Chapter 2 for more about how noise can disrupt and impair communication.)

REMEMBER

The success of videoconferencing (or any) communication channel depends on the people using it and on the rules and structures in place for the communication. This is why some teams are more successful than others in meeting virtually, even if they have the same goal or desired outcome.

Audio-only calls

A step down in richness from videoconferencing, synchronous audio-only channels (for example, phone calls) support audio social cues, such as variations in volume and intonation when people talk (see Chapter 3), but they lack the ability to convey any visual cues (facial expressions and gestures, for example). Even with that limitation, it's richer than text-based messaging.

Audio-only calls offer the following advantages:

>> Two-way communication among participants physically distant from one another

>> A more personal connection than text-based communication

>> Faster back-and-forth compared to email or text messaging

>> The ability to record conversations for later review

TIP

To experience the difference between audioconferencing and videoconferencing, the next time you're in a videoconference, pay special attention to the quality of communication between those who have their cameras turned on and those who don't. Even when someone has their camera turned off, it's better than texting, but the communication and its effectiveness are better when you have a visual of the other person.

Synchronous chat

Synchronous chat is two-way, real-time, mostly text-based communication. It was popularized by platforms like ICQ and AOL Instant Messenger (AIM) in the late 1990s and is now integrated into the workplace through applications such as iMessage, WhatsApp, Slack, and Microsoft Teams.

Synchronous chat is ideal for situations in which you need to

>> Exchange short messages quickly with someone who's physically distant

>> Communicate whenever and wherever you're unable to speak (for privacy or noise reasons)

>> Save a transcript of the exchange for future reference

REMEMBER

A key advantage that synchronous chat has over other text-based communication channels is that it supports immediate interaction. If the information or meaning being communicated is ambiguous, chat participants can express their confusion and ask questions immediately to gain clarity.

Assessing asynchronous communication channels

Asynchronous communication channels are limited by one key factor that contributes to richness: immediate feedback. Of course, feedback is always an option. If you post a video showing employees how to navigate your company's human resources platform, they can't exactly interact with that video in real time, but they can call their HR rep to ask questions. However, with asynchronous communication, delays are baked in.

In this section, I focus on the richness of asynchronous communication channels, presenting them from highest to lowest in richness.

Video

Thirty years ago, communicating organizational messages via video was reserved for businesses, video-production firms, and anyone with the time, money, and expertise to produce quality footage. Now, anyone with a decent smartphone and a few minutes to spare can shoot a video and share it with billions of people around the world!

Although video is asynchronous, it's especially effective for demonstrating how to perform complex tasks. Every day, millions of people head to YouTube to figure out how to do everything from making crème brulé to maintaining and repairing their vehicles. Video can also come in handy in business for everything from training employees to having the CEO calm investor fears. It supports both verbal and nonverbal communication and provides many social cues.

The one potential drawback to video is that it isn't always the most efficient communication channel. For example, if all you need to know is where to find a particular formatting option in your word processor, you won't sit through a 20-minute video on formatting documents just to get the answer. A more convenient option would be to look it up in the word processor's Help system or in the index of a manual on the topic.

Consider using searchable short-form content to help employees wade through training materials more efficiently. (*Short-form content* is any messaging that's clear and concise and can be processed by an audience in a matter of seconds to a few minutes at most.) Microlearning videos are just as effective, if not more effective, than longer-form training content for many tasks. Smart businesses are creating more and more searchable short-form content for training their employees.

Audio

Audio-only is richer than text but not as rich as the combination of audio and video available through videos. Audio carries variations in volume and tone that can convey emotional content and help listeners interpret the meaning of a message that might otherwise be ambiguous.

To appreciate the distinction between text and audio channels, read a transcription of a speech or interview and then listen to the speech or interview. Both are useful. The transcript provides precisely *what* was said, but the audio provides a better sense of *how* it was said, which may reveal the relative importance of key points, the speaker(s) level of commitment, whether something was said jokingly instead of seriously, and so on. In short, audio enables you to "read between the lines" more effectively.

Text/email

Text-based communication (email, texts, reports, articles, whitepapers, and so on) is at the bottom of the richness scale because it is asynchronous, conveys limited social cues, and is difficult to personalize when communicating across a large, diverse audience. Granted, text can be combined with emojis, GIFs, memes, images, and even videos to enrich it, but even with all that, it lacks the nonverbal communication and interactivity of its richer counterparts.

Yet text can be very effective and efficient when you're not in urgent need of receiving a reply and when used in the right situations, such as the following:

>> To disseminate routine, straightforward information or directives or factual data (such as statistics or direct orders)

>> To document information, procedures, or guidelines

>> To delineate the key points in a contract or agreement

>> To enable the audience to digest complex content at their own pace

>> To communicate with individuals who may not all be available at the same time

>> To communicate a clear and consistent message to a large group of people

REMEMBER

Strictly speaking, text-only communication can convey tone and emotion, especially when you know the person well and can make accurate assumptions about their intended meaning and the tone or emotion they meant to convey. However, when you're communicating with people you don't know very well, especially in situations that can get emotional, assumptions are likely to be skewed and can lead to misinterpretations and even conflict. If you spend much time on social media platforms debating contentious issues, you know how susceptible text is to misinterpretation.

TIP

With advances in generative AI (artificial intelligence that's capable of generating text, images, and videos), you can now personalize text, audio, and video messages for distribution to a broad audience. Using applications such as RenderMe (www.rendermedia.ai), you can link your digital likeness to customize scripts to produce videos with mail-merge-like capabilities in record time. Imagine being able to personalize a message to each member of your team with your likeness on video, in your voice, thanking them for their work on the latest project. Rather than send the same generic message to every team member, you can now personalize individual messages in the same amount of time!

IF I HAD MORE TIME, I WOULD'VE WRITTEN A SHORTER MESSAGE

In his "Lettres Provinciales" in 1657, French mathematician and philosopher Blaise Pascal wrote what translates to "I have made this longer than usual because I have not had time to make it shorter." Later, writers paraphrased the quote to create their own renditions, such as "Sorry this letter is so long. If I had more time, I would have written a shorter one." The point is that communication is best when it's not only effective but also efficient.

I'm not immune from pounding on the keyboard and clicking Send on an email that could've been shorter, clearer, and more to the point. It happens to all of us. But truly dynamic communicators understand that sending the best possible message involves some reflection regarding not only words but also the communication channel.

Make it as easy as possible for people to consume your message—whether it's reading it, listening to it, or viewing it. If a simpler medium can accomplish the same goal, use it. Others may not appreciate or even notice the intentionality of your choice of words and communication channel, but you'll notice and appreciate the benefits in how they respond. Just keep in mind, as Pascal noted, it does take extra time. The return on that investment, though, is worth it.

Choosing your channel wisely

When choosing a communication channel, rely on logic instead of emotion or a strong personal preference for a particular channel. I often see people waste considerable time and suffer unnecessary frustration by choosing what they believe is a more efficient means of communication, such as email or text, when a 15- to 30-minute meeting would be more efficient. They choose a channel that's useful for conveyance when their goal is convergence. As a result, they exchange a half dozen or more text or email messages before they realize that they need to meet to get everyone on the same page.

Suppose you're part of a team of four at your workplace that has come up with what you all feel is a way to reduce production costs. You need to work together with your team to pitch this new method of production to your supervisors in hopes of persuading them to allow you to change processes.

You've already worked together over the past few months to refine this production process. Now you need to create a presentation to convince those who have the power to institute the change. You say to your team members in the hallway, "Hey, let's schedule a 30-minute meeting to work on what we need to do for this presentation."

One team member replies, "Do we need to have a meeting? Can't we just do this over email?"

Not wanting to rock the boat, you try to conduct the meeting via email. You send an initial message that describes five essential tasks and requests the team's input.

Then it starts: the Reply All onslaught.

One team member is okay with three of the five but wants two of them changed. Another team member agrees with one of the changes but not the others and recommends a sixth task. And the fourth team member says they'll do whatever the group wants.

Over a dozen emails later (and after much more than 30 minutes has passed), you have no resolution. In fact, you have more questions than answers.

Sound familiar?

You step up and say, "Okay, we can't seem to agree on the basics, and I don't have the time or patience for another dozen emails. Let's meet for 30 minutes to knock out this task list and then divide and conquer."

Now your team agrees on the need for a meeting.

You meet for 30 minutes, agree on six tasks, delegate, set tentative milestones and deadlines, and partner up. You agree to communicate via instant messenger and email to share information and insights and ask and answer questions, and then you all agree to meet in person as soon as the tasks are completed to review and combine everything.

Well, that was certainly much more effective *and* efficient!

The story you just read is one that happens all too often in the workplace. The common mistake of choosing the wrong channel wastes time and stresses everyone involved. And you can avoid it by choosing the right communication channel from the start.

2

Improving Your Interpersonal Communication

Recognize the six levels of listening, sharpen your listening skills, and understand the importance of listening more than you speak.

Take your listening skills to the next level with three advanced listening techniques: paraphrasing, mirroring, and summarizing.

Nurture your natural curiosity to make it your business communication superpower.

Master the fine art of asking questions — to extract the information and insight you need, clarify your understanding, steer conversations, and buy time to formulate more thoughtful responses.

Make your business conversations more meaningful and productive by practicing reciprocity and self-disclosure and finding ways to create mutual meaning.

Chapter **5**

Listening More Than You Speak

Business communication typically focuses on crafting and delivering messages and presentations that have the desired effect on an audience. The focus is rarely on listening, even though listening accounts for a significant portion of every interaction.

If you're engaged entirely in speaking or presenting a message, without devoting at least a portion of your time to listening, you're missing a golden opportunity to learn from your audience and tailor your message to improve the audience's receptivity and understanding. Even if your goal is to persuade others, listening to them first provides you with the information and insight you need to achieve your goal. Think about it: If you don't know what your audience is thinking, you can't possibly address any questions, concerns, or rebuttals they may have regarding your message. You even run an increased risk of saying something that makes them reject what you're saying or negatively impacts what they think of you.

Imagine planning for a battle without giving any consideration to your enemy's forces, weapons, battlefield positions, or possible counter-maneuvers. With some luck and overwhelming force, you could still win, but you'd probably encounter some nasty surprises. For the same reasons, listening before speaking provides you with the intelligence you need to tailor your communications to your audience for the best chance of success.

WHY DON'T SCHOOLS OFFER LISTENING COURSES?

Something that has always baffled me about business schools is that they rarely, if ever, offer or require a course devoted specifically to helping students develop their listening skills. Considering the fact that listening is one of the most critical skills in business, not to mention a major factor in personal success, the lack of attention it is given in education is shocking.

The purpose of this chapter is to give you what a course in listening would entail boiled down to a dozen or so pages. This topic alone could consume an entire book.

In this chapter, I take the spotlight off crafting and delivering messages and shine it on the importance of listening and understanding. Here you discover why listening skills are so valuable, how to prioritize listening over speaking, and how to sharpen your listening skills. The skills you develop in this chapter are sure to make you a much more effective communicator in the workplace and beyond.

REMEMBER

Effective communicators are naturally curious and are skilled listeners. They want to know what their audience is thinking before they open their mouths to speak, before they craft a presentation, and before they send any email or text messages. You can become a more effective communicator by prioritizing listening and developing your listening skills. In this chapter, I explain how.

Recognizing the Difference between Hearing and Listening

If you're like me, when you were growing up, you probably heard a parent, guardian, or teacher say to you, "You're not listening to me."

To which I would often reply, "I heard you!"

Hearing, however, is not the same as listening, which also implies understanding. In my case, the point that the adults in the room were trying to get across to me was that I wasn't receptive to what they were telling me and that I wasn't processing it mentally in a way that demonstrated we had reached a mutual understanding.

The differences between hearing and listening are significant. In this section, I highlight the differences and explain what really needs to happen cognitively for listening to occur.

Moving from mechanical to cognitive processes

The difference between hearing and listening boils down to the difference between a mostly mechanical and a mostly cognitive process. Hearing has more to do with the physical, mechanical process that happens in the outer, middle, and inner ear. Listening has more to do with cognitive processes that occur *between* the ears — in the brain. Throughout the day, your ear registers all the sounds that reach it, but your brain screens out and ignores most of that auditory data so that it can focus on what's important.

In the simplest terms possible, hearing occurs when sounds are perceived through an auditory organ such as the ear (see Figure 5-1). The outer ear acts as a megaphone, directing sound waves to the eardrum and causing it to vibrate. Those vibrations pass through the middle ear to the inner ear, where tiny hair cells inside the cochlea pick up the vibrations and transfer them to the auditory nerve. The signals then travel along the auditory nerve to the brain stem and on to the temporal lobe, where the sound is recorded. That process is hearing.

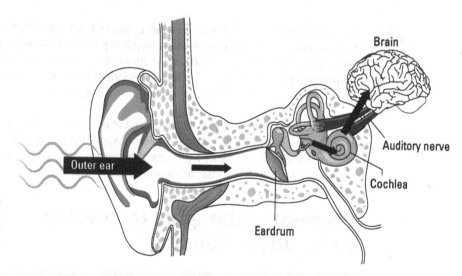

FIGURE 5-1:
Hearing occurs when sound travels from the ear to the brain.

Listening, however, is the process of extracting meaning from those electrical impulses. (See Figure 5-2) Initially, the brain records those electrical impulses in the temporal lobe but doesn't assign them meaning until they reach the frontal lobe. In other words, you can hear what someone is saying without fully understanding it. You've probably experienced this yourself if someone has ever tried to talk to you while you were concentrating intensely on something else; for example, as you were busy weaving through rush hour traffic on a six-lane highway, your bestie was asking you for relationship advice. You heard the words, but they may not have registered in your brain.

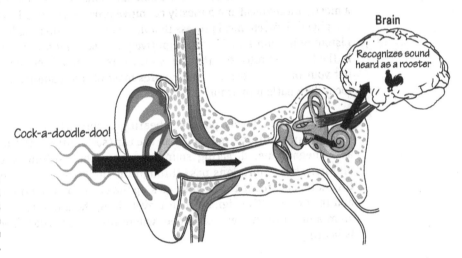

FIGURE 5-2:
Listening occurs when meaning is extracted from sounds in the brain.

REMEMBER

If someone tells you, "You may be hearing me, but you sure aren't listening," they may well be correct. Hearing is only a physical process. Listening is a physical *and* mental process. For example, if you're distracted, you may hear what somebody's telling you just fine, but you're not processing it effectively. It's not registering. And in some instances, this processing doesn't happen at all.

In fact, some people — mostly children and older adults — have a condition called *auditory processing disorder* (APD). A person with APD has healthy auditory anatomy, but their brain doesn't process the signals it receives from the auditory nerve. APD isn't hearing loss; it's a processing complication.

Processing thoughts to develop a fuller understanding

Mental processing often goes beyond converting an audio signal into a thought. It includes synthesizing thoughts and experiences to make sense of the new thoughts in the entire body of knowledge and understanding stored in the brain. For example, when my mom would tell me, "If you don't finish your homework now, you won't have enough daylight later to play basketball with the neighbors," I heard her, but I didn't listen to or process what she said.

I'd reply, "Yeah, Mom, I heard you."

She'd say, "You say you heard me, but you're not *listening*."

And I'd say, tauntingly, "I did listen. You said that if I don't finish my homework now, I won't have enough daylight later to play basketball with the neighbors." So, yeah, I heard my mom. I could even repeat her words back to her.

What happened, though, is that I had stored what my mom said in my short-term memory. The words were in my temporal lobe but didn't progress to my prefrontal cortex, where my brain could analyze them and understand the reasoning my mom was trying to impart. (My annoyance with my mom probably played a role in my resistance to processing what she was telling me.) I didn't realize that my mom actually had my back; she *wanted* me to be able to play basketball with the neighbors! It didn't occur to me until the sun went down and there wasn't enough daylight left to play outside that she wasn't being mean or nagging; she was trying to help me plan more effectively so that I could finish my homework *and* play basketball. (Sorry, Mom. I know now that you were right — I didn't always listen!)

Listening is actually a three-stage process (see Figure 5-3):

1. The physical act of hearing the words

2. Translation of the audio (or visual, if communicating with ASL) signals into words and thoughts

3. Processing the words and phrases into meaning, context, and action

FIGURE 5-3:
Listening is a
three-stage
process.

Most people are pretty effective at hearing (in the first two stages), because those require little effort. The third stage, however, requires paying attention and putting forth some intentional, cognitive effort.

This three-stage process is why ongoing dialogue is important — to ensure that everyone involved in the communication session has a mutual understanding. People need to check in with one another to verify that their thoughts and mental concepts are closely aligned and to address any understandings that are out of alignment. (See the later section "Summarizing to check your understanding" for details.)

Checking for mutual understanding during and after an interaction is one of the most crucial and most frequently overlooked steps in business communication (and in personal communication as well).

Recognizing the six levels of listening

People listen at different levels of attentiveness and cognitive engagement. Various experts in communication have proposed various levels of listening. Here, I offer a comprehensive list of six levels of listening:

» **Ignoring**: No attention is paid at all. The person may be preoccupied with their own thoughts or distracted by something externally, causing them to effectively tune out the speaker.

» **Pretend listening**: The person gives the appearance of listening without being fully engaged. For example, you may maintain eye contact and nod occasionally in agreement, but your mind is somewhere else.

» **Selective listening**: The listener pays attention only to certain parts of what the speaker is saying, typically focusing only on information that interests them or aligns with their preconceived notions.

» **Attentive listening**: Attentive listeners engage with the speaker, ask questions for clarification, and make a genuine effort to understand what they're being told.

» **Empathic listening**: The listener not only makes a conscious effort to understand the meaning of what the speaker is saying but also tunes into their feelings and perspective. Empathic listeners strive to understand the speaker on a deeper level and create a supportive environment for open communication.

» **Generative listening**: At this level, the listener is involved in co-creating new possibilities and insights. Generative listening involves keeping an open mind, suspending judgment, and exploring innovative solutions and ideas that emerge from the dialogue. This level of listening often leads to transformative change, decisive action, and deep collaboration.

Whenever you're in the role of listener, be mindful of how actively engaged you are on a cognitive level. If you're not at the attentive listening stage or higher, you need to tune in. If you're distracted or simply not interested at the moment, consider rescheduling, if possible. You're not doing yourself or anyone else any favors by ignoring them, pretending to listen, or paying attention to only what you want to hear.

Understanding before Responding or Reacting

One of the biggest mistakes people make when communicating in the business world is responding or reacting impulsively to something they misunderstand or don't fully understand. You may have had situations in which you wish you hadn't sent a certain email or text message, or you posted something on social media that you later regretted when you had a better understanding.

To avoid these uncomfortable situations, take the advice of Stephen Covey, author of *The 7 Habits of Highly Effective People* (Simon & Schuster): "Seek first to understand, and then to be understood." Specifically, adopt the following best practices:

>> **Give the other person your undivided attention.** Listen to understand without thinking about how you're going to respond to what they're saying. Stay in the moment.

>> **Give the other person the benefit of the doubt.** In other words, assume the best about the person and their situation instead of assuming the worst. Assume they had good reason to say or do what they said or did, at least until you have a fuller understanding of their situation and motives.

>> **Don't interrupt.** Let the other person speak freely until they've completed whatever they have to say.

REMEMBER

Fighting the temptation to interrupt can be difficult when you believe that the other person is presenting false or misleading information, or is monopolizing the conversation. Try your best to be patient. In many cases, you can learn a great deal from listening that empowers you to respond more effectively.

>> **Listen without judgment.** Set aside any preconceived ideas, biases, or judgments about the speaker and what they're saying. Keep an open mind and remain curious.

>> **Empathize.** Try to put yourself in the speaker's shoes. Consider what you would think and how you would feel if you were in the speaker's position or had the speaker's experience.

>> **Ask clarifying questions.** Demonstrate a genuine interest in understanding the speaker by asking questions about anything that's unclear. Ask open-ended questions (as opposed to yes/no questions) to encourage the speaker to share information and insights you may not even think to ask about.

>> **Check your understanding.** Summarize your understanding of what you've been told to give the speaker the opportunity to correct any misunderstanding and fill any gaps in your understanding. See the later section "Summarizing to check your understanding" for additional guidance.

Listening More Than You Speak (or Think)

In Lin Manuel Miranda's *Hamilton*, Alexander Burr, portrayed by Leslie Odom, Jr, sings these sardonic lines: "[T]alk less, smile more . . . don't let them know what you're against or what you're for." Though these lines are the quintessential essence of politics and straddling the proverbial fence, they deliver sage advice about talking less and keeping your thoughts to yourself — at least until you fully understand what others are thinking and feeling.

When you were growing up, you probably received similar advice from your parents, teachers, or other authority figures who may not have cared much for what you had to say. You've probably heard that you have two ears and one mouth for a reason — so you should listen twice as much as you talked. Or you may have been told, "Better to remain silent and appear stupid than to open your mouth and remove all doubt." (Rude? Maybe. But also accurate in many situations.)

I don't agree with the homespun wisdom about the benefits of keeping one's mouth shut, but listening more than you speak does have its benefits, as I'm about to explain.

Stop planning what you're going to say next

If you're thinking about what you're going to say in response to what you're hearing, you aren't listening at a high level. At worst, you're totally ignoring the other person. At best, you're listening selectively to pick out the information you plan to respond to. Either way, you'll never reach the mutual understanding needed to have a productive discussion.

REMEMBER

Multitasking is a myth. The human brain isn't geared for it. If you try to multi-task, you end up shifting your attention back and forth from one task to the other. If you're thinking about what you're going to say next in a conversation, you can't possibly be fully engaged in listening and processing what you're hearing. If you're thinking about what to say when the other person is speaking, you miss out on some of what they're saying.

TIP

If you're listening to someone and think of something you want to be sure to remember to say, write a note immediately and then refocus on listening. Sometimes, the fear of forgetting the thought drives a person to start crafting their response instead of listening. Eliminate this fear and temptation by writing a brief note — a single word or even a symbol is often a sufficient reminder of what you want to contribute to the conversation.

Finding power in silence and strength in waiting

Silence is a powerful tool in communication. Whether you're speaking, presenting, or negotiating, a pregnant pause can send a powerful message or increase the impact of what you're about to say or have already said. Silence can be equally powerful, if not more so, when you're listening. When you pause to listen, people tend to feel compelled to fill that void. Silence benefits you and others involved in the conversation in at least two ways:

>> Silence gives you time and space to receive and process information.

>> Pausing gives others the time and space to formulate their own thoughts and express them more clearly.

TIP

When you want someone to arrive at their own conclusion about something they proposed, or a question they asked that you're pretty sure they know the answer to, wait in silence. People often need to talk and reason out a problem in their own minds to arrive at a solution. And if they don't come up with the answer on their own, that pause in the conversation may give you all the time you need to come up with the perfect solution. This technique is especially effective in sales. When a prospective customer concludes on their own that what you're selling is the perfect solution for their needs, they feel much more confident in their purchase decision.

However, waiting requires considerable patience and confidence, so be prepared to put forth some effort.

EXAMPLE

When I used to teach undergraduate business communication courses and wanted to engage the class in discussion and not lecture for the entire period, I would pose questions to the students. Sometimes I would get immediate engagement. Other times, I was met with blank stares and silence. These moments of silence could become quite long and uncomfortable, but I would continue to wait . . . and wait . . . and wait. I only had to do this a couple of times. My students quickly picked up on the fact that if they didn't contribute to the discussion, they faced a long and *boring* class.

Stepping Up to More Advanced Listening Techniques

You've mastered basic listening skills. You give people your undivided attention, engage your mind in trying to understand what they're telling you, put yourself in their shoes to understand how they feel, and ask questions to extract additional information and gain insight. What more can you do to improve your listening skills? In this section, I answer that question as I bring you up to speed on a few advanced listening techniques.

Paraphrasing

Paraphrasing involves repeating what the speaker said in your own words to demonstrate your understanding. Paraphrasing is *not* repeating something back word-for-word — that's *parroting*. The idea of paraphrasing is that you demonstrate not only that you listened but that you also processed what was being said enough to come to a conclusion or to ask a thoughtful question. Paraphrasing allows a conversation to advance with mutual understanding. (See "Summarizing to check your understanding," later in this chapter, for phrases to help you better paraphrase what you've listened to in conversations.)

Don't paraphrase after every sentence, only at the end of a major train of thought.

Mirroring, without being a copycat

Mirroring is a technique that involves reflecting back the speaker's actions or emotions. It's a way of physically demonstrating empathy and establishing a bond with the other person. Suppose you're feeling a little down when you visit a friend. Your friend is over the moon about something that recently happened in their life and can't contain their energy when they share it with you. If you're truly listening at an empathic level, your mood starts to improve. Your situation and feelings become less about you and more about your friend, and you start to mirror their emotions. That's a positive example of mirroring in practice.

PARROTING IS FOR THE BIRDS

A friend of mine has an African gray parrot. This bird is 18 years old and has developed quite an extensive and colorful vocabulary. (Really, think of all the things you've said and done at home over the past 18 years and try not to laugh at the thought of a parrot witnessing it all.) And, like any parrot you see characterized on television, in media, and especially in cartoons, it is in fact a parrot; it repeats what it hears, and the owner has little to no control over what it says or when . . usually at the most inopportune times in the most inappropriate contexts.

Though this bird may have some personality and impressive diction, the way it learns and communicates should not be a strategy for you as a human, especially in a business setting. Don't merely repeat back to others what they say. Paraphrase, don't parrot.

Forcing emotions or copying the other person in a mocking way is an example of bad mirroring. When someone leans in to a conversation, you lean in. When the other person become animated, you become animated. When they gesture wildly, you start waving your arms. If you're trying to mirror and you start to feel like you're focusing more on mirroring than you are on listening, or if you're feeling like a copycat, then you're probably doing it wrong and you would be better off not doing it.

REMEMBER

Mirroring can be an effective technique when it comes naturally, but if it's forced, it can do more harm than good.

Summarizing to check your understanding

In any communicative exchange, participants run the risk of *interpretation dissonance*, which is a fancy term for misunderstanding. The meaning the speaker intended to convey differs from the meaning the listeners interpreted. I'm not sure that misunderstandings can ever be eliminated completely — after all, no two people have the exact same life experiences, perspectives, or behaviors — but you can reduce interpretation dissonance significantly as a listener by checking with the speaker to determine whether your understanding is aligned with their intended meaning — that you're on the same page.

Whenever you're engaged in a conversation as a listener, check in periodically with the speaker. Don't wait till the end of the conversation to ensure mutual understanding. Here are some phrases you can use to introduce your summarization:

> Before we move on to the next topic, I want to confirm that we're on the same page. . . .

> Let me summarize what we just discussed to make sure I'm capturing all the relevant points.

> I want to make sure we're aligned before we move to the next stage of this conversation.

> Of everything we just discussed, I would love to know what you feel is the most important first step.

Having these check-ins ensures that you're listening actively throughout the conversation and enables you to leave the conversation confident that you've achieved a mutual understanding.

At the end of any conversation, make sure all parties involved are crystal-clear on any next steps. Better yet, document what those next steps are by writing down answers to the following questions:

>> What's the goal or deliverable?

>> What's our deadline for meeting that goal?

>> What are the measurable objectives we need to achieve to meet our goal?

>> What's the plan?

>> Who's in charge?

>> What are each person's responsibilities?

>> When will we meet next?

Don't assume that everyone understands the plan and their role in executing it. Document the plan and make it explicit so that everyone has a crystal-clear understanding of what they need to do and when they need to have it done. I've seen many meetings end with assumptions that lead to significant losses of time and money due to a lack of follow-through.

Even when you do your best to listen, miscommunication can occur if you don't confirm mutual understanding.

Chapter 6

Leveraging the Communication Power of Asking Questions

Communication can be defined as the exchange of ideas and information through the use of written and spoken language, body language, visuals, and other media. This definition doesn't state directly that questions are being asked, but asking questions and paying close attention to the replies are essential to any successful interaction. In some cases, they're the most important part of an interaction because questions solidify and expand the ideas and information being exchanged and enable relationships to develop beyond the conversation.

Questions serve many purposes. They enable you to engage others in conversation, extract information, deepen your understanding, achieve mutual understanding, evaluate someone's knowledge and skills, promote self-reflection and discovery, and even spark innovative ideas and solutions. In this chapter, I provide guidance on how to nurture your natural curiosity, ask questions to extract information and improve your understanding, and use questions to initiate dialogue and steer a conversation in the desired direction.

Making Curiosity Your Superpower

In any communication scenario, curiosity is a superpower. I'm talking natural curiosity here — a genuine desire to know and understand. I consider it a superpower because of all the valuable benefits it bestows on the most inquisitive people, including benefits in the following areas:

>> **Innovation:** Curiosity drives innovation. Curious people tend to be more innovative and inspire innovation in others. Asking customers about their problems often reveals a need for a new product or service to solve those problems. Asking whether a process your team follows is as efficient and cost-effective as it can be may generate ideas to improve it. Though not everything needs to be questioned, a natural curiosity (not always accepting things as they seem) can be a massive benefit to growth.

>> **Problem-solving:** Curiosity facilitates problem-solving by identifying problems that might otherwise remain unnoticed, by tracing symptoms of a problem to their root cause, and by inventing and evaluating possible solutions. My dad taught me, at a young age, to ask "Why?" at least five times. Now, although this advice later backfired on him and my mom when I wouldn't accept the reply "Because I said so" as a valid reason from them, it did improve all of our communication and understanding because I got to learn the reasons behind the why — even if I didn't always agree with them.

REMEMBER

You don't always need to solve a problem on your own. You may simply be the person who asked the question that made everyone on your team aware of the problem and rallied the team to solve it. But be aware of constantly being the one pointing out issues and never coming to the table with possible solutions.

>> **Understanding:** Curiosity leads to deeper understanding and can help clear up any misunderstandings. Whether you're seeking insight into a specific market, a trend, your customers' needs, your competitors' strategies, your company's culture, or your team's experience, a genuine curiosity can be the impetus for conducting the research and analysis that provides you with that insight. Good questions reveal insights that can drive positive change.

>> **Continuous learning:** Curiosity is the impetus for learning. It's what drives people in business to stay on top of industry trends, technologies, and best practices and to remain future-focused. When you're asking questions with the sincere intent to learn, everyone around you benefits. I tell my team members that the day they don't come to the table with a willingness to learn is the day they don't need to even come to work.

>> **Risk management:** Risk management is a continuous cycle of identifying, analyzing, mitigating, and monitoring threats and uncertainties, and curiosity

helps at every stage in that cycle. When you're curious, you're on constant alert for anything that threatens your organization's success, including its own weaknesses and external factors, such as competitors, changes in consumer behaviors, and disruptive technologies.

I know, you get it now. Being curious is definitely a superpower, and it has benefits beyond what you may have considered. But now you face two challenges — how to:

>> Nurture your natural curiosity

>> Use your natural curiosity in a practical way to obtain the information and understanding you need to communicate more effectively

In the following sections, I suggest two ways to meet these challenges.

Think of yourself as a sleuth

You've probably heard of Sherlock Holmes, arguably the most famous literary detective ever created and the central character in numerous novels penned by Sir Arthur Conan Doyle. As a detective, Holmes was able to solve nearly any case. Aside from his logical reasoning prowess, two qualities that made him successful were his curiosity and his willingness not to make assumptions or to jump to conclusions too quickly. His natural curiosity inspired him to ask all the right questions, challenge assumptions, follow the right trail of clues, and successfully interrogate suspects and potential witnesses.

To nurture your inner sleuth, remain on the lookout for opportunities to practice your investigative skills. Ask questions of yourself and others. Look for problems and seek out their root causes. If you're engaged in an altercation with someone, pause and remind yourself to start asking questions until you fully understand the other person's point of view. Try to identify inefficient or ineffective processes at work or home that could be improved. If you find yourself wondering about anything, start asking questions and researching the topic. In short, practice being curious.

Also, nurture the following skills that are characteristic of the best detectives:

>> **Paying attention to detail:** A supersleuth notices details that others tend to overlook. These small details can make a considerable difference not only in your understanding but also in how you communicate about a situation. Your attention to detail is conveyed in your communication. It ensures that everyone in the conversation has the information and understanding they need to fully engage in a productive way.

>> **Nurturing an analytical mindset:** Analysis enables you to extract meaning from data; identify gaps, inconsistencies, and anomalies in the data you have; and break down and explain complex and perhaps confusing information and present it in a way that makes it more accessible to your audience. The best detectives are able to not only solve difficult criminal cases but also explain the reasoning process they followed to analyze the evidence and draw their conclusion from it. As a communicator, being able to explain the process or thought pattern behind a solution you offer is a strength.

>> **Displaying interviewing prowess:** Capable detectives are skilled interrogators, but I'm not suggesting that you grill people under an intense floodlight to extract answers from them. Being overly aggressive in your questioning can cause people to shut down or give you wrong or misleading information. Always ask questions inspired by your genuine curiosity or interest in knowing and understanding the facts and the situation.

TIP

Listen more than you talk. Ask the question and then remain silent. Take in all the information that someone is willing to share with you — both verbal and nonverbal. Then process, analyze, and report your understanding of the relevant information back to the person to confirm your mutual understanding and give the person a chance to correct any misunderstanding. This approach is especially important when someone's actions (nonverbal communication and gestures) don't match their words (verbal communication).

>> **Maintaining adaptability:** Great communicators, just like great detectives, need to be able to adapt to what people say *and* how they say it (their preferred communication style). For example, if you're asking questions and not receiving the level of interaction you expect or the information you need, change your approach. One way to adapt is to switch from asking close-ended questions to asking open-ended questions. (See the nearby sidebar, "Closed-ended and open-ended questions," for an explanation of the difference between the two.)

Challenge your assumptions

A common adage in the United States warns that "when you assume, you make an ass of you and me" (ass-u-me). Though this clever play on the word's spelling is memorable, it's also highly relevant to the topic of communication. Making assumptions can lead to numerous negative consequences in both business and personal interactions, such as these:

CLOSED-ENDED AND OPEN-ENDED QUESTIONS

Questions fall into two traditional categories: Close-ended questions ask respondents to choose from a distinct set of predefined responses, such as "Is the report ready for review [yes or no]?" or "We have that model car in four trim options: base, premium, limited edition, and touring. Which would you prefer?" Open-ended questions require more thoughtful, detailed responses; for example, "Can you walk me through your team's approach to solving complex problems?" or "How would you improve our customer service?"

Close-ended questions are geared toward gathering information. Open-ended questions are designed to extract insights. Effective open-ended questions prompt the audience to start thinking beyond a single piece of information or data. It challenges them to consider information in a certain context and use it to make a complex decision or come up with a solution. Here are some general open-ended questions you can use to pivot conversations to get more detail on any topic you choose:

What do you feel about _____?

What are your thoughts on _____?

What is your experience with _____?

What is your opinion on _____?

What would you do if _____?

What could be improved with _____?

What change would you make to _____?

>> **Communication breakdowns:** When you assume, especially incorrectly, your presentation or conversation can be taken in an entirely different direction than the one you intended. Suppose that the marketing team assumes that the product features they're promoting are those that the product development team shared in a meeting two weeks ago. However, the product development team continued to make changes based on customer feedback and now, everything the marketing team has started sending out to customers is all wrong.

>> **Bad decisions:** False assumptions result in making decisions based on wrong information or misunderstandings. For example, assuming that all you need is a website to generate interest in your business, you invest thousands of dollars in building a website that draws little traffic — a total waste of money that could have been used for more effective marketing efforts. Similarly, assuming that you have all the information in a situation without confirming that you do can cause significant problems.

>> **Conflict:** Making false assumptions about who was responsible for saying or doing something that harmed you or your organization in some way, or about their intent, can result in unnecessary tension, cause costly distractions, and damage relationships with team members, clients, customers, and others within and outside your organization. Conflict itself isn't bad — it's how people grow. However, unnecessary conflict — caused by making assumptions — can cause problems you don't anticipate. (I cover more about conflict in Chapter 16.)

REMEMBER

Beware of anything you believe to be true that's not based on solid information and facts, including what you're told and haven't observed or experienced yourself. Ask yourself, "What evidence do I have that this is fact?" If you have no evidence, or the evidence you have is weak, gather more information and insight to confirm or refute what you assumed to be true. This is where being a supersleuth comes into play! Challenge your own assumptions before making decisions.

Asking Questions to Extract Information and Clarify Your Understanding

Curiosity is a desire to know and understand. It's necessary, but without follow-through, it's insufficient for gaining knowledge and understanding. You have to act on that curiosity by asking questions and processing the information you receive to ask even better questions. As a sentient human being, you already know how to ask basic questions. You've been doing it (nonverbally, anyway) from before the time you uttered your first words. But you can hone that skill to become a more effective communicator.

REMEMBER

Think of asking questions as an art. In this section, you begin to learn the brushstrokes.

Understanding the distinction between information and knowledge

Information is data or facts that are organized, structured, or presented in a meaningful context. *Knowledge*, on the other hand, encompasses understanding, insight, and the ability to apply information effectively to complete a task or achieve an objective. Consider the distinction in the context of learning a second language. You can know all the information required to communicate in that language — the vocabulary, grammar, and so on — and still be unable to communicate effectively with someone in that language. To carry on a conversation, you'd need the knowledge gained from experience, reasoning, and reflection. You'd need to connect the language to your existing knowledge about the world and understand the meaning of words and phrases in the context of the real world.

Another way to appreciate the difference between information and knowledge is to compare examples in the context of sales and marketing (see Table 6-1).

TABLE 6-1   ## Information versus Knowledge

Information	Knowledge
Statistics	**What the numbers mean in a situation**
Sales increased 25% Q1 to Q2	Though sales revenue increased 25% from quarter to quarter, this is 20% below the projected amount in our company's annual growth strategy plan.
[Sounds good, right? But with knowledge, you gain insights to the data.]	
Price	**The value the product or service provides**
Subscriptions start at $200 per month	Our competitors' plans start at $50 per month and provide you with 15 minutes of content. Though our plans start at a higher monthly rate, our base plan gives you immediate access to all features and 75 minutes of content. That starts at $200 a month.
[Okay, but what is that rate compared to others?]	
Term (Timeline)	**What can be achieved in a specific period**
No minimum contracts	We have no minimum contract term because we want you to be happy using the service with the ability to cancel at any time. What we find, though, is that customers who have the most success with the platform are active within the first three months of service.
[You're missing an opportunity to give meaning to the data, as you'll see in the next cell.]	

The difference between information and knowledge is vast. The way humans record and recall information versus how they use it to understand concepts and motivate action are very different processes. The way people listen for information and the way they listen to acquire knowledge are also two very different processes. For example, if you ask your supervisor, "What time are we meeting tomorrow?" you're then listening for a specific bit of information, such as "10 A.M." However, if you ask, "Why are we meeting tomorrow?" you're then listening to acquire knowledge so that you can prepare for the meeting. Your supervisor replies, "We'll be brainstorming ideas for improving our productivity." Now your brain doesn't merely record a bit of information to recall it later — instead, begins to think about ideas to share with the team.

REMEMBER

To move an audience to any type of action, which is the point of most communication in a business setting, you need to make sure that people are listening not merely to capture and regurgitate information but also to apply that information in a specific context or choose a certain course of action.

Asking questions to extract information

Questions that merely extract information are the most basic. You're simply requesting a fact or a data point. These are usually Who/When/Where questions; for example, "Who's leading the project?" and "When do you need the project completed?" and "Where are we planning to build new stores?" These questions and others like them are simply fact-based questions. The responses to them don't increase your knowledge or understanding or persuade you to change your thoughts or behaviors or follow a certain course of action.

Asking questions to gain knowledge

Questions people ask for the purpose of gaining knowledge require more complex responses. These are usually What/Why/How questions (see Table 6-2). For example, you might ask, "What are the key factors that drive sales of our product?" or "Why are we seeing a sudden increase in incident reports from Plant 5?" or "How can we increase employee retention?" These questions are phrased to elicit responses that increase your knowledge and understanding. The responses to them have the potential to change your thoughts or behavior or persuade you to follow a certain course of action.

TIP

When you're trying to increase your knowledge and understanding of your communication partner who is merely giving you information, ask knowledge questions to steer the conversation in the desired direction. The ultimate goal is to gain insight into your communication partner's needs and desires so that you can present information in a favorable (convincing) context.

TABLE 6-2

Information Questions versus Knowledge Questions

To Gain Information	To Gain Knowledge
Who	What
Where	Why
When	How

EXAMPLE

Suppose you're selling car insurance. Before you even present the policy to your clients, they say, "All we need to know are the deductible and premium amounts." Those are two facts. The clients are probably planning to compare those numbers to their current policy to make their decision, but you know that those two pieces of data don't tell the full story; the policy you're offering has extra protections and a vanishing deductible along with other benefits your prospective client isn't considering. You need to steer their minds in a different direction — to change their knowledge and understanding. So, after giving them the two numbers they requested, you ask, "When you're comparing policies, what's most important to you: the premium or the deductible?" This question acknowledges the two concerns the clients raised and gives you more information to figure out the next question to ask. With this answer, you'll be given data that can help you make a stronger case to broaden their understanding, which can make them more open to considering the policy you're presenting.

Seeking clarification with follow-up questions

Follow-up questions enable you to dig deeper, uncover underlying issues, narrow the scope of your inquiry, or guide a conversation to a specific objective. They're especially useful when you need additional information and insight to clarify your own understanding before expressing your opinion or delivering your presentation.

EXAMPLE

Go back to the car insurance example in the earlier section "Asking questions to gain knowledge." You ask your clients, "When you're comparing policies, what's most important to you: the premium or the deductible?" They reply, "Both are equally important." Now you're back at square one. You didn't elicit the thoughtful response you had hoped for. Fortunately, all is not lost — you can always ask a follow-up question. That first question was a close-ended question, so, to encourage your clients to open up, you decide to follow up with an open-ended question.

"That's understandable," you say, "because both are important factors when selecting a policy. Let me rewind a second and ask another question: What made you decide to shop around for other policies in the first place?"

They respond this way: "Well, we've been with this company for a few years and haven't filed a single claim or had any traffic tickets, and our premium for the same policy just increased substantially. So we decided it was time to start investigating other options."

That response provides valuable information that you can use. You now know that the premium is the clients' biggest concern and that they haven't filed a claim or had any traffic violations in several years — an important detail that may qualify them for a lower premium.

You confirm what you heard and then push a little further by saying, "It sounds like the premium is what's most important to you, but the deductible is also important. Because you haven't filed a claim or had any traffic violations in several years, I can probably reduce the premium I initially quoted you. How do you feel about a deductible that decreases each six-month period you go without filing a claim?"

Notice that you could have asked close-ended questions, such as whether they knew about policies with deductibles that decrease over time, but by asking an open-ended follow-up question, you're likely to extract a more thoughtful response. They reply, "If we had had that benefit with our previous policy, we wouldn't be shopping for a new policy. Tell us more about that."

DITCH THE SCRIPT

Think of the worst sales call you've ever received. You know the one — the caller strictly followed a script. Even when you responded with an answer that was totally irrelevant and intended to disrupt the caller's line of questioning, they proceeded to ask the very next question. The person wasn't interested in having a conversation; they had a job to do, and maybe a quota to meet.

Obviously, that person was not an adaptable communicator! You don't want to be like that person. When you're communicating with others, strive to engage in a conversation with them. You may have written some notes, but be prepared to go off script and listen when the people you're communicating with have something to say that they truly need for you to hear.

There is no one-size-fits-all script for communicating with unique (and complex!) human beings. Humans want to be treated as individuals. Though you may have guidelines for a conversation, being able to pivot and to personalize a conversation to your communicative partner is a vital skill.

Bam! You have the conversation right where you want it. You're about to drop the knowledge that will help them make the decision that, had you given them just the number price on the policy, wouldn't have provided you the opportunity to close the sale.

Using Questions and Guardrails to Initiate and Guide Conversations

Although the primary purpose of asking a question is to get an answer, you can also use questions to initiate conversations and steer them in the desired direction. In this section, I explain how to use questions and guardrails to encourage people to open up and to guide them in subtle ways toward the desired destination.

Asking safe questions to get the conversation moving

You can obtain insight from people only if they choose to share it, and people share only when they feel safe. To get people to start talking and open up, consider asking them what they think, feel, or have experienced by posing questions such as these about your chosen topic:

» What do you think about _____ ?

» What's your opinion of _____ ?

» How does _____ make you feel?

» What has been your experience with _____ ?

These questions are safe because they do not have any wrong answers. People can freely answer them with no fear of being incorrect. They're also open-ended questions, so they prompt people to share their knowledge and insights. And, they get the ball rolling, so you can start to steer the conversation in the desired direction with follow-up questions.

EXAMPLE

Imagine that you're meeting with your brand-new team. All of you were brought together to achieve a specific goal, and none of you has ever worked together. You were asked to be the leader of this initiative, and you need to take charge. Thinking that you're being a good leader, you ask your team, "Where do we start?"

Surely, this question will show that you are open-minded and you seek other people's input! But the room goes silent. Nobody's sharing. Why? Well, in some situations, especially when working styles, leadership styles, and trust have not been established, many people are afraid to speak up, for fear of saying something wrong.

Realizing that your technique didn't work, you decide to switch gears and ask a safe question instead: "What are your thoughts on the project outline?" That question has no wrong answer. You're asking for someone to give their opinion. By asking that question, you're taking pressure off the team members and giving them space to share what they think without fear of saying something wrong. You're getting the same result you wanted when you asked that first question, "Where do we start?" but you're approaching it in a different way that's less threatening to your audience.

Adding guardrails to limit the scope of a question

Guardrails enable you to place limits on responses and steer a conversation in the direction you want it to proceed. Conveniently, they also set up your respondents for more success because they make your question more specific. You typically add guardrails to a question. For example, rather than ask, "What's your opinion of the best place to start this project?" you ask, "Based on your experience in process management, what's your opinion on the best place to start this project?" The guardrail in this case sets the parameters and the expectations for the person's opinion. It also recognizes the expertise of people you have in the room with you, which is always a good communicative strategy and a strong leadership move!

Guardrails can also be helpful in building on responses by seeking alternative viewpoints. For example, after the expert on process management offers their opinion, you can say something like this: "Now that we've heard how a process manager would proceed based on their experience, what do you, as a member of the quality control team, think of that approach?"

Using questions to transition to other topics

A good communicator knows when the time has come to move on but is also aware that everyone in the conversation needs to move together naturally. Shifting abruptly to the next topic breaks the flow of the conversation. To transition smoothly, take the following steps:

1. **Recognize the current state of the conversation.**

2. **Introduce the new topic.**

EXAMPLE

Suppose you've been discussing the parameters of a project, but before nailing down all the parameters, you'd like a better understanding of how your colleagues work so that you can distribute tasks in a more targeted manner. In this situation, you want to acknowledge the current topic and then introduce the new topic, so you say something like this: "I realize we haven't exhausted all the project parameters yet, but would you be okay talking about our respective working styles so that we can better divide and conquer and then come back to the parameters?"

Here are two more examples of how to transition smoothly from one topic to another:

> That's a really useful perspective on [current topic]. What do you think about [new topic]?

> I appreciate the insights on [current topic]. I'd really like to know more about your experiences with [new topic].

You can then build on the transition by asking a follow-up question that links the two topics. For example, after transitioning from project parameters to working styles, you may ask one of your team members, "From what you just shared about your working style, which project parameter would make the most sense for you to take on?"

Great job! You not only asked a question that will give you a useful answer, but you also linked the topics. Now your conversation truly has come full circle.

Chapter **7**

Holding Productive and Meaningful Conversations

Conversations are the building blocks of personal and professional relationships, serving as the foundation on which people build and maintain connections. Whether you're having a casual chat with a friend or a structured meeting with colleagues, your ability to hold a meaningful conversation can determine the success of your relationships and endeavors. Yet, despite the importance of conversations, many people do not fully grasp how to make them both productive and meaningful.

This chapter is designed to help you become a better conversational partner — one who listens actively, shares openly, and engages authentically. You learn how to balance speaking and listening, how to offer and solicit information effectively, and how to ensure that your conversations lead to clear and beneficial outcomes for all parties involved.

By reading this chapter, you'll be able to engage in conversations that leave each participant feeling heard, respected, and valued while achieving the desired outcome. You'll better understand the dynamics of reciprocity, self-disclosure, and the necessary give-and-take that foster deeper connections and mutual understanding. By mastering these techniques, you'll be able to transform your interactions into opportunities for growth and collaboration.

Appreciating the Value of Reciprocity, Self-Disclosure, and Give-and-Take

Effective communication is not just about conveying information; it's about creating an exchange— a dynamic interplay that involves giving and receiving. This section introduces the concepts of reciprocity, self-disclosure, and give-and-take, and explores the foundational principles that are essential for holding productive and meaningful conversations.

Embracing reciprocity

Reciprocity, which is a core element in relationship development, refers to the mutual exchange of information, emotions, and assistance. In the context of conversation, reciprocity means interacting in ways that make all participants feel equally heard and valued. It's about ensuring that the conversation occurs in a shared space where each participant contributes and benefits equally and no one dominates the discussion.

To foster reciprocity in conversations, start by actively listening to the other participant(s). Show genuine interest in what they have to say by asking clarifying questions or making comments that reflect an understanding of their points. Genuine active listening not only makes others feel respected and valued but also encourages them to engage in the conversation more openly and honestly.

Moreover, reciprocity involves being responsive to the needs and feelings of others, in part by adjusting the tone, style, or direction of the conversation based on the cues provided by your conversation partner(s). (See Chapter 3 for more about adapting to other people's communication styles.) For instance, if you notice that a topic is causing discomfort or disinterest, redirect the conversation in a way that makes the topic more relevant to the needs and interests of your communication partner(s), or change the topic.

REMEMBER

In Robert Cialdini's book *Influence: The Psychology of Persuasion* (Harper Business), he describes six fundamental principles of influence, one of which is reciprocity. As Cialdini points out, "People generally feel obliged to return favors offered to them." In the context of conversations, this principle suggests that the more you contribute to a conversation, the more others will feel inclined to contribute. However, you need to be careful not to monopolize a conversation by trying to give too much. Allow others to contribute equally. If they're shy, you may need to put in a little extra effort to encourage them to open up.

Building trust and reciprocity through self-disclosure

Self-disclosure involves sharing personal information about oneself in a way that is appropriate and relevant to the interaction. By opening up, you invite trust and intimacy, which are vital for deepening relationships, and you invite others to reciprocate by sharing personal information about themselves.

However, self-disclosure must be balanced and timely. Sharing too little can make you appear distant or disengaged, whereas sharing too much too soon may overwhelm others or come across as inappropriate or manipulative. The key is to gauge the level of intimacy in the relationship and disclose personal information gradually and reciprocally, ensuring that your openness is met with a similar openness from the other person.

Giving and taking more or less equally

Though there is some romanticism in the cliched statement "It is better to give than to receive," if you only give-give-give in conversation, you're setting yourself up for failure. Both giving and receiving are equally important for building trust and nurturing relationships. Think about it: Nobody can give without having a willing recipient; giving works only when someone else is on the receiving end of the transaction. And, if giving is better than receiving, the recipient is truly the more noble participant in that exchange, and that's not the case. In the best relationships everyone gives and receives more or less equally.

Likewise, the most productive conversations are those in which the participants give and receive equally, more or less; each person contributes to the flow of information and ideas. I'm not saying that each and every conversation has to be 50-50. What I'm saying is that your conversational history over time should be fairly balanced. This balance helps maintain engagement and ensures that both parties find the interactions rewarding. To achieve an equitable give-and-take, be mindful of the amount of time you spend speaking versus listening. (See Chapter 5 for listening tips.) Aim to contribute to the conversation without overshadowing the other person's opportunity to speak.

FROM GOOD TO BAD: A FIRST DATE

A first date is one of the most simultaneously exciting and terrifying scenarios. It's also a situation in which reciprocity and self-disclosure are, if the date is going well, evident in spades.

I'll never forget a blind date I once went on — set up by a good friend whose coworker, she thought, would be a great match for me. We met in a tapas lounge at a small cock- tail table — perfect for conversation. He started off by sharing that he was pleasantly surprised by some of the information my friend had told him about me — repeating it to me and asking some questions (he'd clearly paid attention to *her!*). I answered a cou- ple of questions and, knowing that I also wanted to learn about him and knowing the importance of reciprocity and self-disclosure, I said, "I'm loving your questions, and I also want to ask you some, too!" To which he replied, "Of course! But we're already on this train of thought, so let's keep talking about you, and we can switch to me in a little bit."

Well, that "little bit" never came. I pushed. I tried to navigate the conversation. I tried saying, "What about you? What led you to start your career in the fitness industry?" But I never got much more than a one-sentence answer.

Though my blind date excelled at asking questions and listening to me, he did not recip- rocate in kind, failing to self-disclose anything of true substance. By the time the check arrived, I was drained from trying to get any bit of information out of him and went home defeated — feeling as though I had just survived a grueling interview!

Needless to say, a second date didn't happen.

I'm sure you've had experiences like this — when people didn't share, when their answers seemed sketchy, or when they provided little, if any, detail. Gives you the "ick," yeah? Well, it did me. And it definitely didn't engender any trust!

Additionally, try to maintain a balance between offering information and asking questions. Though sharing your thoughts and experiences is important, asking questions shows that you value the other person's perspective and encourages a two-way dialogue. (See Chapter 6 for more about asking questions.)

REMEMBER

Of course, some conversations may need to be more one-sided in the short term. For example, during an interview, the interviewer is asking most of the questions and listening more than talking (or should be). But in these cases, the expectation is well established. In other instances, if you need the conversation to be one- sided for some time, establish that expectation upfront. For example, you may start the conversation by saying, "Before we get started, let me share what I've been told about this new initiative."

Being a Good Conversation Partner

One-sided conversations aren't conversations — they're interrogations! To have an effective conversation, strive to establish a communication partnership with others. Most business-related conversations have an objective — to solve a problem, reach a mutual understanding, resolve a conflict, complete a project, and so on. Good communication partners work together for their mutual benefit and the benefit of the team, organization, or customer or to achieve a mutual objective. In this section, I offer tips and techniques on how to become a good conversational partner, which can enhance both your personal and professional interactions.

Cultivating two-way interaction

To be a good conversational partner means to engage actively and empathetically, recognizing that every conversation is a two-way street. This role requires attentiveness, flexibility, and a genuine interest in understanding your conversational partner(s). When engaging in conversations, follow these guidelines:

» **Practice active listening.** Active listening doesn't mean memorizing and regurgitating what you've been told. It's more than just hearing words; it's about trying to understand fully the underlying meaning and emotions being expressed. Show that you're listening by nodding, maintaining eye contact, and offering verbal affirmations or confirmations of what you've heard. Active listening helps you respond more thoughtfully and makes the speaker feel valued. (See Chapter 5 for more about active listening.)

» **Engage with empathy and sensitivity.** Try to put yourself in the other person's shoes, especially when discussing sensitive topics. Empathy enables you to connect on a deeper level and navigate the conversation with care, avoiding misunderstandings that could lead to conflict or discomfort. If you can tell someone is uncomfortable or sensitive about a topic but you need to get to the point, recognize that by saying something like this: "I realize that this isn't an easy subject to discuss, but we need to sort this out if we're going to have any chance of meeting our objective."

» **Be as clear as possible.** Know your communication partner and present information in as clear and well-organized a manner as possible. (See Chapter 12 for tips on organizing information.) Avoid using unfamiliar jargon or acronyms, use examples and visuals to illustrate your points (see Chapter 22 for more ideas on communicating complex ideas), and encourage your partners to provide feedback, especially when they're confused or they disagree. Most of all, keep it simple.

>> **Be concise.** Being concise serves two functions. First, it demonstrates respect for the other person's time. Second, it avoids overwhelming the person's brain with more information than can be processed at one time. If you have a lot of ground to cover, take frequent breaks or divide the material you need to cover into multiple sessions.

>> **Ask more open-ended questions.** Encourage a richer dialogue by asking questions that require more than yes-or-no or multiple-choice answers. Open-ended questions stimulate deeper thinking and show that you're interested in a detailed response, giving your conversation partner(s) opportunities to express themselves fully. (See Chapter 6 for additional guidance on asking questions to promote productive discussions.)

WARNING

If you're a manager or team leader, be extra careful about shutting anyone down or discouraging them from sharing an idea, unless you have good reason to do so and are prepared to share that reason. Dismissing an idea summarily by saying, "That's just not possible" or "That's just not the way we do things here" is the equivalent of telling a child, "Because I said so." Encourage open exchanges; don't discourage them by penalizing people for sharing their ideas.

Putting the principle of reciprocity into practice

If you've ever watched beach volleyball, you know it's the most exciting during an intensive and extended volley — the passing of the ball back and forth over the net. Bump, set, spike! Bump, set, spike! The partners scramble to reach the ball before it strikes the sand and place it in play for the next hit. For a volley to happen, each team has to be working together in unison to make the exchanges possible. Player 1 dives to the sand to dig the ball, keeping it in the air for Player 2 to set the ball high, giving Player 1 enough time to regain their footing and spike the ball over the net. In the next exchange, it may be Player 2 eating sand, Player 1 setting, and Player 2 spiking.

A good volley is much like a good conversation. And a good conversation involves reciprocity — the give-and-take — in a conversation. The concept arose from social psychology, where studies demonstrated that when someone does something for someone else, they create an obligation — a social contract — to return the favor. For example, when someone compliments you on your outfit, you feel compelled to do the same, or something equivalent, for them.

The principle of reciprocity plays a crucial role in the dynamics of any conversation. You can reciprocate in a conversation through the exchange of words, gestures, emotions, information, depth of disclosure, and so on. The goal is to maintain a balanced interaction in which all participants feel equally involved and valued.

RETHINK WHAT'S POSSIBLE

Telling someone that something is "not possible" is a dangerous action. Unfortunately, business managers do it all too often. When you tell someone that something is not possible, you typically see one of the following two reactions:

- The person becomes more determined to prove you wrong.

- The person's spirit is broken.

Either reaction damages workplace productivity.

In the first case, you have an employee focused on the wrong tasks — restoring equity, looking for a new job, or focusing so hard on what's "not possible" that other tasks fall by the wayside.

With the second, you get an employee who feels undervalued, underappreciated, or, worse, underutilized. By saying something is not possible, you're telling someone that their thoughts aren't worth merit, that the innovation isn't worth consideration, and that they shouldn't bring new ideas to the table.

If you catch the words *not possible* slipping out, here is a simple fix: Add the phrase "unless . . ." to your sentence. For example, "it's not possible unless you/I/we can find a way to [name your goal]."

This phrase shows the employee some cause-and-effect and challenges them to be creative about offering a way to meet the stated goal. Many new ideas could come to the surface from this simple addition.

Don't discourage innovation by using limiting language. Instead, let your employees help you rethink what's possible.

Here are some ways to promote reciprocity in a conversation:

» **Maintain a healthy balance between talking and listening.** Dominating the conversation can lead to a disengaged partner, and being overly passive may place the burden of maintaining the dialogue on the other person. Strive for a balance with both parties contributing meaningfully. Don't be a conversational bully!

» **Share insights and information generously but also encourage others to share their thoughts and feelings.** This exchange fosters a richer, more diverse conversation and can lead to unexpected insights and solutions. (See Chapter 6 for more about asking questions.)

>> **Pay attention to the cues your conversation partner is sending, and be ready to adjust the direction of the conversation accordingly.** If a participant seems disinterested or uncomfortable, you may need to change the topic or ask them what they would prefer to discuss. Being able to adapt and adjust your communication is the sign of a savvy conversationalist. If you're concerned that changing or directing the conversation may seem insensitive, you can always explain your reasoning. For example, "I understand that this topic is important to cover, and I want to make sure we have ample time to do the conversation justice. Can we pivot to another topic for now and come back to this one when we have more space to devote to it?"

>> **Express appreciation for the other person's input and ideas.** A simple "thank you" can go a long way in acknowledging their contributions and reinforcing the positive aspects of the interaction. "Thanks for sharing your perspective" and "I appreciate that you're telling me about this" are both good ways to easily recognize someone else, and an even better way is citing a benefit that you or the team will receive because of the information shared or exchanged.

>> **Demonstrate that you value the conversation and the relationship by following up on discussed topics or promises made.** This step could be as simple as sending a thank-you note or an email summarizing key points or following up on what you committed to doing. If you don't follow up on something, at least let your partner know that they shouldn't expect to hear back from you so that they don't feel ignored or ghosted.

>> **When someone gives, give back.** I'm not suggesting that you return all those gifts you received on your birthday, or even that when someone gives you something or does something for you, you must return it in kind. Do look for an opportunity, though, to provide something of equivalent value to that person to demonstrate that you respect the relationship. The give-take balance in conversations and relationships is one of value, not objects.

Strengthening Relationships with Self-Disclosure

The act of self-disclosure plays a pivotal role in the cultivation of deep and resilient relationships, in both personal and professional contexts. *Self-disclosure* involves revealing personal information to others, which fosters a sense of intimacy and trust, creating a foundation for strong and lasting connections. In professional settings, self-disclosure can transform superficial interactions into meaningful relationships, enhancing collaboration and teamwork. Why do you think companies invest so heavily in team-building activities? Because they're designed to encourage self-disclosure, which strengthens bonds and enhances collaboration.

By sharing personal experiences, challenges, and aspirations, communication partners can bridge the gap between mere acquaintanceship and genuine connection, fostering an environment in which open communication and mutual support are the norm.

However, engaging in self-disclosure is not without risks and requires a delicate balance. It demands sensitivity to the context and timing of what's shared, ensuring that it's appropriate and welcome by all parties. Effective self-disclosure also involves a reciprocal exchange in which both parties feel safe to share and listen, thereby avoiding one-sided conversations that can lead to discomfort or disengagement.

In this section, I offer guidance on how to make self-disclosure a more natural part of your discourse and use it more effectively to strengthen relationships with your communication partners.

When managed correctly, self-disclosure not only strengthens existing relationships but also paves the way for new ones, enhancing personal interactions and building a collaborative and supportive network.

Following the ebb and flow of the conversation

The ebb and flow of dialogue is what makes conversations engaging and productive and creates an environment in which the participants feel safe and comfortable disclosing personal information. When conversations occur at just the right pace and rhythm, they move beyond mere transactions of information to become transformative experiences that can deepen relationships and enhance understanding. Self-disclosure becomes a natural part of the conversation instead of feeling awkward and forced.

Although the ebb and flow of a conversation develops naturally, you can influence it in the following ways:

>> **Tune in to the conversation's pace and rhythm.** Recognize when to interject your own thoughts and when to step back and give others space to express themselves. The art of conversation lies in this properly timed dance of listening and speaking. Effective communicators are those who can sense the right moments to contribute and to pause, facilitating a fluid exchange

that respects everyone's need to be heard and understood. This sensitivity is developed over time and, with practice, becomes an instinctual part of engaging in meaningful discussions.

>> **Check regularly for mutual understanding.** For example, summarize what the other person has said before adding your own perspective. Checking for mutual understanding demonstrates respect for each person's contributions and ensures that everyone is on the same page.

>> **Encourage everyone to contribute.** If someone's being ignored or is simply holding back because they're shy, look for opportunities to engage them in the conversation. Ask what they think about what another participant just said or pose an open-ended question to extract their input on a topic. You don't want to put anyone on the spot and make them uncomfortable, but someone who's just listening and not contributing can become a distraction if it goes on too long.

WARNING

Don't push too hard for reciprocity or self-disclosure or try to encourage someone to share too much too soon (before they're ready). Doing so can lead to discomfort and withdrawal rather than the openness you seek. Remain sensitive to everyone's comfort level.

TIP

Achieving a cadence that's conducive to self-disclosure isn't always easy, especially if one or two people are monopolizing the conversation. To prevent and intervene in these situations, consider the following options:

>> **Set ground rules before the onset of the conversation.** Encourage everyone to be mindful of the amount of time they're speaking and to allow others to contribute without interruption.

>> **Politely redirect the conversation.** For example, when someone has been talking for some time and has already made their point, you could say, "That's an interesting point. I'd love to hear what others think about it."

>> **Use nonverbal cues.** For example, rather than maintain eye contact with the speaker who's been oversharing, turn your attention to another participant who hasn't contributed or subtly gesture to indicate that it's someone else's turn to speak.

>> **Intervene diplomatically.** If a gentle redirect doesn't do the trick, you may need to remind the "air hog" that, although you appreciate their input, others need to be given a chance to participate.

Through mindful practice and conscious effort, anyone can master the ebb and flow of a conversation, turning everyday interactions into opportunities for mutual discovery and connection. This cadence of mutual sharing is the cornerstone of not only effective communication but also the development of relationships that are built on genuine understanding and respect.

Getting personal, even in a business setting

Though this book is focused on communication in business, communication is an activity that's most effective and efficient when the participants establish and maintain strong, healthy, semipersonal relationships. Although much of your business communication focuses on task-based messaging, the more you get to know your colleagues as people, the more effective you can be in your collaborations.

In the complex choreography of crafting communication, the saying "sometimes you have to give to get" underscores the importance of the give-and-take, the back-and-forth, and the reciprocity of conversations. When building trust and cooperation are key, such as in situations for team collaborations, leadership, and client interactions, focus not only on the task at hand but also on the humans working together on these tasks. To foster a genuine connection and encourage openness, individuals must be willing to share not just factual information but also their personal insights and vulnerabilities. This act of self-disclosure sets the stage for deeper and more meaningful interactions.

WARNING

Don't give to get in a manipulative way. When I say the words *give to get*, I'm referring to the fact that sometimes you need to take the lead and be the first to share or to demonstrate trust. Going first can be particularly effective in new relationships when trust has yet to be established, or in strained relationships when trust has been compromised and needs to be rebuilt. However, giving to get in a manipulative way can lead to distrust and undermine relationships and productivity.

Creating Mutual Meaning

Creating mutual meaning involves co-creating ideas, solutions, perspectives, and proposals rather than merely transmitting them from one party to another. It requires two or more individuals thinking as one, as you might carry on an internal debate in your own mind before making a complex decision.

To create mutual meaning, you and your communication partner must be in sync. In this section, I share practical techniques for establishing common ground, checking in with one another, and gaining agreement on next steps.

Checking for confirmation

Mutual understanding does not occur automatically; it requires active effort and attention to ensure that all participants in a conversation have correctly interpreted what they've discussed. Here are two effective techniques for checking in:

>> **Paraphrase:** Restate in your own words what others said. Paraphrasing not only confirms you're understanding but also gives the other person an opportunity to clarify any inaccuracies in your interpretation. For example, in a business meeting, after a colleague presents a new strategy, you may say, "Let me make sure I understand correctly. You're suggesting we increase our marketing budget to target a younger audience, and you're asking for my help in crafting this pitch to the management team?" This strategy prompts immediate feedback and ensures that everyone is on the same page. Then you can move on and discuss the type of help your colleague wants and the actions that both parties need to take.

>> **Summarize and request feedback:** If you've covered several points, summarize those points, share your summary with your communication partner(s), and request their feedback on your summation. Summarizing not only helps to confirm understanding but also encourages engagement and makes the conversation a two-way street, where feedback is actively sought and valued. It also ensures alignment on goals and next steps and can help to eliminate any redundancies.

Agreeing on next steps

Concluding any meeting with clear, actionable steps is crucial. This practice ensures that all participants know exactly what is expected of them after the meeting, reducing the chance of misunderstandings and ensuring that the momentum of the conversation carries forward.

Each action step should be specific, measurable, and assigned to a specific individual with a set deadline. For example, concluding a project planning meeting might involve agreeing on steps such as these: "Sara will complete the budget review by next Tuesday and send an update email to the team" or "Sam will coordinate a look and feel for the campaign with the design team by the end of the week and report back in our next meeting." As a leader, you can set these action steps. Or, you can be strategic and let others set their own action steps and clarify as needed.

SETTING S.M.A.R.T. GOALS

The concept of SMART goals is generally attributed to George T. Doran, a consultant who published a paper titled "There's a S.M.A.R.T. way to write management's goals and objectives" in 1981. SMART stands for Specific, Measurable, Attainable, Realistic, and Timely:

- **Specific:** What are you trying to accomplish? Saying something like "Improve sales" or "Increase sales in my top accounts" isn't specific enough. Instead, be specific: "Increase sales by 20 percent in the second quarter of this year within the top 10 percent of my existing clients."

- **Measurable:** Tie the goal to a quantifiable metric — a number. You need to have a measurable metric to determine whether you have achieved your goal.

- **Attainable:** The goal must be one you can achieve; otherwise, what's the point? Do you have the time, money, expertise, and other resources needed to attain the goal? If not, can you acquire those resources? How?

- **Realistic:** Given all factors in the organization and in your professional role, is this goal realistic? If the goal is not realistic, what do you need to do to make it so? Or, do you need to change the goal?

- **Timely:** Start with the end in mind and work backward to identify a timeline to meet your goals. In some iterations of SMART goals, the *T* stands for *time-bound* — it has a specific deadline. As the saying goes, "A goal without a deadline is merely a dream."

TIP

Document the agreed-upon next steps so that you and your communication partners have something in writing to hold each other accountable. Life happens — other projects, issues at home, and various other challenges and distractions. Document your takeaways and commitments and distribute them to everyone who participated in the discussion.

Clear directives are essential for accountability, and they ensure that every participant leaves the meeting with a precise understanding of their responsibilities. This approach not only maximizes productivity but also enhances the sense of teamwork and commitment to shared goals because everyone has "visibility" on what each member is doing and verbal commitments to getting it done.

Employing these strategies effectively can lead to more productive conversations and meetings, better project outcomes, and stronger interpersonal relationships within and between members of a team.

3

Owning Your Message with Confident Communication

Discover several simple ways to adjust how you communicate in business to make people more receptive, improve your chances of eliciting a positive response, gather useful information about the people you meet, and strengthen the impact of your messages.

Understand how your audience's willpower affects their ability to take on more information, change course, or modify their behavior — and find ways to use that willpower to your persuasive advantage.

Lay the groundwork for effective, efficient communication by encouraging your audience to tune in and preparing them for what you're about to tell them.

Build a positive reputation and spread the word about your knowledge, skills, and experience, all without feeling as though you're bragging about yourself.

Add effective networking techniques to your repertoire, avoid common networking mistakes, and inspire your colleagues and clients to sing your praises so that you don't have to carry all that burden yourself.

Structure an effective presentation and prepare and practice well in advance so that you're ready to deliver calmly and confidently when you step in front of your audience.

Chapter **8**

Making Simple Communication Changes for Significant Impact

Business communication is a complex topic, but you can communicate much more effectively by making some minor adjustments. Simple changes in wording and genuine interest in people can make others more receptive to everything you say and more open to giving you what you request.

In this chapter, I reveal basic techniques and tips to improve communication effectiveness and efficiency without investing significant time and effort.

Making People Less Defensive and More Receptive

Regardless of how strong and confident people may appear on the outside, they're generally less so on the inside. If you say anything about them that might be interpreted as critical or condescending, many people grow defensive and may even go on the offensive to protect their ego.

To avoid making people feel as though they're being attacked, blamed, or criticized, make a conscious effort to start reframing "you" statements into "I" statements, as I explain in the following sections.

REMEMBER

Communicating with confidence is more about achieving mutual understanding than merely getting what you want. Understanding ensures that everyone is moving in the same direction to deliver the best outcome, which is usually in everyone's best interest.

Using the I+verb framework

One of the simplest, most subtle, and most effective changes you can make in your day-to-day communication is to start framing statements with the *I+verb* construction, as in the following examples:

"I noticed that ____."

"I need ____."

"I'd like to know ____."

"I understand that we ____."

Using the I+verb framework fosters understanding, respect, and empathy in the following ways:

>> Enables you to express how someone or something made you feel without placing blame.

>> Strengthens your position. People are less likely to argue with you when you're merely expressing how you feel or what you think.

>> Promotes listening, understanding, and collaboration over conflict. When you start with *I*, you're essentially asking the person for understanding, empathy, or help. You're pulling them in rather than pushing them away.

>> Clarifies communication. Starting with *I* often forces you to make a clear and more accurate statement than if you start with accusations and generalizations.

>> Conveys respect. Using the I+verb framework sends a message that you're open to conversation to gain further understanding instead of using a "you" statement, which someone may interpret as placing blame.

>> Models an effective communication technique. When you communicate what you feel, think, want, and need, you increase the likelihood that other participants will take the same approach.

The I+verb framework positions the conversation as one that's now in response to your observation, need, want, or knowledge. This changes the dynamic of how others can respond. For example, you created a quarterly report for your department, and your supervisor criticized the way you organized and presented the data. You may be tempted to say something like, "Well, how would you have done it?" but after reading the previous text, you decide to rephase it as an I+verb statement:

> "I would appreciate insights on how I can present that data more effectively. Do you have any recommendations?"

This rephrasing communicates that you're proactive, you're seeking improvement, and you're prepared to make adjustments based on your supervisor's feedback. It comes across as less defensive and accusatory and more collaborative than starting with "you."

If you prefer your way of organizing the data over more conventional approaches, that's okay, but you can phrase your opinion to make it less confrontational by saying something like this:

> "I would like to explain why I organized the data the way I did. And, if a more effective arrangement is possible, I'm certainly open to it."

This approach allows you to express your opinion in a nonconfrontational way and positions you as someone who exercises judgment yet is open to suggestions.

When you own your message, you steer the dialogue away from confrontation and toward collaboration, which is likely to result in a superior outcome.

REMEMBER

Avoiding "you" statements

When I was growing up, I'd freeze like a deer in headlights whenever anyone in a position of authority would use my full name. If one of my parents said, "Jill Suzanne Schiefelbein, you better get down here!" I was in TROUBLE (yes, all caps). The feeling I'd get in the pit of my stomach when I'd hear my mom use my middle name is one that, even as a 40-something adult, I want to avoid. And it would always be followed up by a word I try to avoid — *you*.

I get the same feeling whenever someone points the verbal finger of blame in my direction with statements like the following:

> *"You* didn't do this right."

> *"You* need to have more patience."

> *"You* should change your attitude."

When you read those statements, do you picture someone shouting or conveying disappointment? That's exactly what goes through the minds of others when they hear statements like these, and I see leaders at all levels making that common mistake more often than I'd like.

TIP

Whenever you need to deliver constructive feedback, avoid the temptation to start with the word *you*, and instead rephrase your statement using the I+verb framework. This technique is subtle and quite effective. For example, rather than say, "You need to do better," say something like, "I noticed that your attention has shifted this month."

Now you're stating your observation. You're even giving it a timeline for when you noticed a change. And instead of issuing a command, you're identifying a behavior and encouraging discussion. You're giving the other person a chance to open up about what's going on. If you don't receive a response, you could follow up by asking, "What has changed?" Questions like these are even more effective if you express them in a tone of genuine curiosity and concern.

Your team members, employees, and, quite frankly, most people in your life will respond more favorably and openly to this approach than they will to a "You need to do better" command or "What's the matter with you?" question.

REMEMBER

Don't get me wrong — starting off a sentence with *you* isn't always a bad choice. But when you're trying to encourage someone to change or to approach a conversation with an open mind and a willingness to collaborate on a solution, pointing the verbal finger of blame isn't the way to go.

Many people are programmed (by negative encounters with authority figures from early in their lives) to physically and emotionally react to the word *you*, and not in a good way. Even if what follows the *you* is neutral or positive, the body and brain are already bracing for negative information to follow, and when braced for negativity, they take a little while to adjust. (See Chapter 9 for more about how the body and brain respond to communication.)

Steering clear of generalizations

The only thing worse than starting a statement with "You . . ." is to start it with "You always . . ." or "You never . . ." Generalizations are rarely accurate and typically result in exaggerated claims that the target of the accusation immediately objects to and can easily prove wrong. Then, you're in the awkward position of having to backpedal and qualify your statement, at which point you've pretty much lost the argument and derailed any conversation you hoped to have.

In short, don't use *always, never, nobody, everybody,* or any other gross generalizations unless, of course, you use the word in a statement that's absolutely true and poses no risk of derailing a conversation.

Getting to Yes Faster

Nobody likes a premature ask. You know the type — someone who hasn't earned the right to make requests of you but does it anyway, putting you in the awkward position of saying no and then often feeling guilty about it or saying yes and later regretting it.

Maybe it's desperation, overconfidence, or oblivion — whatever it is, most people don't respond well to it. However, when you're in a jam and truly need someone's help to get out of it, you may find yourself in the awkward position of having to ask.

With a few subtle shifts, you can get to the yes you're looking for faster, as I explain in the following sections.

Subtly framing your requests

According to Robert Cialdini, an internationally known researcher and the author of *Influence: The Psychology of Persuasion* (Harper Business, 2006), the key to influencing others to respond positively to your requests is to practice the "subtle framing of requests." These are Cialdini's techniques for subtly framing requests:

>> **Provide opportunities to reciprocate.** People generally don't like to feel indebted to someone else. And when someone does a favor, the beneficiary often feels a responsibility to return the favor. That's the principle of reciprocity. The best approach is to help others *before* making a request so that the person you're asking feels that they owe you. The next-best approach is to offer reciprocity rather than ask for a favor without offering anything in return.

>> **Provide social proof.** If your friend likes something, you're more likely to like it, too. You make decisions based on evidence around you, and often that evidence comes in the form of what your friends, members of your social and professional networks, and others you hold credible think. Include in your request information about others who've already responded positively to your request and, if available, their reason(s) for saying yes. People tend to be more willing to lend their support when they see that others support the initiative.

>> **Leverage authority.** Although overplaying this hand if you're using your own authority can backfire, demonstrating support from others who have authority can frequently work in your favor. If you have relevant credentials or affiliations to support the legitimacy of the request or your ability to achieve the proposed objective, include that information. For example, if you're trying to change the culture in your organization and you have a sponsor on the leadership team, use that person's position of authority to your advantage.

>> **Encourage consistency.** Humans stick to patterns of action — such as taking the same route home or creating morning routines. And when they deviate from those patterns, they often experience an internal conflict. Present your request in a way suggesting that answering "Yes" would be consistent with the person's past decisions, commitments, or behaviors. For example, mention that the person supported a similar initiative in the past that turned out to be quite successful.

>> **Create a sense of scarcity or urgency.** If you're presenting a limited opportunity, highlight the fact that you're making it available to only a limited number of people or for only a limited time. Salespeople frequently use (and overuse) this technique, but you can expand its use to different situations and use it more subtly (and sparingly) to encourage a prompt response. Don't manufacture scarcity or urgency if it doesn't exist.

TIP

Start with small asks and work your way up to bigger asks. Whenever you get someone to make a choice, any choice, and they say yes, it lowers their barriers to saying yes to subsequent choices you ask them to make.

Providing choices

One way to lower the psychological barriers preventing people from responding positively to a request is to provide them with options. Here's an approach that works well:

1. **Brainstorm potential choices.**

   You can do this alone or with the person you're asking for help. Involving the other person early in the process can make them more likely to comply with your request.

2. **Prioritize options.**

   Identify options that are most attractive to you and the person you're asking. Dismiss any options that aren't likely to achieve the desired outcome.

3. **Present and discuss the options.**

   Discuss the pros and cons of each option and answer any questions the other person may have.

4. **Choose and commit.**

   Choose the best option you can both agree to and commit to following through on it.

Removing all reasons to say no

An effective way to get to yes is to remove all reasons the other person has to say no. Anticipate every possible objection the person may have to what you're proposing and be prepared to counter it with your own data, reasoning, and solutions. If the person is already too busy, find a way to reduce their workload. If they argue that your proposal would be too costly, provide a budget showing that your plan would actually pay for itself. If they doubt that what you're proposing will be effective, present case studies showing other organizations that are successfully implementing your solution.

"NOBODY PUTS BABY IN A CORNER"

If you've ever watched the 1987 movie *Dirty Dancing*, you're familiar with the classic line "Nobody puts Baby in a corner." For the uninitiated, *Dirty Dancing* is a story about Frances "Baby" Houseman, a young woman (played by Jennifer Grey) who falls in love with dance instructor Johnny Castle (played by Patrick Swayze) at an upscale summer vacation resort in the Catskill Mountains. Her parents don't approve of the relationship or their daughter's infatuation with "dirty dancing," so they prohibit her from seeing Johnny.

The final night at the resort, everyone gathers for the season finale — the talent show. Baby and her parents are seated near the wall with Baby in the corner. Johnny approaches their table to request a last dance of the season with his partner and says, "Nobody puts Baby in a corner." Baby rises from her seat and accompanies Johnny to the stage, where the two of them commence to dirty-dance to the award-winning tune "I've Had the Time of My Life" (performed by Bill Medley and Jennifer Warnes, 1987).

The moral of the story is that nobody with any talent, imagination, or intelligence should be kept in a corner — forced to do what others want them to do or demand that they do. Tight control over others rarely leads to positive, sustainable results. By giving people choices, you give them some degree of freedom, which encourages them to be more cooperative or compliant.

Provide data, testimonials, or other evidence to back up your claims, build your credibility, and eliminate any skepticism.

Focusing Less on Names and More on Pertinent Details

Many people in sales and management are obsessed with remembering the names of everyone they meet and addressing people by name during every subsequent interaction. Nothing's wrong with that. In fact, remembering a person's name is necessary for showing respect and consideration, but it's not sufficient.

To significantly improve your ability to communicate with others, get to know more about them — their professional and personal goals, their work interests and hobbies, their family, or what they value most.

Nurture a genuine interest and curiosity about everyone you meet. Ask them questions that inspire them to talk about who they are and what they do and how they hope to achieve their dreams and aspirations. The more you know about someone, the more effectively you can personalize your message to optimize receptivity and understanding.

In this section, I explain how to keep the focus on pertinent details that matter to your audience, whether you're presenting to an individual or a group.

Avoiding cheesy sales talk

Old school sales strategies encouraged salespeople to say the name of a prospective customer *ad nauseam*. This age-old advice seems to have originated from Dale Carnegie's classic self-help book *How to Win Friends and Influence People,* in which he wrote, "Remember that a person's name is to that person the sweetest and most important sound in any language." Though that may be true, repeating a person's name can become downright annoying (and that's definitely not what Mr. Carnegie had in mind). Imagine visiting a vehicle dealership to check out the new models and engaging in this conversation with Sam, the cheesy salesman:

"Hi, I'm Sam. What's your name?"

"Hi Sam, I'm Jill."

"Well, hi, Jill. What are you looking for today?"

"I'm looking for a small SUV that gets at least 30 miles a gallon. Do you have anything like that?"

"Jill, I have just the thing for you. Come on over here, Jill, and let me show you some of these new models. What would you feel about driving home in a new SUV today, Jill?"

Did you cringe while reading that exchange as much as I did while writing it? Well, imagine how you'd feel living it! Like most things in life, too much of anything, even the sweetest sound in your native language, can be a bad thing. And it can make a person uncomfortable. That's why I caution any of my clients who have been to any type of cookie-cutter sales training or persuasion training to be leery of trying any single strategy too much. As the saying goes, "All things in moderation, including moderation."

Another overused sales tactic is to use fear to pressure people into making a decision before they've had the opportunity to fully consider their options or the ramifications of moving forward. These tactics may work in the short term, but the long-term consequences can damage your reputation. Here's another example from the vehicle dealership:

"I'm here to get a feel for the models that fit my budget and lifestyle. What do you have in the smaller sport utility vehicle range that gets at least 30 miles per gallon?"

"Jill, you've come to the right place. And did I mention that we're featuring a great promotion this weekend only? We're offering a low APR if you purchase a new vehicle and trade in your old vehicle with us."

"No, you didn't mention that, but I saw it on a television ad. I came here specifically to see if you have any vehicles that meet my requirements in stock and give them a test-drive."

"I'll see what we have on the lot. Even if we don't have them in stock, you can sign today and put down the deposit, Jill, and I'll be able to get you locked into that low APR."

. . . Sam checks inventory . . .

"Jill, we don't have any of those models in stock, but let's try the next model up so that you can get a feel for how it drives. I don't want you to miss out on this low APR offer."

. . . Jill gets visibly frustrated . . .

"I'm not going to put down a deposit on a car I haven't tested. As I said when I walked in . . ."

Notice that the customer's question wasn't directly answered — at all. I don't know about you, but this type of exchange exhausts me.

Sam also committed a grave error in all types of sales and persuasion — focusing on what he thinks is important and ignoring what Jill is telling him is important to her.

Listening is an often overlooked but crucial business communication skill that the most effective leaders appreciate and practice. (See Chapter 5 to find out more about sharpening your listening skills.)

Admitting what you don't know

Not knowing everything is okay. That's right. I give you permission. And you know what else? I give you permission to admit out loud — in front of other people — that you don't know everything. Acknowledging that you don't know everything projects honesty, humility, and confidence. The transparency of this simple act increases people's trust and confidence in you.

If you don't know something you should know, you may need to navigate the situation more delicately. However, even in these situations, admitting that you don't know something you should know is better than pretending you know something you don't. It can still be a trust-building opportunity. When this is the case, you can use a phrase like: "That is an important question and I want to make sure my figures are accurate before I answer. I'll get back to you before the end of the day."

In the following sections, I present techniques for escaping uncomfortable situations in which you should know something you don't know or can't recall. These techniques are useful when you need to buy yourself time to think through your response, you don't know an answer and want to get the information from someone who does, or you want to be a great leader by giving credit to others in the room.

Pivoting to someone else

Not being able to recall something when put on the spot doesn't make you a dummy. It can happen to anyone. It just means that you need a minute to compose yourself, engage your brain, and recall the information. This is a great opportunity to pivot and bring in someone else on the team who has more expertise than you, has a better perspective on the current topic, or can use a chance to shine (even if you know the answer).

Regardless of the reason, a simple strategy is to combine the I+verb framework from earlier in this chapter with the name of the person you're pivoting to and the reason you're calling on that person. Here are a few examples:

"I think Sara is more qualified to answer this question, based on her experience with running charitable fundraisers."

"I would love to hear Juan's insights on this question, as he has succeeded in these activities in previous roles at other companies."

"I believe Robin's insights would be valuable here, since they led a team of interns to produce the award-winning campaign for our competition last year."

You don't have to call attention to the fact that you don't know the answer or can't recall information. You simply pass the baton and give a reason that the person you're passing it to is qualified to present the information or answer the question.

Tabling a topic for later

If a request or question that comes to you is off-topic or a topic you plan to cover later, say so tactfully. For example, if you're discussing a proposal to transition to a new software development methodology and someone asks about filling a key vacancy on the team, you may say something like, "That's a topic we need to discuss in a separate meeting. Let's plan to meet about it early next week."

WARNING

Table a topic or question only if you plan to come back to it at some point. If you put it off until a later time and never address it, you're essentially dismissing the other person's concerns and contributions, which can make them less likely to contribute to future discussions and can harm your reputation.

Returning the serve

Sometimes, bouncing a question back to the audience for their opinion is a helpful strategy to use to collect your thoughts and think about how to respond to a question or a request for information. If you're struggling to answer a question, you may say something like, "If any of you have relevant information or insights you're willing to share, I'd like to hear it."

Purging "Sorry" and "Just" from Your Vocabulary

To instantly communicate with greater confidence and power, remove two tiny words from your vocabulary: *sorry* and *just*.

Helen Appleby, an executive business coach and the author of *The Unwritten Rules for Women's Leadership* (Rethink Press, 2020), told me about a client who wrote

Sorry and Just on sticky notes, drew a circle around each word with a line through it, and stuck the notes to the edge of her computer screen. These notes served as constant reminders not to use those words in any communication she was preparing to send.

How are these two words harming your communication and confidence, and what can you do about it? I'm glad you asked.

Stop saying "sorry"

Apologizing when you sincerely regret making a mistake or causing harm is noble, but when overused, it conveys weakness and a lack of sincerity and quickly becomes annoying. To communicate more confidently, revise your autopilot apologies into more direct statements or requests, as shown in the following examples:

Sorry	Not Sorry
I'm sorry to send this again, but _____.	I am resending this from a different email account. Please respond by the end of the day.
Oh, I'm sorry, but I didn't receive _____.	I did not receive the information you're referring to.
I'm sorry I'm late, but [insert excuses here]	I appreciate your waiting for me.
I'm sorry I couldn't hear.	Could you please repeat that? I need to hear that one more time.

Jettison "just"

Unless you're referring to a temporal matter, as in "just in time," remove the word just from your vocabulary. This one-word shift brings more confidence and conciseness to your messaging, as demonstrated in these examples:

Just	Un-Just-ed
I just want to check in.	I want to check in.
I think if we just do X, then _____.	If we do X, then _____.
If she'd just change Y _____.	If she'd change Y _____.
Just get it to me by _____.	Get it to me by _____.

See how superfluous the word is? People have a tendency to toss it into expressions to make them feel softer, nicer, or more polite. In reality, it's just (used intentionally to prove a point) taking up extra space.

TIP

To see for yourself whether you overuse the words *sorry* or *just,* search your Sent email folder(s) for those words and make a conscious effort not to use them when communicating over other media, including phone, face-to-face, videoconferencing, text, and social media. You're likely to be surprised at how easily those words flow off your tongue and through your fingers — and how unnecessary they are.

IN THIS CHAPTER

» Recognizing the challenge of capturing and maintaining your audience's attention

» Priming your audience to make them more receptive to your message

» Getting your audience focused and motivated

» Setting expectations and getting buy-in for virtual communications

Chapter **9**

Setting the Stage for Effective Communication

I f you've ever been to a concert or a play or another live performance, you're familiar with customs for eliminating distractions and ensuring that the audience is in the proper frame of mind when the performance commences. At a theater performance, for example, doors open a half-hour before curtain, and everyone is expected to settle into their seats five to ten minutes before the show commences, with cellphones turned off or silenced. Audience members receive a playbill that includes a cast list and an outline of the play (acts, scenes, intermission) and introduces the actors. The director may even include a note in the playbill that contextualizes what the audience is about to experience. Lights dim to indicate that the performance is about to begin. The director or one of the actors may appear on stage to deliver a pre-show announcement. A period of silence follows, curtains open, the performance begins.

Likewise, before you initiate a conversation, presentation, or performance of any kind, you want to be sure your audience is in the right frame of mind — attentive and receptive to what they're about to experience. You want their minds free of distractions and laser-focused on what you're about to say, whether you're presenting to an audience of 1 or 10,000.

In this chapter, I explain how to set the stage for effective communication. I describe what you're up against — highly distracted minds — and provide guidance on how to clear those distractions. I present practical tips for getting the audience to focus and making their minds more receptive to your message. And I provide additional suggestions specifically for virtual meetings and presentations. By the end of this chapter, you'll know exactly how to put your audience's mind into an attentive and receptive state.

Challenging the Status Quo

Whenever you're delivering a message, you're challenging the *status quo* — the existing situation. That means you're having to overcome whatever's going on in your audience's mind — distractions, assumptions, existing knowledge (correct or incorrect) about the topic, emotions, beliefs, and more. If you're merely presenting information, you're asking the audience to change or add to what they know. If you're engaged in persuasion (including sales), you're asking them to change what they already think or believe or change their current situation by adding something else to the equation. In either case, getting people to change their thoughts or behaviors can be a monumental challenge.

Consider what happened during the COVID-19 pandemic. Many people were forced to work from home, which, in many cases, drastically changed their daily routines. Some adjustments were welcome: No commute — yay! Others weren't so welcome: No physical separation between work and home — ugh! Organizations required time to restructure. Policies and procedures needed to change. New styles of leadership had to evolve.

Eventually, everyone adjusted, but it took time to alter the status quo and for those routines to become the new normal. Even when change is welcome, it's challenging. People need to modify their deeply ingrained mindsets and develop new ways of thinking. They need to adapt to the new status quo.

In this section, I explain why change can be challenging and how to use this understanding to become a more effective communicator.

Understanding why changing the status quo can be difficult

Over the course of a day, a person's ability to absorb and process new information and make decisions is diminished. That's not just me talking — that's according to Roy F. Baumeister, a prominent social psychiatrist known for his research on willpower and the concept of *ego-depletion* — the idea that over the course of a day, people expend willpower from a limited pool of mental resources, and as these resources are depleted, people gradually lose self-control.

Self-control is what people need in order to overcome their natural resistance to change. When willpower is depleted, people begin to lose self-control. They become more easily distracted and vulnerable to temptation and less receptive to any proposal that requires them to exert extra effort—mentally or physically—to effect the proposed change.

But what does this have to do with communication? I love that you're curious! Because when you're trying to get someone to take on more information, or change a course of action, they have to *decide* to do this. Decision-making requires willpower. In the next section, I delve into this topic a bit more.

REMEMBER

Willpower is the energy that people exert to exercise self-control and make decisions. Over the course of a typical day, everyone's willpower wanes.

Using willpower (or the lack of it) to your advantage

In business communication, keeping an eye on your audience's willpower gauge can work to your advantage in two ways:

>> If your audience has a high level of willpower, they're better equipped to make rational decisions, even when those decisions may not be aligned with what they perceive to be easier or more pleasant for them. For example, if you're asking your team to change their approach to product development, they'll need a high level of willpower to agree to accept the additional effort that implementing the change will require (not to mention the willpower needed to understand the changes in the first place).

>> If your audience has a low level of willpower, they're more susceptible to giving in to temptation. This is why some approaches to sales involve wearing down prospective customers. The more information a customer must

process, and the more small decisions they make, including the decision to continue to sit through a long sales presentation, the less willpower they have to exert self-control and say no, and the more apt they are to agree to buy whatever appeals to their comfort and pleasure.

After reading this section so far, you may think, "But if low willpower means my audience will accept my communication, why is this bad?" Well, it's a short-term gain but with long-term consequences (kind of like this beer I just cracked open while making edits to this section — it feels good in the moment, but tomorrow it's unlikely to help me in any way). You can also think of it as *buyer's remorse* — the regret a customer often feels after making an emotional or impulsive decision (often with a lack of willpower).

REMEMBER

In short, if you're asking your audience for something that requires their self-control, approach them when they have a full tank of willpower; for example, early in the day or after they've been able to take a break and refresh their minds. You can also use certain strategies to preserve or build willpower (see the later section "Preserving and restoring willpower and self-control").

Recognizing factors that deplete willpower

Getting to know the factors that deplete willpower gives you a better sense of what could be impacting your ability to communicate with your audience. Several factors deplete willpower, including these:

>> **Exerting self-control:** Resisting temptation or distractions

>> **Regulating emotions:** Suppressing anger or frustration or controlling impulses and reactions

>> **Making decisions:** Even decisions made on autopilot, such as opening a door to enter a room or stepping on the brake to stop at an intersection

>> **Exerting oneself physically:** Intense or prolonged physical exercise or work

>> **Exerting oneself mentally:** Engaging in challenging cognitive tasks or prolonged periods of intense concentration

>> **Not getting restorative sleep/rest:** Insufficient quantity or quality of sleep

>> **Dealing with distressing conditions:** Noise, uncomfortable temperatures, poor lighting, or clutter, for example

Preserving and restoring willpower and self-control

You can use your knowledge of willpower and self-control to become a more effective communicator. For example, if you're delivering a long presentation, you can give your audience an outline before you begin so that they know what to expect and can follow along. If you begin to sense that they're losing their willpower to pay attention, you can take a break and give everyone a chance to recharge their batteries, so to speak, before proceeding to the next slide.

Your willpower is also important for effective communication. You can increase your own willpower to become less susceptible to rhetorical tactics designed to capitalize on a lack of willpower. Here are a few ways to preserve and restore *your* willpower:

>> **Set clear, achievable goals.** Having a clear purpose focuses your attention so that you're less likely to waste mental resources spinning your wheels.

>> **Develop routines.** Routines transform decisions into habits, empowering you to accomplish more in less time with less effort. Routines also help preserve willpower because you're not consciously processing decisions.

REMEMBER

Successful athletes, corporate executives, business leaders, and entrepreneurs frequently write about the routines and habits they've developed that are often the keystones of their success. Follow their lead. Routines optimize efficiency and conserve willpower. (To find out about my morning routine, see the nearby sidebar, "The coffee pod conundrum.")

>> **Break goals into objectives and tasks.** Smaller objectives and specific tasks can make large goals feel less overwhelming.

>> **Prioritize tasks.** Focus on completing tasks that require self-control during times when your energy and willpower are highest. For many people, this is earlier in the day when they're well-rested and haven't yet encountered many decision-making challenges.

THE COFFEE POD CONUNDRUM

When I'm home and not traveling for business or leisure, I have a highly regimented morning routine: Wake up. Do the biology thing. Put a pod in my Nespresso machine. Return to my bedroom to make the bed and get dressed. Go back out to the kitchen. Take my daily vitamins. Grab my coffee (of which I have the exact same variety every weekday). Sit outside (or facing the window if the weather doesn't cooperate). Write in

(continued)

(continued)

my gratitude journal. Head back to the kitchen to rinse out my coffee mug, place it in the sink, and mix up my daily greens drink. Head to my desk, green drink in hand, and read market updates, business news, and tech updates from the newsletters I follow. When I open my list of tasks for the day (which, of course, I wrote out the night before), I'm ready to get cranking.

I'm like a robot every morning, and I embrace this regimented routine because it requires zero willpower. It's a routine — a deeply ingrained habit. However, a single deviation from this routine can significantly zap my willpower.

One week, when I was away on business, a friend stayed at my place. I told her I had only one rule: Make sure to have coffee available when I return home! Well, she enjoyed herself, drank the coffee I had on hand, and — considerate person that she is — replaced it when it ran out.

Unfortunately, the morning after I returned home, I had a rude awakening. When I reached for my usual coffee pod, I didn't see the pods I always bought. In their place was a *variety pack!* I had to pause, refocus, and engage my brain in making a choice. My willpower took an instant hit.

In the grand scheme of things, this was a minor glitch in the matrix. But for me, in that moment, it was a disruption, and it shows how even a factor as inconsequential as a coffee variety can impact the brain's status quo.

Prepping Your Audience's Brain for What You're About to Tell Them

Presenting new information or ideas to an audience is like planting seeds: If you want seeds to sprout, take root, grow into hearty plants, and produce an abundant harvest, you need to prepare the soil in advance. If the soil is too wet, too dry, too cold, too compact, or void of nutrients, those seeds won't have a chance. Likewise, if your audience isn't prepared to accept what you're about to tell them, the information and ideas you impart won't be received or processed as effectively as they could be.

Imagine taking your normal route home from work or school and encountering an unexpected road closure. Suddenly, your brain must disengage from whatever it was thinking and reengage to figure out a new route. You're having to burn willpower to solve an unexpected problem. However, had you received notification of the road closure in advance, you would have been prepared to identify a detour, and you'd follow that new route and not give it a second thought.

The moral of this story is that whenever you're about to present an audience with new information or a new idea, prepare them for what you're about to tell them. In this section, I present several ways to make an audience more receptive to your message.

Focus your audience

Whether you're having a one-on-one conversation or presenting to a group, focus everyone's attention on the here and now and the subject matter you're about to present or discuss. To minimize potential distractions, narrow the scope for your audience to one or more of these categories:

» A period of time

» A project or task

» A situation or issue

» A goal for the conversation or presentation

Try starting with a statement such as, "I need 30 minutes of your time to nail down milestones and deadlines for the new product rollout" or "The goal of our call today is to establish benchmarks for the new website." If you're uncertain about the purpose of a call or meeting, you can start by saying something like, "Before we talk about the new website, let's discuss what we hope to accomplish during this call." You can then collaborate on setting a goal for the call.

By restricting your communication to a specific period of time, a specific project or task, a specific situation or issue, or a specific goal (or all of these), you're more likely to have a productive conversation, meeting, or presentation.

WARNING

Multitasking doesn't work. People who claim to multitask shift their attention back and forth from one task to another and are actually 100 percent focused on only one task at a time. By being specific about what you want your audience to focus on and the time commitment you're expecting, you're creating a sense of tunnel vision focused entirely on the situation or issue you want to address.

WARNING

Don't assume that everyone's on the same page. If you're going to assume anything, assume that nobody's aligned. Be explicit about the goal of your communication and your expectations. One of the biggest mistakes people make in business communication is assuming that everyone involved is on the same page and has the same goals and expectations.

Get agreements upfront

When people make a commitment, especially publicly, they're more likely to follow through. When you need your team to focus on a task or you need a colleague to dial in on a conversation, get agreements or pre-commitments before you begin. These agreements or commitments function as guardrails; if anyone deviates from what was agreed upon, you can steer the conversation back to where it needs to be.

Suppose that you're scheduled to meet with a team member about their performance on a recent project. Before providing feedback, establish parameters for the discussion. For example, you may start with a statement like this: "I know the purpose of today's meeting is to discuss your performance on project X, but I want to approach this more like a conversation rather than a one-perspective review. Can we both agree to contribute equally to the meeting so that we can work together to find the best path forward?"

Check in with your audience

If you have an opportunity, before initiating your conversation or presentation, even if it's only a few minutes in advance, check in with your audience. Make sure everyone is comfortable and understands the purpose of the session and is able to participate in the necessary manner. If anyone requires more context, provide it. If anyone has questions, answer those questions.

REMEMBER

If someone has unanswered questions, their brain will likely be focused on that instead of on whatever you're about to present. The more you can do early on to eliminate distractions and fully engage your audience, the better.

Have you ever been to a party and noticed people looking in your direction and laughing while providing no indication of what they're laughing about? (Come on, it can't be just me!) It may have nothing to do with you, but if you think that there's even a remote chance that they're laughing at you, it will likely weigh on your mind for a large part of the evening.

The same is true for your audience. The human brain isn't geared to handle uncertainty, so it works overtime to fill any gaps in understanding, and it may fill those gaps with false assumptions, misinterpretations, and mistaken conclusions. If your audience has any uncertainty, they'll be distracted at best, and at worst they'll have preconceptions that'll interfere and maybe even undermine their ability to understand and accept the information and ideas you're about to share.

WARNING

If you're presenting to a small group, avoid the common mistake of making this request of your audience: "Please hold all your questions to the end." When I hear a presenter say this at the beginning of a meeting, it drives me nuts. It's okay when you're delivering a presentation to a large audience in an auditorium, especially if you need audience members to line up to use a microphone to be heard, but when you're presenting to a small group, it takes away a perfect opportunity to gain a better understanding of your audience.

TIP

If you're in a small group meeting and someone asks a question that derails the conversation or interrupts a point, consider saying, "Let me finish this segment first, and then I'll answer that question" or "Once I finish this portion, I think your question will be answered in what I plan to present."

If you're asking someone to make a decision based on what you're presenting and they have a question — an uncertainty — the best course of action, in many cases, is to answer that question immediately so that their brain can refocus on your presentation. You don't have to pause midsentence. Finish your train of thought, and then answer the question and move on.

REMEMBER

Communication is a two-way street, and understanding evolves through your interactions with your audience. Be prepared to modify your message as your understanding of what your audience needs evolves.

A QUICK TIP FOR SALES SUCCESS

Whenever you're selling anything, you're asking someone to step outside their comfort zone — to add something to their life or change their routine (to change their status quo, as explained in the earlier section "Challenging the Status Quo").

When you know this fact, you can approach sales more as a conversation and less like a presentation. For example, if you're a real estate agent trying to sell a four-bedroom home, think twice about highlighting the fact that it has four bedrooms. The person you're selling to may want a house with two bedrooms, an office, and a workout room. Start by asking questions and gathering information, and then you can tailor your presentation to your customer's needs and desires more effectively.

Likewise, if you're selling a business product or service, don't start by launching into all the features and benefits. Start by encouraging your customer to talk about their situation and the challenges they face, and how their life would look if only they could overcome those challenges. Using the information and insights they share, you're better prepared to show how *your* solutions solve *their* problems.

Putting It All Together

Setting the stage for outstanding communication is a two-step process:

1. **Assess your audience's willpower, how it will impact your ability to communicate with them, and how you'll use your understanding of willpower to communicate your message most effectively.**

2. **Prepare your audience to be attentive and receptive to what you're about to present or discuss.**

The following example illustrates what this two-step process looks like in a real-world scenario.

EXAMPLE

Suppose you're planning to meet with your team to discuss the results of a survey from your customers about a recent product launch so that you can reinvent the next campaign. This strategy requires your team to be factual and innovative — two qualities that require willpower.

Step 1: Thinking of your audience, you know your team is exhausted from the previous two weeks leading up to the launch and from taking customer calls and feedback post-launch. As a result, team members are likely to be in reporting or complaining mode and not have an innovative mindset. Their willpower is low. Read Chapter 12 for more information about knowing your audience.

Step 2: Knowing that your team's willpower is depleted, which compromises their self-control, you need to get everyone on the same page, focused on the same goal, so you prepare your team with this statement:

> "We're here today to dive into customer feedback and figure out ways to use that feedback to drive innovation and improve our next launch. I understand that you have all received feedback — both positive and negative — and have been working insanely hard. I don't want to spend time and energy airing our frustrations, beating ourselves up, or placing blame. I'd rather we focus on making constructive comments based on the feedback we received and use what we've learned to drive innovation and improve future product launches. We can vent all those other topics at happy hour tonight! Can we all agree that we'll keep the conversation focused on that goal? [get agreement] Great! Now, if during this meeting we start to wander off course, every one of you has permission to point this out respectfully so that we can realign and move forward together."

This statement is effective in three ways:

» It gives public recognition to the fact that the team has worked hard and expended a great deal of mental energy (so they're likely low in willpower).

» It focuses the team on a unified goal and gets agreement upfront about how the session will be conducted.

» It encourages the efficient use of time and energy by allowing team members to bring the meeting back into focus if it starts to veer off course, thus conserving willpower.

Congratulations! The stage is now set for a productive and successful meeting.

TIP

When participants in a meeting lose focus, simply stop the meeting briefly and remind everyone of the agreed upon goal. You may say, "The issue you bring up is certainly valid, but I believe it is outside the scope of this meeting. Can we table it for now or reframe it in a way that aligns with our goal?"

Virtual Conversations: Calling Attention to Paying Attention

Virtual meetings have some unique challenges with respect to keeping everyone focused and engaged. You have cameras and microphones to consider and the ability to chat and exchange emojis in real time. To ensure that everyone is aligned and in agreement on how the virtual meeting will be conducted, here are a few phrases you may want to start with:

» "Let's agree to silence all notifications for the next 30 minutes so that we can avoid distractions as much as possible to honor everyone's time."

» "Please leave your camera on during this meeting so that we have instant feedback and can do quick visual polling."

» "Can we all agree to use the thumbs-up emoji in chat to upvote someone's question so that we can cover the most useful questions first?"

» "Feel free to use the chat feature throughout the presentation to comment and expand on ideas."

Chapter 10

Talking about Yourself without Bragging

A chieving success in nearly any field of endeavor involves some degree of tooting your own horn. However, most people don't like to call attention to themselves or brag about their achievements. And in many cultures, especially those that value *we* over *me*, self-promotion is taboo. Yet ensuring that others know what your strengths are is important for professional opportunity and advancement.

How do you let your light shine for the world to see without feeling or appearing boastful?

In this chapter, I answer that question.

Understanding Why Bragging Feels Icky and Shifting Your Mindset

Unless you're an attention-seeker, you probably don't enjoy being put on the spot to talk about your education, skills, and accomplishments. Why? I can think of several reasons:

>> You've been indoctrinated to value humility, so you tend to downplay your achievements to avoid appearing arrogant or boastful.

>> You're afraid of being judged harshly by others for being self-centered or self-absorbed.

>> You suffer from *imposter syndrome* — uncertainty about your own abilities that leads to fear of being exposed as a fraud.

>> You're reluctant to draw attention to your success because it may over-shadow, or be perceived to overshadow or undermine, the achievements of others.

>> You believe that your work should speak for itself.

>> You think that people will or should notice how wonderful you are (and it's not up to you to tell them).

Each of these reasons is a false and self-limiting belief. The good news is that these are all perceptions, so you can challenge and replace them with facts.

First, realize that telling people what you do and what you've accomplished, especially when you're asked to do so, is not bragging. It's educating. As long as you stick to the facts and don't embellish or exaggerate, all you're doing is providing information that enables others to get to know you and make well-informed choices about the people they want to work with. This distinction between bragging and educating is important in making you feel more empowered to talk about yourself.

REMEMBER

Some people have the attitude that their work will speak for itself, that — if they do good work and consistently meet or exceed expectations — they don't need to promote themselves. Though I wish this were true, it's not. Much of the work you do goes unnoticed. This isn't to say that you need to shout from the rooftops every little detail about what you're working on. But it does mean that you need to be aware of the work you're doing and what about that work is important for others to know. Then start thinking strategically about how you'll communicate about your work to others.

Educating Others about You

Educating others about you is like sales: It's not about the product; it's about what the product can do to provide value to the customers. It's not about selling yourself to someone you want to work for or with; it's about enabling the stakeholders to make a well-informed choice of whether you're the best solution to meet their current and future needs. It's less about promotion and more about education. Educating others about you allows you to approach self-promotion more along the lines of writing a whitepaper than creating an advertisement.

In this section, I provide you with some strategies to communicate about your abilities and accomplishments discreetly, without appearing to be self-centered or boastful, so that you're prepared to embrace opportunities to talk about yourself and your work when they arise.

REMEMBER

You'll have no shortage of casual opportunities to promote yourself in the world, and I don't want you to miss any of them. Be prepared to seize these opportunities when they appear.

Delivering facts that show results

One way to take the edge off when talking about yourself is to stick to facts and steer clear of opinions. Suppose that you're a consultant who helps companies improve their productivity and you're talking with the CEO of a company that manufactures computer chips. Rather than say that you "knocked it out of the park" in helping a client achieve their productivity goal, you may say something like this: "You know, 60 percent of the average worker's time is spent coordinating workflow. At the company I'm currently advising, we reduced that to 20 percent and achieved an overall increase in productivity of 35 percent."

TIP

Keep a running list of your projects and accomplishments and make a conscious effort to work them into your conversations whenever you're talking about your work. For example, if a leader in your organization says to you, "I heard your team did a great job of transitioning to the new sales management system," you can respond with more than a simple "Thank you." Instead, you may say something like this: "Thank you! That new system is much improved, and my team ensured a seamless transition. Conversions are already up 150 percent over the prior month!" This reply shows that you appreciate the compliment, you followed up to track the results, and you have a genuine interest in the company's success, all without bragging. A response like this one leaves a lasting impression and opens the doors to future conversations and opportunities for yourself and your team.

Featuring others

Don't hesitate to sing the praises of others when the opportunity presents itself, especially if you're a supervisor or team leader. Doing so benefits you, as well as others, in the following ways:

>> Strengthens your position as leader by showing that you appreciate every team member's contribution. When your team members see that you're team-focused and willing to give credit where credit is due, they're more likely to be committed to you as their leader.

>> Demonstrates your generosity and consideration of others. By sharing the credit, you're celebrating everyone's accomplishments, not just yours. You can brag a little more about your team's achievements without appearing to brag about yourself.

>> Conveys the sense that you're focused on and committed to the work, successful outcomes, and organization's success. You're less concerned about who gets the credit.

>> Projects confidence, showing that you don't feel threatened by the knowledge, talents, and skills of others.

Suppose that you're a team leader, and an executive in the organization approaches you in the break room to commend you for your work on winning the latest client contract. Resist the temptation to simply say, "Thank you!" Use this opportunity to educate leadership about what you and your team accomplished and to introduce your talented colleagues. For example, you may say something along the lines of, "Thank you so much! It was an honor to lead a team that worked incredibly well together and contributed to the success of the campaign. Maria was instrumental in gathering the necessary documentation, and Robert was clutch in providing deep research on the client that allowed us to work better examples into the pitch. It was definitely a team effort!"

This richer response enables you to not only graciously accept the accolade but also claim your leadership role and give credit where it's due to team members. Featuring others is an excellent way to capitalize on an opportunity to give people more information and insight into what you and your team do and are capable of.

Don't be afraid to talk positively about others. Many people believe that doing so diminishes or distracts from their own value. This belief is ridiculous. You've probably heard the adage "People support what they create." When you build a team, you have a responsibility to support each team member on their path to success. In addition, your success is largely a product of theirs; they created you to a certain degree, so they'll support you as long as you continue to earn their respect.

Highlighting outcomes

One way to engage in self-promotion without bragging about yourself is to shine the spotlight on outcomes instead of personal achievements. Focus on results that benefited your team, the department, or, even better, the entire organization. By focusing on outcomes, you can seize opportunities to make people aware of the role that you and your team played in making that outcome possible, but you have the added advantage of educating others on how that outcome benefited them. The message is powerful yet subtle.

Suppose that the leader of another team tells you, "Great job on hitting your quarterly goals." You have a golden opportunity here to highlight outcomes by saying something like this: "Thank you so much! Our team was so happy to not only meet the goal but also beat it. Now the service department can afford that new Help desk software they've been wanting. That'll streamline customer experiences across the organization and hopefully free up more resources for R&D. This is an exciting time for our organization!"

You may have noticed a pattern developing across these responses. It's pretty simple:

1. Start by recognizing the compliment. (A simple thank-you is sufficient.)

2. Immediately pivot to the fact of the achievement: "I was thrilled to . . . " or "We were happy to . . . "

3. Finally, wrap up with how this ties into a bigger picture, beyond just you (how it benefits others): for example, "I'm looking forward to seeing how this impacts the productivity of the sales team" or "I'm eager to find more ways to contribute to our customers' success on other projects."

4. (Optional) Add a call to action! For example, "If any other projects involving this new system integration are in the works or happen to arise, I'd love to be considered for them" or "As I'm developing my skills with this new project, I'd welcome other learning opportunities to improve my leadership skills."

REMEMBER

Teams and even entire departments often operate in isolation. If you can show how your team's success ripples through the organization, you have a powerful tool for breaking down silos and increasing awareness about your team's importance as well as your own value in the bigger picture.

TIP

Similarly to how you wouldn't say a simple thank-you when receiving a compliment (now that you've read these strategies to educate others), don't "simply" give a compliment! When you find out about a colleague's success or achievement, don't rush to be the first to congratulate them. Seek first to understand the full scope of their accomplishment and the award or promotion they received so that you can express clearly and in some detail your understanding and appreciation of what they accomplished. For example, if someone on your team wins an award from a professional association, research the organization, the significance of the award, and the criteria used in the selection process. Knowing the details enables you to prepare a more heartfelt congratulations.

Asking for help and showing the results

"A friend in need is a friend indeed" also applies to colleagues. Seeking help from a supervisor or peer can be an expression of respect. It provides a valuable networking opportunity by giving you a chance to talk about yourself and your goals. And, it may even result in a mentorship or sponsorship! To seek help and follow up in an effective way, take the following steps:

1. Identify the person you think can help you the most.

2. Let that person know what you're seeking to accomplish and how you think they can help.

Prepare a request that includes the following details:

- A brief introduction to yourself: your name, company/department, and position/role. (You can shorten or omit the introduction if you already have a relationship with the person, but be sure to state what's relevant to your request.)

- A description of the specific goal or project for which you're seeking guidance or other assistance.

- A brief explanation of why you need help or the obstacle preventing you from achieving your goal or completing the project.

- Why you believe this person is best qualified to help you. Can this individual help you with funding, expertise, connections, leadership? What qualifies this person to provide you with what you're requesting?

  Better yet, use the "I + verb" framework presented in Chapter 8 to highlight this person's unique qualifications. For example, rather than say, "You have expertise in x y z that can help me," say something like this: "I admire the work you've done on x y z and feel that it can benefit me in this task."

- A detailed description of what you're asking the person to do. For example, are you asking for a few hours a month, assistance in writing a grant proposal, introductions to other people who may be able to provide assistance, or funding?

3. **Assuming that the person agrees to assist you and you agree that what the person offers you has value, act on the recommendations you receive. (Or, be prepared to explain why you didn't — no excuses!).**

   One of the biggest mistakes you can make is to ask for advice and not follow it. If you decide not to follow through on what you're offered, explain why.

4. **Collaborate closely and keep your partner/mentor apprised of your progress.**

   This follow-up step is vital, and it's where most people who ask for help drop the ball. People like to know when they've made a difference, and showing them that they have done so can strengthen your relationship.

Asking for help is perhaps my favorite strategy for self-promotion and education because it's kind of like buy one get one free: You get to not only talk about yourself, your accomplishments, and your goals but also seek out help that may result in either a mentorship or a sponsorship. Such a great communicative strategy!

Suppose that you want to become Six Sigma-certified and need help making the case for professional development funds. (Six Sigma is a methodology for improving business processes.) You know you have skills in project management, strategic thinking, and analytics, but you've struggled to secure the funds and the time away from the office to pursue certification. You realize that a manager in another department, Sarah, is Six Sigma-certified, and you think she may be able to help you. Your request might go something like this:

> Hi, Sarah. My name is Logan, and I'm a project manager over in manufacturing. I was looking through the company's directory for people who are Six Sigma-certified and noticed that you received your certification last year after being with

the organization for two years. I'm entering my third year with the company, and I have success in managing a number of projects but know that I can improve. I think this certification would take my skills to the next level and benefit the organization as a whole, but I've been struggling to secure the funds and time off to pursue certification. Would you be willing to have a brief conversation with me about the path you took to achieve this goal?

This request demonstrates that you've done some research, that you have skills and results to bring to the table, and that you have a specific need. This is a much stronger "ask" than simply saying "Hi, Sarah. I see you're Six Sigma-certified. Could you help me become certified, too?"

Assuming that Sarah is willing to either meet or share information with you, following up is critical. After you use some of the advice or information Sarah shares, circle back to let her know precisely the information/advice you found useful, how you acted on it, and the outcome you achieved. Here's an example of what you might say during a follow-up contact:

Hey, Sarah. Thank you so much for the advice you gave me about mapping the criteria of Six Sigma-certification with my performance review metrics. I did exactly that in making the presentation to my supervisor and was successful in getting permission to start the program next quarter. I am so grateful for your insights, and I'll keep you posted on how my certification progresses. Again, I appreciate you helping me clear this first hurdle.

Notice that the follow-up is specific about the advice that was given, the action taken, and the outcome. In this format, I have no doubt that Sarah would be willing to help again if you requested her assistance. I also imagine that *you* would be willing to help anyone else who is trying to achieve the same thing by paying it forward.

Networking in Meaningful Ways

Networking is all about putting yourself out there — letting people know who you are and what you do — but it's effective only if you're doing it for everyone's mutual benefit. In fact, networking can backfire if you're doing it purely for selfish reasons. Just think of the number of times you received a LinkedIn request to connect from someone you had never heard of. The other day, I received a request to connect from a coach looking to help me "publish my first book." Given that I have four published books and multiple other publications, this message was purely for selfish and spam reasons, and I wouldn't accept that request or grant this person access to those in my network.

Networking in meaningful ways involves establishing mutually beneficial relationships. Before inviting someone to network with you, be sure you have a compelling reason to add them to your network. Likewise, don't agree to network with someone unless they provide you with a compelling reason to do so. Focus on quality connections over quantity.

In this section, I present several techniques for having productive conversations that can bring mutual benefits now or in the future and for avoiding costly networking mistakes.

Finding genuine connections and alignments

When engaging in conversations in networking situations, go beyond the surface-level questions of "What do you do?" and "Who do you work for?" Instead, try to make genuine connections and identify opportunities for forming strategic alliances. Here are a few topics of conversation that can help you connect on a deeper level with networking candidates and identify potential strategic alliances:

>> Passions and hobbies outside of work

>> Challenges/obstacles you've encountered in your careers and in your personal lives

>> Career goals and paths

>> Industry trends and innovations

>> Books, podcasts, webinars, and other educational materials you've found to be relevant and fascinating

>> Mentorship (asking about their experience with mentors and sharing your own)

>> Community involvement

>> Travel experiences

>> Potential future partnerships or collaborations

TIP

Expand the conversation beyond the usual shop talk to discover other possible alignments. Rather than network for self-promotion, use it to uncover potential partnerships or alliances — ways that you can advance or promote one another. By diving deeper, you naturally uncover openings to educate others about yourself.

Suppose that you're a rising star in the sales department for a local Christmas light installation company. You're attending networking events in your area because, obviously, you want to score some new clients. However, you know that if you show up spewing a sales pitch and handing out your cards like a dealer in Vegas, you'll trigger a stampede toward the exits. Instead, you strike up a conversation with a complete stranger and discover that they're in sales for a medical device company in the area. You ask, "Why medical devices?" and they launch into a story about how their father received an early diagnosis of pancreatic cancer, thanks to the cutting-edge equipment available at his area hospital, and that was crucial in saving his life.

Now what? If this person asks you what you do for a living, you can't possibly tell him that you sell Christmas light installation services. Fortunately, you recall that your company donated Christmas lights to the local cancer clinic, so you have a meaningful connection. You respond by saying, "Wow, cancer survivors like your dad are true warriors. Last year, my company donated Christmas lights to the New Hope Cancer Clinic. I got to talk to several of the patients, and our installation team had the opportunity to see firsthand the importance of bringing little joys to those patients and their families."

My guess is that you'll both remember that conversation and connection much more than if you merely mentioned that you both sell things. Meaningful exchanges like this one are far more impactful than the usual conversations about title, role, and company name.

Matchmaking to expand your reach

Networking offers a unique way to expand your reach by expanding the reach of others. When you have an extensive and diverse collection of contacts, you naturally begin to identify opportunities for creating mutually beneficial relationships among people in your network. So-and-so needs a software developer, and you just happen to know one. You just learned that a project manager friend of yours is out of work, and that CEO you know over at Ace Pharmaceutical is looking for a good project manager. All you need is to connect the two and you're a hero to both.

Don't share anyone's contact information without their permission. When you're making introductions, pitch the potential opportunity to both parties and ask them both for permission to share their information with the other party. If they give their permission, then you can pass along their contact information.

TIP

Reinforce your own strengths in these introductions! I can show this technique in more detail by continuing the example from the earlier section "Finding genuine connections and alignments." You sell Christmas light installation services. You know the medical director at the New Hope Cancer Clinic, and now, after this event, you know a person who sells a medical device that's helpful for early detection of cancer. Bam! You've made a connection in your head.

Now, to continue the conversation with your new networking connection, you ask whether they've sold any devices to the New Hope Cancer Clinic, and they say, "Not for lack of trying. I've been there a half-dozen times and can't get past the receptionist."

Since you personally handled the account for the cancer clinic's holiday decorations, you offer to make an introduction. Your new contact says, "That'd be awesome! Here's my card."

The next day, you contact the medical director and mention your meeting with the medical device rep (while you were attending a networking event to support the local Chamber), and you share a few details about the device. The medical director says, "That sounds interesting. Do you have contact information?" You share the rep's contact information and ask whether the medical director wants you to facilitate a conversation. Then you call the rep and share your update.

All the while, you're bringing a third person into the conversation, demonstrating your sincere interest in the success of both parties and your attention to detail, and facilitating a meaningful and mutually beneficial connection. What a terrific position to be in, and what an amazing way to showcase what you're capable of accomplishing! The next time either of these people needs Christmas lights installed, you know who they're going to call!

Avoiding these networking no-no's

You can do more harm than good for your business or career by making these common networking mistakes, so avoid them:

>> **Speed dating:** You fly through the room shaking as many hands as possible as you tell everyone about yourself and shove your card in their hands. This approach makes people feel targeted and uneasy about talking with you or even being associated with you. If they politely accept your card, they will likely toss it to the side at best and throw it in the trash at worst.

>> **Tuning out:** You introduce yourself and ask a question, but, ten seconds into the answer, your mind has left your body and is scouring the room to identify the next person you want to meet. In addition to being rude, tuning out is pointless: You'll never recall the person or the conversation. Remain engaged at all times, listening with an open mind and an open ear for opportunities that could benefit the other person. (See Chapter 5 for more about developing listening skills.)

>> **Asking for too much too soon:** Take time to build a relationship before requesting any big favors. As discussed in Chapter 8, in the section about getting a yes response faster, a premature request can have disastrous consequences.

>> **Monopolizing the conversation:** Focus on asking questions and encouraging the others in the conversation to open up about themselves. You'll get your chance to share.

>> **Remaining in your comfort zone:** Be courteous to anyone you already know, but don't spend all your time talking with them. Focus on expanding your network and meeting new people. Or, if you're new to networking, work with your existing connections to meet people together.

>> **Not following up:** When you meet someone through your networking efforts, that's the beginning, not the end. Be sure to exchange contact information. Email or text your new contact the following day to remind them of who you are and where you met. If appropriate, ask the person to meet to get to know them better or keep in touch in other ways.

Take an other-centric approach. Try to find ways to assist the other person before exploring ways that they can benefit you and grow your network.

Inspiring Your Colleagues and Clients to Sing Your Praises

Better than any self-promotion is an endorsement or a testimonial — praise from others who've experienced or observed you. It's the difference between an advertisement and a product review. So how do you make that happen? How do you get people to speak well on your behalf? In this section, I explain how to leverage the power of mentorships, sponsorships, coaching, and clients to spread the word about who you are and what you do, and how others can benefit from what you have to offer.

Word-of-mouth is the most powerful form of advertising, and this applies to self-promotion as well. The more people talking you up, the better.

Leveraging the promotional power of mentorships

A *mentorship* is a relationship between two people in which the mentor shares knowledge, experience, and guidance with the mentee. In either role, a mentorship can help you promote yourself or your business.

By no means is your mentor or mentee obligated to actively promote you, but the relationship you develop and the conversations and experiences you share give you opportunities to educate your mentor or mentee on your values, knowledge, insights, and abilities. Assuming that you make a good impression, that person will think and speak highly of you and share opportunities that come along whenever they deem them a good fit for you. Mentors and mentees can also play a more active role in promoting you by serving as a source for letters of recommendations, references, endorsements, and testimonials and by introducing you to people in their networks.

Here are a few suggestions for leveraging the promotional power of mentorships:

>> Focus on nurturing the relationship and let the promotional opportunities develop organically from it.

>> Demonstrate a commitment to learning and growth. Taking a proactive approach makes a positive impression.

>> Attend events with your mentor (if invited) so that you gain exposure to people in your mentor's network.

>> Seek opportunities to provide value in return. When appropriate, offer your knowledge, insights, and skills to further your mentor's success. The most productive mentorships are mutually beneficial.

Promoting yourself through sponsorships

A *sponsor* is someone — typically, within your organization or industry — who takes an interest in and plays an active role in advocating for and advancing your career. Your sponsor vouches for you, speaks positively on your behalf, recommends you for positions and opportunities that you're well suited for, and may even arrange for you to receive the funding and other resources you need for additional training/education or to succeed in whatever projects, tasks, or initiatives you're working on.

You may not even know you have a sponsor. For example, you may be promoted and never realize that someone you met from another department recommended you.

To take full advantage of sponsorships, follow these suggestions:

» Do your best to identify your sponsors so that you can at least thank them and possibly collaborate more closely with them to your mutual benefit.

» Thank your sponsors whenever you discover that they've done something on your behalf.

» Stay in close communication so that you can find out more about your sponsors and they can find out more about you.

Sponsorships can develop into incredibly strategic and synergistic relationships. Leveraged properly, they can expand your positive reputation and opportunities exponentially.

TIP

My client and friend Helen Appleby has written an informative book, *The Unwritten Rules of Women's Leadership* (Rethink Press, 2020), in which she outlines effective approaches for pursuing mentorships and sponsorships.

Expanding your reach with coaches

A *coach* is someone you recruit (or hire) to provide the guidance and support to excel at something, such as personal branding, time management, conflict resolution, or parenting. One of the benefits a coach brings to the table is an objective perspective on what you're doing and how you're doing it, along with insight on changes you can make to be more effective or efficient.

Experienced coaches generally have a broad network of clients, and although they need to keep their coach-client relationships confidential, they may, with your permission or at your request (and with the permission of their other clients), share career or business opportunities, make introductions or referrals, or even recommend you for certain positions. Don't hesitate to ask for a coach's help in promoting you. Although the coach may not be obligated to further your career success, that's often part of their job, and even if it's not, they may be happy to do it for you.

WARNING

Don't ask for what you haven't earned. Be sure that you're following the advice in this chapter (and in other areas of this book) for listening, communicating proactively, following up, and giving credit where it's due.

COACH ISN'T ALWAYS RIGHT

I played a lot of team sports growing up. One summer between fifth and sixth grades, I was bored with slow-pitch softball, so I started playing little league baseball. I was the only female player in the boys league in my hometown. I started the season pretty strong. I was a solid second baseman and the fifth batter in the lineup. If you know anything about baseball, you know that the better batter you are, the higher up you're placed in the lineup. And I was thrilled with my placement.

About midseason, my coach decided that he could improve my swing. He told me I could get a lot more power behind my swing if I changed the way I was holding my bat at the start of my swing. I tried what he recommended and wasn't comfortable with it. Coach kept telling me that the more I practiced, the more comfortable I'd become, and eventually I would be hitting better than ever.

Alas, this prediction never came true. By the end of the season, I was batting last on the team, and my average had dropped considerably.

The moral of this story is that coaches (and mentors and sponsors) aren't always right. If someone you respect gives you advice that doesn't work out for you, don't hold it against them. Be prepared to go back to the way you were doing things or try something different. And be prepared to share your experiences with them for why you made the pivot.

Asking clients for recommendations and referrals

If you're in business for yourself, your access to mentors, sponsors, or coaches may look a little different (because you don't have a full organization of colleagues and leaders to interact with), but you do have plenty of access to clients, who can be a valuable source of recommendations and referrals. Without being too pushy, ask your clients to help promote your business. Here are a few suggestions to encourage clients:

>> **Request a referral, recommendation, or testimonial soon after you've had a positive interaction with them.** In my speaking contracts, for example, it's actually one of the terms and conditions so that my team can follow up and collect them.

>> **Be specific about the skills, qualities, and experiences you'd like for them to highlight.** When seeking nominations for a recent award, I made the request to clients and industry colleagues with a list of what about my skill set and experiences I wanted to stand out in the application.

>> **Make it easy.** Refer clients to a platform, such as LinkedIn or a page on your website, where they can easily post their recommendation or testimonial. You can also offer to write a draft for them that they can edit. Many of my clients have found this strategy helpful because they want to provide something that will be valuable to my marketing team.

>> **Express your gratitude soon after they share their recommendation or referral(s).** If applicable, let them know the positive outcome of their recommendation or referral. For example, you may write a note saying, "Thanks for recommending me to Ms. Atkins. We spoke briefly and she's now one of our clients!" Or, depending on your business structure, you may want to send a thoughtful gift.

IN THIS CHAPTER

» Breaking down presentations into two types: informative and persuasive

» Following a basic presentation structure: beginning, middle, and end

» Laying the groundwork for a successful presentation

» Using visualization to inform, inspire, and motivate your audience

» Delivering your presentation with confidence — practice required

Chapter **11**

Calm, Cool, and Confident: Making and Delivering Presentations

The ability to create and deliver effective presentations is a vital skill for professionals across all industries. Whether you're sharing insights with colleagues, delivering sales presentations to prospective customers, or pitching ideas to stakeholders, presentations are essential for conveying information and driving desired outcomes.

In this chapter, I introduce you to the two basic presentation formats, explain how to structure an effective presentation, reveal what to do before delivering your presentation that can make it better, explain how to use visualization to your advantage, and provide guidance on how to practice your delivery to improve your confidence and poise.

Comparing Presentation Types: Informative versus Persuasive

In the realm of business communication and public speaking, presentations generally serve two purposes: to inform or persuade. Each of those purposes is unique and shapes the way information is delivered and received:

>> **Informative presentations** primarily educate the audience. They focus on delivering facts, explanations, instructions, and insights to enhance the audience's knowledge and understanding. The content consists primarily of factual data and information, statistics, and instruction. And, the presentation is structured in a way to deliver the content logically, using examples and illustrations to clarify. For example, an informative presentation may detail the features of a new software update, explain the principles behind a business process, or provide step-by-step instructions for following a new company procedure. These presentations are often characterized by a neutral tone.

REMEMBER

Neutral tone doesn't mean monotone! People learn best when they're engaged and having fun, so look for ways to make even (or especially) your informative presentations interesting and engaging.

>> **Persuasive presentations** aim to change minds or behaviors or prompt the audience to take a specific action, such as buy a product, subscribe to a service, support a candidate or a cause, or secure stakeholder buy-in for a proposed initiative. They go beyond merely informing to influencing, and they typically blend factual information with emotional appeals to sway the audience. For example, a sales pitch for the latest technology product doesn't just list and describe features (as an informative presentation is likely to do) but also emphasizes the benefits of purchasing the product, perhaps appealing to the customer's desires for convenience, simplicity, or comfort.

Understanding these differences is important for any communicator. By knowing the underlying purpose of a presentation, you can tailor your message more effectively to a specific audience and choose and structure your content in a way that's better suited to achieving the desired outcome. With a clear view of your presentation goal — to inform or to persuade — you're ready to start structuring your presentation and making well-informed choices about the content to include in your message.

Structuring Your Presentation: As Simple as 1-2-3

Every presentation is unique, but what they all have in common is their structure — a beginning, middle, and end — or, more specifically, an engaging introduction, a well-organized body, and a compelling conclusion with a strong call to action. Using this simple structure, anyone can create a powerful presentation that drives home the intended message and motivates the audience to learn and/or act.

REMEMBER

Crafting an effective, impactful presentation involves both art and science. The science is what gives the presentation its basic structure. The art is the creativity you bring to everything within that structure. In this section, I focus on the science (the structure) of business presentations, which may seem restrictive at times. However, keep in mind that this basic structure provides you with an incredible amount of leeway to be creative and cater to the unique needs and communication styles of a broad range of audiences.

Introduction: Starting off on the right foot

The introduction of the presentation sets the tone for the rest of it. In a standard presentation structure, the introduction contains three parts:

>> Gaining attention

>> Stating your purpose

>> Previewing what's to come

Gaining your audience's attention

Whether your goal is to inform or persuade an audience, you need to capture their attention first. You can *hook* an audience (like you hook a fish) by telling a compelling story, sharing an intriguing quote or a startling fact or statistic, telling a relevant joke, asking a provocative question, or making a bold statement. You may think of other creative ways of your own.

WARNING

Start with a joke only if you're sure it'll draw a laugh and only if it's relevant to the content of your presentation. Don't start with a joke merely to calm your own nerves or to get the audience to relax. You want the joke to reinforce or set up your message, not detract from it.

TIP

A helpful way to gain attention is to tell a story that simultaneously establishes your credibility. For example, if you're delivering a presentation to your new team to promote agile development (developing products incrementally in short cycles called *sprints*), you could tell a story about how your team at a previous company became far more innovative after adopting this approach. This story would set the stage and establish your credibility at the same time.

Stating your purpose or thesis

After gaining your audience's attention, state the purpose or thesis of your presentation. (A *thesis* is a main point, opinion, or theory that you prove or support in the course of your presentation.) Your overall purpose may be to inform, persuade, educate, train, report, pitch, motivate, celebrate, solve a problem, build relationships, or something else, but be specific. Clearly state the purpose of your presentation — the outcome you're hoping to achieve. For example, you might say, "By the end of my presentation, you'll be kicking yourself for not subscribing sooner."

Stating your purpose or thesis gives your audience a compelling reason to pay attention.

Previewing what's to come

After stating the purpose of your presentation, give your audience a road map so they know what to expect. For example, you may say something like this:

> Before diving into the details, I'd like to provide you with a brief overview of what I'm going to cover. I'll start by discussing the current market trends in our industry and the challenges and opportunities they present. Next, I'll delve into our company's strategic response to these trends, including our new product initiatives and market expansion plans. Following that, I'll examine our recent performance metrics and key achievements and highlight areas for improvement. Finally, I'll open the floor for questions and discussion to address any concerns or insights you may have. By the end of our time together, I hope you'll have a clear understanding of where we stand as a company and where we're headed. Without further ado, let's get started.

Think of the overview as the foundation and frame of a home you'll be building over the course of your presentation. This mental framework provides an underlying structure on which your audience can hang all the details you're about to present.

Body: Serving the main course

The body of a presentation is the portion between the introduction and the conclusion, in which you elaborate on key points, discuss relevant information, and present supporting evidence, analysis, instruction, and other content. What you include in the body can vary considerably based on the topic and the purpose of the presentation, but it needs to follow a clear and logical progression, with each point building on the previous one to maintain audience engagement and understanding. In this section, I cover various ways to organize a business presentation and persuade an audience.

Choosing a conventional organizational structure

Structuring your presentation content logically makes it more accessible to your audience. By following a predictable pattern, you make it easier for the audience to organize the content in their own minds. As you begin to conceptualize your presentation, consider organizing your content using one of the following conventional structures:

>> **Chronological** organizes information in a time-based sequence, which is ideal for presenting timelines, project updates, progress reports, and historical overviews.

   For example, your team just completed a project and, as the project manager, you're giving a post-project analysis. You decide to walk your team through the project from start to finish. You cover the reason the project was initiated, the selection of the team, the planning phase, the execution, key milestones, challenges your team encountered along the way, and the end result.

>> **Spatial** arranges information according to its location or layout, which is suitable for presenting maps, floor plans, organizational charts, supply chains, and so on.

   For example, during a strategy session on workplace optimization, you want to propose new office layouts aimed at enhancing productivity. Your presentation walks through the current office setup and then transitions to proposed layouts: the main workspace, break rooms, meeting areas, and recreational areas. Each section of the office is discussed in terms of changes and expected impacts on employee interaction and productivity. During the presentation, you walk people through the new layout.

>> **Topical** breaks down the subject into related themes or categories, offering flexibility and clarity when addressing complex subjects with multiple subtopics.

   For example, you're an HR manager and you need to conduct a training session covering new employee benefits. You organize the presentation into topics: health insurance, retirement plans, professional development, and wellness programs. Each section details the specifics of the benefits, eligibility, and enrollment. This structure enables employees to grasp the range of benefits available and understand how to access each one.

» **Problem-solution** outlines an issue and follows with a proposed solution. This structure is particularly effective for persuasive presentations, enabling you to establish a need and propose a solution for meeting that need. (See Chapter 13 for details about structuring a persuasive presentation.)

For example, you've just been chosen to lead a project team and you have been given your first objective — to present strategies to increase sales by 25 percent in the next quarter. Based on your previous experience in sales at other companies, you know that a strong customer relationship management (CRM) platform would be beneficial and you're hoping to convince the leadership team to approve funding for it. You present the problem — not having easy access and a quick view of customer data — and then provide your recommendation — implementing a CRM platform.

» **Cause-effect** explores the relationship between events or conditions and the factors that produced them. This structure is effective for analyzing and explaining trends, predicting consequences, and identifying and explaining the root causes of problems.

For example, during a quarterly review, you, the sales manager, need to explain why your team failed to meet the sales target. Your presentation starts by identifying recent changes in the market and competitor activities as causes. It then links these to effects such as decreased customer engagement and reduced sales. You conclude by proposing strategies to adapt to these market challenges and recover lost sales.

» **Compare and contrast** involves analyzing and explaining the similarities and differences between options, strategies, products, solutions, and so on to highlight their differences and their advantages and disadvantages. This structure is useful for presenting product comparisons and competitive analysis and leading decision-making sessions.

» For example, as a member of your marketing team, you've been chosen to deliver a presentation on the advantages and disadvantages of different marketing channels — social media, print, television, search engine, email, podcasts, influencers, and so on. You decide to compare and contrast the different media channels in terms of reach, cost-effectiveness, and audience engagement to enable your team to make well-informed choices.

Organizational structures aren't mutually exclusive; your presentation may combine two or more structures. For example, a problem-solution presentation may begin with a chronological timeline of how the problem arose or a cause-effect analysis of the underlying conditions that gave rise to the problem. Keep these structures in mind and let the content drive your decisions about the most effective way(s) to organize it.

Using rhetorical strategies to sway your audience

In persuasive presentations, the classical appeals of ethos (credibility), pathos (emotion), and logos (logic) play a critical role in influencing an audience's perception and reaction. These three modes of persuasion, articulated by Aristotle over two millennia ago, remain foundational in crafting effective speeches and presentations, especially persuasive presentations but even when your purpose is to inform.

Understanding and applying these modes of persuasion can significantly enhance your credibility and the impact of your presentation:

» **Ethos** refers to the credibility or the character of the speaker. Early in your presentation and throughout the course of it, you need to establish your knowledge and expertise on the topic. Establishing ethos involves more than just listing qualifications; it's about demonstrating knowledge, experience, and a strong command of the subject matter. For instance, a business leader discussing innovative strategies may share personal success stories, reference established works, or cite professional experiences that contribute to their standing as a trusted authority on the topic. You can also convey ethos by projecting confidence and poise. By solidifying your credibility, you not only command attention but also foster trust, making your audience more receptive to the material and your insights and perspective.

    If a previous speaker introduces you, that person may establish your ethos for you. Your ethos also grows with your reputation.

» **Pathos** is the quality of a presentation that arouses emotions, which often influence decision-making. Pathos can be engaged through storytelling, vivid language, and the strategic use of visuals and sounds that resonate with the audience's emotions. For example, a nonprofit organization seeking donations to aid disaster relief might share heart-wrenching images and stories of affected individuals, aiming to evoke sympathy and prompt the audience to pledge money. However, though pathos can be a powerful tool in persuasion, use it judiciously and ethically to avoid manipulation and ensure that emotional appeals are backed by facts and genuine intent.

» **Logos** is the quality of a presentation that appeals to logical minds. It consists of reasoning and empirical data that support a position or claim. In a business context, you can enhance logos by presenting research reports, trends, statistical evidence, and logical arguments that highlight the benefits and practicality of a proposed plan or product. For example, a tech company may use data-driven presentations to demonstrate the efficiency and cost-effectiveness of a new software solution, appealing to the logical, analytical mindset of potential corporate buyers.

REMEMBER

Logos not only enhances the persuasiveness of a presentation by appealing to the intellect but also helps to ground emotional appeals (pathos) and bolster the speaker's credibility (ethos).

Effective persuasive presentations often blend all three of these appeals. A speaker may begin by establishing ethos, move on to engaging the audience's emotions through pathos, and then anchor their message in logos. For example, in a business conference, a speaker may start by outlining their expertise and background (ethos), use a compelling narrative about a client's challenges and triumphs (pathos), and conclude with compelling statistics and case studies that offer concrete evidence of their proposal (logos).

Understanding the differences between ethos, pathos, and logos and how to integrate them can transform presentations, making them more compelling and effective. This integration ensures that the message not only resonates on an emotional level but is also underpinned by credibility and logic, making for better presentations, whether your goal is to inform or persuade.

Conclusion: Delivering your call to action

The conclusion of a presentation is critical because it synthesizes the information presented and reinforces the main points. As with the introduction, think of the conclusion as also containing three sections: a summary, a reinforcement of the main message, and a call to action:

» **Summary:** Synthesize into a single sentence everything you covered, if possible — a few sentences at most. For example, you may say something like, "As you can see, we are facing an urgent and complex challenge in dealing with the impacts of inflation on our sales. Fortunately, we can overcome that challenge by working together to implement my proposal."

» **Reinforcement:** Restate your goal or purpose clearly and succinctly. For example, if you're in HR and you just delivered a comprehensive overview of benefits to employees, highlight those benefits in a way that reinforces your organization's commitment to their health, safety, and well-being.

REMEMBER

Follow the rule of three: Tell your audience what you're going to tell 'em, tell 'em, and then tell 'em what you told 'em. Repeating your main points at least three times is a classic technique for reinforcing your message, and it fits with the overall presentation structure I recommend in this chapter — beginning, middle, and end.

>> **Call to action (CTA):** Your CTA for an informative presentation may be as basic as providing your contact information for any follow-up questions or concerns or providing links to additional resources. For persuasive presentations, the CTA encourages the audience to change their mind or behavior or follow a certain course of action, such as adopt a new business strategy, register for a service, or support the proposed initiative.

REMEMBER

Make your CTA clear, compelling, and actionable, providing the audience with a sense of urgency and purpose. For example, after a presentation on the importance of cybersecurity, you may conclude by urging the company to adopt a specific security solution and outlining the steps to begin the process immediately.

TIP

Delivering a strong request isn't always easy. Here are five strategies for crafting a CTA that resonates and motivates your audience to act:

>> **Be clear and specific.** Leave no room for ambiguity about what you expect the audience to do next. Specify the action you want them to take, the steps for taking it, and any deadlines. For example, rather than say "Consider our product," say "Sign up for a free trial by the end of this week."

>> **Create a sense of urgency.** To compel your audience to act swiftly, incorporate a sense of urgency in your CTA. You can convey an urgent need by highlighting what they stand to gain by acting quickly or what they may lose by delaying.

REMEMBER

Before delivering an urgent CTA, have in place all the logistics that enable your audience to act immediately. For example, if you're asking colleagues to share their ideas or feedback, distribute notebooks so that audience members can jot down their ideas on the spot. Alternatively, have a designated area with whiteboards or a suggestion box, or offer an email address or web page where audience members can send or report their feedback conveniently.

>> **Align with the audience's interests.** Tailor your CTA to align with your audience's goals, challenges, or needs. By demonstrating how the proposed action serves their interests or solves a problem for them, you enhance the appeal of your CTA. For example, if you're addressing a group of managers, emphasize how adopting a new tool could save time and reduce operational costs.

>> **Use engaging language.** An engaging and motivational tone can enhance the effectiveness of your CTA. Use strong, action-oriented verbs and confident language to inspire and energize your audience. Make them feel empowered to take the action you propose and optimistic about the outcomes. Make sure your audience realizes what's in it for them.

>> **Repeat your CTA.** Repetition can reinforce your message and make it more memorable. Mention your CTA early in your presentation to plant the idea, elaborate on it as you proceed, and finally, restate it powerfully at the end to ensure it sticks with your audience.

By incorporating these strategies, you can craft a CTA that not only captures attention but also drives your audience toward the desired action, maximizing the impact of your business presentation.

Preparing for Presentation Success

Presentation success relies on more than the structure and content of the presentation. It extends to factors beyond the presentation itself, such as spatial arrangement, lighting, acoustics, and technologies. In this section, I provide guidance on how to ensure that these external factors facilitate and support your presentation rather than complicate and detract from it.

Setting the stage for your presentation: Environmental considerations

Setting the stage for your presentation applies regardless of whether you're delivering your presentation from a physical stage. After all, you may be presenting to only a few people sitting around a table in a conference room or to a virtual audience. Setting the stage simply means making sure the environment is suitable for you, your presentation, and your audience and ensuring that everything works — audio system, lighting, computer, presentation software, Internet connection, projector, and so on.

In this section, I explain how to choose and configure a space, check it to ensure everything's working as expected, and plan for the unexpected. This section focuses on physical environments; I cover virtual environments in the next section.

Choosing and arranging a space

When you're planning a presentation, consider the expected size of your audience, the desired ambience (mood), and how intimately you want to connect and interact with your audience. With these considerations in mind, take the following steps:

1. **Choose a suitable venue.**

   Choose a venue that's sized for the audience you anticipate. Empty seats can change the audience's energy. You don't want a large auditorium with stadium seating if you're going to present to a dozen people (or fewer). Also consider factors such as acoustics, lighting, availability of audio/visual equipment, convenience of parking and restroom facilities, and space for any breakout sessions or interactive activities.

2. **Arrange the furniture (if possible and practical).**

   To facilitate and encourage engagement and interaction, arrange seats in a circle or U shape around where you'll be presenting. You can reserve a seat for yourself at one point in the circle or in the best position for everyone to see you. Keep in mind that arranging chairs in a classroom style (all chairs facing forward, toward the presenter) creates a formal setting that discourages dialogue and interaction.

   Also arrange furniture in a way that makes the room easy to navigate, especially for anyone in the audience who has difficulty moving.

REMEMBER

   The physical proximity between the speaker and the audience affects communication dynamics. In larger rooms, speakers must rely more on vocal projection and visual aids to connect with the audience, whereas, in a more intimate setting, nuances such as facial expressions and gestures become more impactful.

3. **Remove any physical barriers between the speaker and the audience, such as a podium, desk, or table (unless everyone will be seated around the desk or table).**

   Physical barriers can have a negative impact on the audience's perception of your presentation. They can make the audience feel as though they're sitting in the principal's office being chastised for breaking a school rule or that you're hiding behind a podium.

4. **Provide comfort.**

   It may seem obvious, but make the space as comfortable as possible in terms of seating and temperature, and provide amenities such as refreshments. Let everyone know where the restrooms are located.

5. **Enhance the visual appeal.**

   Consider the aesthetics of the space, and look for opportunities to use décor to create a welcoming and engaging environment. You can also use signage and décor to reinforce your brand or the theme of your presentation.

MUST YOU STAND TO DELIVER?

To help you appreciate the importance of arranging a presentation space, let me tell you a story from when I was teaching business communication to undergraduate students at Arizona State University. For their final project, students had to conduct, in teams, a communication audit of a fictitious organization, essentially acting as consultants. After conducting this audit and writing their report, students were to present their findings to the board of directors of this fictitious organization — me and two other business professionals who volunteered their time. The conference room had one rectangular table and 12 chairs. The two business professionals and I were seated in a line on one side of the table.

Each student group would enter the room, look around, and stand on the opposite side of the table to deliver their presentation. When they were done, I invited them to sit down. I then asked whether they were more comfortable sitting down, to which they replied, yes, it was a little weird standing to present to three people in so small a room.

I then asked, "Why did you stand to give the presentation? Why didn't you sit down?"

Inevitably a student would say something like, "Because you're supposed to stand when you give a presentation."

"Who says?" I'd ask. And they would look at me in silence.

(I, too, found it awkward to be seated with two other people listening to four people standing in front of me to deliver their presentation.)

The thought of giving a presentation often creates an image of somebody standing in front of a roomful of people who are all sitting passively while absorbing knowledge. But the most effective presentations feel like — and often are — conversations. And, if your environment enables you to level the physical playing field, don't be afraid to take advantage of it!

Checking the acoustics: Testing — one, two, three

Poor acoustics (sound quality) can hinder communication, making it difficult for the audience to hear and understand the presenter, which can lead to disengagement. Acoustics aren't generally a major consideration in small venues, such as an office or conference room, but you should still check out any space where you will speak. Here are some suggestions for checking the acoustics:

>> In a large, unfamiliar venue, check with the venue's manager to find out about any acoustics issues you need to be aware of.

>> Check the room size and shape. Large rooms or those with high ceilings are more likely to have problems with echoes. Clap your hands or yell and listen for echoes or reverberations, indicating that sound is bouncing off hard surfaces. Having more people in the room reduces the effect. Acoustic treatments such as sound-absorbing panels, carpeting, and curtains can also help.

>> Listen for any noises that could distract an audience, such as the low hum of an air conditioner or noise from nearby traffic (ground or air).

>> Use sound equipment, if necessary, such as a microphone, an amplifier, and speakers, and be sure to test the equipment beforehand, regardless of whether it is yours or is provided by the venue.

TIP

Even if you have a booming voice, you may benefit from using sound equipment, especially in a large venue. If a meeting planner sets up a microphone in a room, don't ignore their subtle suggestion; they probably put it there because they know you'll need it to provide the best quality experience for your audience.

Taking the technology for a test-drive

Test any technology you're going to need to deliver your presentation, including microphones, amplifiers, and speakers; projectors and screens; the computer and software you'll be using to deliver your slide show; your laser pointer (if you use one); and your Internet connection. If all your presentation files are in the cloud and you can't connect to the Internet to access them, you'll become flummoxed, especially if you didn't plan for such an emergency. Also, be sure you have power cords and connectors for all the equipment. If possible, connect all the equipment the day before your presentation and take it for a test-drive.

Don't check technology merely to see whether it works but also to become comfortable using it, especially if you're using unfamiliar equipment, such as a microphone or projector provided by the venue.

WARNING

Always have a Plan B. I've seen many presenters over-rely on technology. What happens when the technology doesn't work and you can't show your slides? These presenters often fail. The best presenters always have a Plan B and know exactly what to do if the technology fails. For example, they may have printouts of key slides that they pass out in an emergency.

REMEMBER

Don't try to dazzle your audience with technology. Technologies should supplement, not supplant, your presentation.

Using a slide deck

Slide show presentations are a staple in business environments, offering a visual complement to spoken words that can significantly enhance the impact of your message. To ensure your slide show presentations are effective, here are some essential tips to follow:

>> **Keep it simple.** Slides should be clean and uncluttered. Use simple backgrounds and avoid overcrowding slides with too much text or too many images. A good rule is to focus on one main idea per slide.

>> **Maintain consistency.** Use a consistent layout, font style, and color scheme throughout the presentation. This uniformity helps maintain a professional appearance and keeps the audience focused on the content instead of the design.

>> **Use high-quality graphics.** Incorporate high-resolution images and professional graphics. High-quality images boost your credibility and enhance the visual appeal of your slides, and can help explain complex information more clearly than text alone. (See the next section for more about using graphics and other media to enhance your presentation.)

>> **Limit bullet points.** Too many bullet points can overwhelm your audience. Limit yourself to a few, if any, bullet points per slide and expand on them verbally. This approach keeps your slides clean and maintains their focus on listening to you instead of reading the screen.

Seeing too much information on a single slide can overwhelm your audience and detract from your presentation. Human attention is triggered by change. When you change a slide, the first thing people do is look at the slide. Then the majority will read the slide. Finally, they'll tune back into you as the speaker. Keeping your slides simple with one main point or strategic animation can help keep the audience's attention focused on you as the speaker.

>> **Use animations sparingly and in sync with your narration.** Animations can be effective for drawing attention to specific points, but overuse can be distracting. Use animation to build your visuals step by step as you explain them. For example, if you're presenting a flowchart that outlines a process, introduce each step sequentially with animation, syncing your verbal explanation with the appearance of each new element of the flowchart. This approach keeps the audience focused on what you're discussing at any given moment and prevents them from reading ahead or getting lost.

>> **Use color and contrast effectively.** Use color and contrast to draw attention to key points and organize information visually. Colors can highlight differences, show relationships, and indicate importance. For example, in a pie chart representing sales of different products, use contrasting colors for each

segment to clearly differentiate them. Highlight the best-selling product with a brighter color or a larger slice.

>> **Practice your timing.** Run through your presentation multiple times to practice the flow and timing. Make sure each slide is displayed long enough to be absorbed by the audience but not too long. Slides should change quickly enough to keep the presentation moving forward at a comfortable pace that maintains the audience's engagement.

>> **Prepare for technical issues.** Always have a backup plan in case of technical difficulties. Consider having backup equipment, a copy of your presentation on a different device, and/or a printed outline of your presentation.

>> **Ensure accessibility.** Make sure your visuals are accessible to all audience members, including those with visual impairments. Use color schemes that are colorblind-friendly, and provide textual descriptions for graphics when appropriate. Avoid combinations like red/green in your charts, and ensure sufficient contrast between text and background colors. Include alternative text for graphs and images when sharing slides digitally.

WARNING

Don't look at your slides when giving a presentation. *Your slides are not your audience.* If you need to glance at a slide to get your bearings, don't speak as you're doing so, because the direction of your voice will change, which can prevent some people in the room from hearing you clearly. If you need to look at a slide, set your computer to Speaker mode so that you can have that information in front of you. You're presenting to your audience — to the humans in the room — not to the technology. Don't use your slide show as a crutch to help you remember what you should know.

Incorporating visuals and other media

A picture may not be worth exactly 1,000 words, but graphs, illustrations, videos, and other visuals can be quite effective in communicating information and insights, and they're often far more effective and efficient than words. You just need to know how to use them properly. Here are a few suggestions:

>> **Integrate visuals seamlessly with your text.** Your visuals should complement your words, not compete with them. Introduce each visual element as it comes up and explain what the audience is looking at and why it's important. For example, if you bring up a graph, guide the audience through it by stating, "Here you can see how our market share has increased significantly over the past three years, outpacing our main competitors."

>> **Choose the right visual.** Match the visual to the data or concept you're presenting. If you're presenting sales growth over several years, for example,

a line graph would effectively show trends and patterns. For a breakdown of market share among competitors, a pie chart would provide a clear visual representation of each competitor's proportion. If you're trying to help someone visualize an outcome, use an image or a mocked-up model.

>> **Leverage multimedia elements.** One of the most powerful aspects of using technology in presentations is the ability to integrate diverse multimedia elements. Audio, video, and animation can transform a mundane presentation into an engaging experience that captures and retains the audience's attention and can engage, entertain, educate, and transform an audience all at the same time. For instance, a short video clip that illustrates your points can provide a break from the spoken content, giving the audience a visual understanding of the application of complex concepts. Similarly, animations can demonstrate processes or highlight changes over time, making abstract ideas more concrete and understandable.

Prepping for virtual presentations: The same but different

A *virtual presentation* is one that's delivered to an audience online rather than in person. To meet the growing need to communicate and collaborate from diverse locations, virtual presentations have become a staple in the modern business environment. The tips in the following three sections can help you deliver effective virtual presentations. See Chapter 23 for additional tips and techniques to create engaging and successful virtual meetings.

Test your technology beforehand

Before a virtual presentation, conduct a complete run-through with the platform you'll be using. Check the platform for updates at least two hours before your presentation. Check your Internet connection, audio clarity, video quality, and any sharing tools. Testing helps to avoid technical issues, such as an inability to share your screen or interruptions due to poor connectivity, which can undermine your credibility and distract from your message.

Manage your presentation space

Set up your webcam at eye level and ensure your lighting is frontal to avoid shadows on your face. (That window you have behind you? It shines a backlight that darkens your face. So close those blinds!) Keep the background professional and distraction-free — possibly, using a branded virtual background if your camera quality allows for it without distorting anything. This setup helps maintain a professional image and keeps the focus on you and your presentation.

Use visuals wisely and keep slides clear and uncluttered

When explaining complex data, use clear and concise charts or infographics rather than large tables filled with numbers (see Chapter 23 for details). Simplicity helps the audience grasp your points quickly without getting lost in details that are hard to follow on a screen. Also realize that using slides with too many details or a font that's too small can detract from your audience's ability to follow along.

Design your slides with minimal text highlighting key takeaways. Use large fonts and adequate spacing. For instance, rather than a slide full of paragraphs explaining a product's benefits, use icons next to short, impactful statements, such as "Increases efficiency by 50%." Visuals should enhance your presentation, not overwhelm it. Avoid clutter by limiting the amount of text, using clear labels, and displaying only data that's relevant to your point.

Take advantage of the advanced features of remote presentation applications

As remote work environments become more common, technology has bridged the gap between speakers and audiences across the globe. Applications such as Zoom, Microsoft Teams, and Google Meet provide additional features that improve accessibility and facilitate engagement. I encourage you to explore these features, which include the following:

» **Screen sharing:** Presenters and participants can share their screens, enabling them to perform live demonstrations and showcase slides, documents, web pages, and other content.

» **Interactive polls and surveys:** Presenters can conduct live polls, surveys, and quizzes during the presentation to gather audience feedback, evaluate the audience's understanding of the topic, and generate discussion.

» **Live chat:** Participants can communicate with the presenter in real time, facilitating discussions, Q&A sessions, and collaboration.

» **Virtual whiteboard and annotation tools:** Digital whiteboards and annotation tools (text boxes, arrows, shapes, and highlighting) enable presenters to draw, sketch, or share handwritten notes in real time, encouraging and facilitating brainstorming and collaboration.

>> **Breakout rooms:** Presenters can divide participants into smaller groups for discussions, activities, and workshops.

>> **Audience engagement features:** Participants can use emojis and other icons to raise their hands, applaud, or express other reactions during the presentation. These and other engagement features can help you evaluate the audience's interest and adjust your presentation on the fly.

>> **Accessibility features:** Closed captioning, screen reader compatibility, and language translation can make a presentation more accessible to a broader audience.

>> **Recording/playback:** You can record a session for later playback, creating a valuable resource for reference and for sharing with others.

Leveraging the Communicative Power of Visualization

Visualization goes beyond what the eye can see. It involves creating mental images in a person's mind. Some people use visualization to control pain, improve performance, and promote healing. For example, one of the most accomplished Olympic swimmers of all time, Michael Phelps, is known to have used visualization as part of his training regimen. He would visualize every aspect of the race, from the dive off the blocks to the turns and the final stroke to the wall. He would imagine himself swimming flawlessly, feeling the water glide past him, and seeing himself touch the wall first.

As a presenter, you can use the audience's ability to visualize to create images in their minds that improve their understanding, evoke an emotional response, and motivate them to take action. Here are a few tips for creating vivid and impactful images in the minds of your audience:

>> **Use descriptive language.** Use words to paint a picture, create a scene, or re-create an experience in the minds of audience members. For example, rather than simply describe a new product as innovative, describe its features and benefits and how it revolutionizes the user's ability to perform an otherwise complicated or frustrating task.

>> **Incorporate storytelling.** Use narrative techniques to tell a story that resonates with your audience. A good story involves characters, conflicts, and

resolutions that reflect the themes of your presentation. For example, you could share a customer success story of a client who faced a specific challenge, chose your solution, and experienced remarkable results. Describe the client's initial struggle in detail, the decision-making process, and the joyful outcome.

>> **Use and/or create relatable characters.** When telling stories, introduce characters your audience can relate to; for example, "Meet Sarah, a longtime user of our product, who discovered a unique way to integrate our software into her daily workflow, turning what used to be a chore into a quick, pain-free task." Characters in an engaging story enable the audience to understand and, in some cases, relive the character's experience.

>> **Use comparisons to simplify and clarify.** Similes, metaphors, and analogies compare the unfamiliar with the familiar, helping to clarify complex ideas by linking them to everyday experiences (see Chapter 23 for details). If you're explaining a complex tech solution, you might say, "Think of our artificial intelligence (AI) solution as the ultimate consultant, drawing from an ever-growing knowledge base to deliver accurate and current information and insights from across the industry, answer questions on demand, and identify problems before anyone in your organization senses trouble."

>> **Invoke the senses and emotions.** Engage multiple senses in your descriptions — not just sight but also sound, smell, taste, and touch. Sensory language makes your content more engaging and memorable. Suppose you're explaining the new design of the office space. Rather than say it's an open-concept design, you could say: "As soon as you enter the new office space, the warm, inviting glow of the sun through the large windows and the soft hum of collaboration fill the air, creating an environment that energizes everyone who walks in." This example may be a little over the top, but I'm exaggerating to prove a point.

>> **Use dynamic verbs and active voice.** Dynamic verbs and an active voice contribute to a more vivid presentation by creating a sense of action and involvement. For example, if you're reporting on your team's progress for the quarter, which exceeded expectations, instead of simply saying, "We exceeded our goal by 25 percent, you could say, "Our team didn't just meet the target — we shattered expectations by adapting quickly, responding to customer feedback, and innovating under pressure." (By the way, this is a good example of self-promotion. For more information, read Chapter 10.)

By integrating these techniques into your business presentations, you can more effectively paint a picture with words, enhancing your audience's engagement and comprehension and evoking a little pathos while you're at it.

Practicing Your Presentation to Improve Your Confidence

You've likely heard the saying "Practice makes perfect." Well, I don't think there's any such thing as perfect, but practice does help you appear more prepared and confident. Even as a seasoned presenter, having spoken on very large stages for over 20 years, I always rehearse each and every presentation multiple times. I practice not only to hone my skills with the latest technologies but also because I'm learning something new every day that can improve my performance.

I encourage you to practice every presentation multiple times before delivering it. Here are five strategies for optimizing the performance boost you gain from your practice sessions:

>> **Practice under similar conditions.** Ideally, practice in the same venue where you'll deliver your presentation using the same equipment you plan to use. If anything goes wrong, you want it to go wrong during a practice session.

>> **Speak it out!** Practicing your presentation out loud is fundamentally different from merely reviewing your notes silently. Speak through your entire presentation as though you were in front of your audience. This technique helps you refine your speaking pace, tone, and articulation. Speaking also enables you to identify areas that may trip you so that you can make adjustments.

>> **Time yourself.** Use a timer to keep track of how long each section takes, making sure you stay within your allotted time without rushing through important points.

>> **Get specific feedback.** Before delivering your presentation to the intended audience, present it to colleagues or a mentor and ask for their feedback. They can provide insights on clarity, flow, content, and other specific elements of your presentation.

TIP

Set expectations for the type of feedback you want. Have certain people pay attention to your visuals, others to your message, and others to your delivery. The more specific you are about the type of feedback you seek, the more valuable the feedback you'll receive.

>> **Record and review.** Use video recording to capture your practice sessions and then watch them. Watching yourself can reveal habits such as unnecessary hand movements, filler words, or awkward pauses, which you can then make a conscious effort to eliminate. Watching yourself as an audience member also helps you refine your message and improve your nonverbal communication. Set up your smartphone or camera to record a practice session. As you review the recording, pay attention to your body language and eye contact, and to how well you engage with the imagined audience. Notice and work on smoothing out parts where you seem unsure or where your delivery lacks enthusiasm.

TIP

For a deep analysis of your presentation skills, record yourself speaking, and then watch that recording with the sound turned off. If you don't sense any emotion, confidence, or energy from your physical movements alone, you know you have to work on your nonverbal delivery.

WATCHING IN SILENCE: THE ULTIMATE HUMILITY PLAY

When I was in my early 20s, before digital cameras were the norm, I received a recording of myself doing a presentation on VHS. (For those of you who don't know what VHS is, I'm guessing you never had the fun experience of going to Blockbuster to rent a movie; let's just say it's an antiquated piece of recording technology.)

I started that speech strong, but I quickly noticed that I was making the same repetitive gesture with my hands — as if I were clapping . . . over and over again. Pretty soon, that's all I could look at! This repetitive gesture definitely detracted from my message and delivery. And, once I saw it, it was much easier to correct.

4

Persuading and Driving Results

Analyze your audience so that you can target your message for maximum impact and anticipate and address any possible concerns or objections they may have.

Choose the most effective direction — upward, downward, or lateral — for any given business communication and craft your message accordingly.

Leverage the power of Monroe's motivated sequence to lead an audience along a predetermined path from identifying a need to understanding the solution you're proposing — and, ultimately, responding positively to your call to action.

Avoid four common mistakes that plague persuasive presentations.

Negotiate more effectively in a business setting to get more of what you want with respect to compensation, workload, resources, and anything else that improves your success, professionally or personally.

Chapter **12**

Knowing the People You're Trying to Persuade

The first rule of communication is this: *Know your audience.*

Tailoring your message to resonate with your audience and their specific interests and needs improves engagement and receptivity. It enables you to adapt your language, tone, and content to align with their level of understanding and their cultural, educational, and professional backgrounds and preferences. It helps to achieve clarity while you build rapport with your audience and earn their trust. Ultimately, knowing your audience enables you to have more meaningful interactions and communicate more effectively and with greater impact.

In this chapter, I explain how to analyze an audience. I go beyond demographics to enable you to determine more about what they think, how they feel, and how they're likely to respond to you and your message. I also provide guidance on how to communicate upward, downward, and laterally so that you can tailor your message and delivery more effectively to your colleagues and organizational leaders.

Finally, I delve into how knowing your audience empowers you to achieve the ultimate goal of persuasive communication — to change minds and behaviors or, as I like to say, to change the status quo.

Only amateurs communicate without first analyzing their audience and assessing their needs, interests, and preferred communication style. After you've developed a long-term relationship with an individual or a group, audience analysis can proceed quickly. If you're planning to present to someone new and unfamiliar, analysis can require considerably more time and effort. However, the more comfortable you feel around an individual or group, the more susceptible you are to making assumptions that can lead to miscommunication, so always consider your audience before engaging with them. Assumptions can result in severe misunderstandings.

Analyzing Your Audience

Bias in communication is inevitable. That's right. Any act of communication coming from a human being is inherently biased to some degree, even when the communicator has the best intentions. Messaging generated by artificial intelligence is not immune to bias because humans program and train the system that generates it. In addition, the audience is biased in what they choose to pay attention to, accept, or reject and the way they interpret the message. Bias is why understanding an audience is important. Conducting an audience analysis before engagement gives you deeper insight into your audience's biases, and your own, so that you're better able to craft a message that achieves your communication goal.

In this section, I introduce you to two basic approaches to audience analysis that can help you understand which types of bias may be present in your audience: demographic analysis and psychographic analysis.

Conducting a demographic analysis

Demographics are data you can find about people from a census, such as age, location, gender, ethnicity, education level, employment status, annual income, and so on. In organizations, you can extend demographics to include other data that may be relatively easy to access, such as tenure with the company, position, and previous work experience.

Demographics can provide valuable insights into an audience that enable you to communicate more effectively with them. For example, if you're recruiting talent to expand operations, demographics can help you attract the right people by shedding light on characteristics such as the following:

>> **Age:** By knowing the age range of the candidates, you can highlight benefits and qualities about your organization that are likely to appeal to them. Older candidates may be drawn to an organization that values and rewards experience, whereas younger candidates may be seeking positions that offer opportunities for education and professional growth.

>> **Ethnicity:** If you're trying to increase diversity in your workforce, you may want to focus on crafting inclusive messages that respect and appeal to candidates from varied backgrounds.

>> **Location:** Based on what you know about the recruits you're trying to attract, you may want to highlight certain qualities about your organization's location(s); for example, that you have locations around the world (for workers who value travel), that your headquarters are in the heart of a bustling metropolis (for those who want to live and work in a trendy urban setting), or that you offer flexible work arrangements (to attract digital nomads).

>> **Education level:** The educational background of candidates often reflects their qualifications and suitability for specific roles, whether it's a high school diploma, a technical or associate's degree, a bachelor's or master's degree, or certifications in specialized areas of knowledge and expertise. Education level can also help you choose the level of language to use when communicating with potential candidates.

Avoid using demographic analysis exclusively. It tends to put people in boxes in which they may not fit, and most people don't like to be treated that way. Demographics have some validity in terms of planning communication, but they're limited in scope — they provide an incomplete picture of any individual in your audience and can lead you to make erroneous assumptions.

Digging deeper with a psychographic analysis

Psychographic analysis, as its name suggests, has more to do with the mental processes and activities (the psychology) of an audience than with the statistical characteristics of a population. It involves analyzing traits, such as beliefs, values, tendencies, ideals, desires, lifestyle choices, and so on. These traits, which reflect thoughts and behaviors, are often much more applicable, precise, and valuable in the context of communication than are demographics, but they're also more difficult to figure out.

To understand the difference between demographic and psychographic analysis, compare the level of insight each one provides. A demographic analysis, for example, may be able to tell you whether someone is a registered Democrat or Republican, but it doesn't tell you the person's position on a specific issue. A psychographic analysis, however, can provide that type of insight. Although someone may be a specific ethnicity or belong to a certain generation, assuming that they all believe the same way would be disastrous and is definitely not the case.

Most researchers and practitioners agree that psychographic analysis provides more valuable insights than those provided by demographic analysis when the purpose of the analysis is to craft a persuasive message. The reason psychographic analysis is superior is that when you're trying to persuade someone, you're essentially attempting to cause them to change their current mental state (their status quo), as explained in the later section Chapter 9 "Challenging the Status Quo." Accomplishing this feat is significantly easier when you're able to position your message in a way that resonates with your audience's existing beliefs and values.

Suppose that your office policy prohibits remote work. You know from your experience during the pandemic that you can do much of your job better and more efficiently while working from home, and you're trying to convince the management team that having a more flexible work policy would benefit everyone involved. You're aware that everyone on the management team has young children and values being present in their lives, often taking personal time or leaving the office early to attend sporting events and other after-school activities.

Knowing that management values their family time, you decide to use that value to petition for a more flexible workplace policy. Rather than merely deliver data on productivity and workplace trends, you decide to frame your case in the context of what management values most. At the core of your presentation, you show how someone in your position could actually put in more focused hours at work while still supporting their children at after-school events by using the time saved from not having to commute to and from the office. With this approach, you can deliver a data-driven, values-based presentation that appeals to your audience at both a rational and an emotional level — a combination that's sure to increase your chances of success.

Using Communication Direction to Your Advantage

You would say all sorts of things to your best friend that you would never consider saying to one of your parents or grandparents or some other authority figure.

Why communicate with different people in such different ways? Because communication direction matters. And it matters just as much in business as it does in every other setting. Consciously or subconsciously, you communicate one way to superiors, another way to subordinates, and a completely different way to peers. More formally, communication direction falls into the following three categories (see Figure 12-1):

>> **Upward:** To superiors

>> **Downward:** To subordinates

>> **Laterally:** To peers

In the following sections, I share tips and techniques for each of these communication directions.

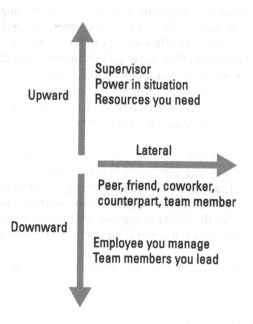

Upward

Supervisor
Power in situation
Resources you need

Lateral

Peer, friend, coworker,
counterpart, team member

Downward

Employee you manage
Team members you lead

FIGURE 12-1:
Communication
directions.

Communicating in the wrong direction can create noise, which can diminish your audience's receptivity or understanding of the message you're trying to convey. See Chapter 2 for more about noise.

Here are a couple of tips that can make you more persuasive regardless of communication direction.

>> **Prioritize listening.** Listening provides valuable insight into the situation you're discussing and your audience's needs, desires, thoughts, and emotions,

all of which enable you to deliver a more persuasive proposal. Seek feedback from everyone involved, and listen carefully when they offer information and insight.

>> **Offer something of value.** WIIFM (what's in it for me?) is an important consideration regardless of communication direction. Demonstrating how your proposal or your request is likely to benefit the person(s) you're trying to persuade is always an effective technique.

Upward communication: Finesse required

Upward communication involves interacting with someone who's in a higher position than you, has more power than you, has money or other resources you need or desire, or stands between you and access to such a person (acting as gatekeeper). In a business setting, it typically involves communicating with a supervisor, manager, boss, or boss's boss, but it can extend to peers who perceive themselves as more powerful or influential. (You know the one — that coworker who thinks they're holier than thou and can do no wrong. Yeah, that one). Upward communication can even occur in a temporary situation, when you need something from someone in a specific moment; even if the person is a peer or subordinate, in that instant, when you need something that person can provide, you're in a position in which upward communication is strategic.

When you're in a situation that calls for upward communication, ego plays a role, and catering to that ego can go a long way in getting what you need — but that's not all bad. Don't feel that you're having to demean yourself by stroking someone else's ego. Think of it as a reconnaissance mission. Whenever you're catering to someone's ego, you have the ability to uncover what motivates them and others, which is valuable insight you can use in future persuasive situations.

In the following sections, I offer a few tips for managing upward communication successfully.

Demonstrate respect

Keep in mind that the person you're communicating upward to has something you need or want, has the power to prevent you from getting it, and is in that position for a reason. Respect that position and the knowledge, expertise, and effort that were required to earn it. I'm not suggesting that you kiss up. I'm just saying that higher-ups generally deserve a little respect.

Suppose that the supervisor of another department has knowledge and experience that you think could help you make a more powerful presentation to your supervisor. You can approach this person respectfully by giving them credit where credit is due. You may say something like this: "Taylor, I know you have a lot of expertise in securing funds for professional development for members of your team. I'm working on putting together a proposal for my supervisor, and I would appreciate it if you'd be willing to share some of your valuable experience in this area so I can prepare my presentation."

Taylor is likely to be far more receptive to this message, carefully delivered in the form of upward communication, than if you were to say something like, "Hey Taylor, I'm trying to persuade Jodie to make some funds available for professional development. Can you help me with my pitch?"

Cut to the chase

With upward communication, get to the point quickly. Don't waste your time or theirs with small talk or superfluous details and lengthy narratives — none of that's needed! For example, when you're asking Taylor for help, as discussed in the previous section, you don't need to lay out everything you already tried to persuade Jodie, how frustrated you are that she doesn't appreciate the value of professional development, the specific types of professional development you think would benefit your team, or any other gratuitous details. Be prepared to provide additional information if asked, of course, but keep your request direct and specific with a clear purpose. Cutting to the chase also demonstrates respect for another person's time.

Show how your proposal will benefit the organization or individual

When you're talking up to someone, linking your proposal to the interests of the individual or the organization can work to your benefit. Suppose that you're talking to someone who has a vested interest (a financial stake) in your company. Though they may have an ego that needs stroking, they also have interests in the organization's success and the financial gain they hope to realize from their financial investment in the organization.

In this case, showing the positive impact that what you're proposing can have on the organization's success and its bottom line (profit) can be very effective, so you say something like, "The professional development I'm proposing for my team will not only provide us with the skills we need to do our jobs better and faster, but it will enable us to deliver more innovative products to market faster, increasing the company's overall profitability." When you can show a mutual benefit for your request (or go all in by focusing exclusively on how the organization and its stakeholders will benefit) then you're well on your way to persuasive success.

Downward communication: A balancing act

When you're the one who "holds all the cards," meaning you're in a position of power and in charge of making decisions that affect the actions of others, you often find yourself in situations involving downward communication. Typically, these situations involve persuading subordinates to provide something you need or desire, such as their cooperation, time, effort, or expertise. Downward communication isn't about ordering people around; it's more effective when you persuade — rally the troops. In this section, I present three techniques for improving the effectiveness of downward communication, all of which require balance — a little give-and-take.

Don't take your power for granted. Assuming that someone will be persuaded solely by your position or your resources tends to create an environment in which subordinates concede reluctantly rather than proceed enthusiastically. Effective leaders understand how to work with, manage, and motivate each person individually.

Explain your rationale

Leaders often bemoan the fact that military-style management (ordering people around) isn't as effective as it used to be. I've heard older managers say something along these lines: "You used to not have to give a reason for somebody to do something. If you were a manager, people just did what you told them to do!" Well, that's definitely no longer the case. Increasingly, those you lead and manage want to know the bigger picture, and they're not afraid to ask questions. This change isn't necessarily bad. People are generally motivated to perform better when they understand the rationale behind what they're being asked to do.

When you're communicating downward, look for opportunities to explain your rationale or provide insight into the big picture — how what you're asking a subordinate to do contributes to the overall success of the team, the project, or the organization. This approach not only inspires and motivates subordinates but may also spark a discussion that leads to more innovative ways to meet the same objectives more effectively and efficiently.

For example, ever since you started allowing team members to work remotely three days a week, you notice that innovation has suffered. Team members are no longer bouncing ideas off one another. Your office environment isn't as fun and vibrant as it once was, and the team is losing its cohesiveness. You could change your team policy to prohibit or strictly limit remote work to one day a week, but that might discourage some team members. Instead, you lead a team meeting to share input on how to strengthen team culture. The team unanimously agrees that both socializing and collaborating on projects in close physical proximity to one another makes the team more cohesive and innovative. As a result of your meeting, team members are likely to be more receptive to the idea of spending additional time together in the office. They realize that they had more fun and were more innovative when they could call impromptu meetings and collaborate in person.

Approach the situation with a curious mind

Effective leaders are curious. They don't assume that they have all the answers or even all the relevant data. When you're communicating in a downward direction, gather as much data as is reasonable about the situation, and remain curious as you engage in conversation with your subordinate(s). Don't assume you already know everything you need to know. Ask questions until you're fairly certain that you fully understand the situation.

Suppose a member of your team is struggling to meet their sales goals. You may be tempted to draw your own conclusions — the person doesn't have the right stuff, isn't putting in the necessary time, lacks motivation, whatever. You're tempted to say something like this: "Your sales numbers are the lowest on the team. If you don't meet your goal for the next quarter, I'll need to find someone who can." That's a reactive stance — you get data, draw your own conclusion, and react.

A more effective approach is to enter the conversation with a natural curiosity and gather information and insight from your salesperson before drawing any conclusions. So, you say something like, "As I was looking over the sales numbers for the past quarter, I noticed that you're 25 percent short of your goal. What's going on?"

This open-ended question allows and encourages your subordinate to share information or insight they have about any underlying issues. Maybe they're dealing with a challenging situation at home. Maybe they need additional information and training about a new product your company just introduced to the market. Perhaps they would benefit from a mentorship with one of your other sales reps. You probably won't know what's going on or have any idea of how to remedy the situation until you get your subordinate to open up.

You'll never find out what you don't know if you assume you already know everything.

Listen and be prepared to respond to complaints and excuses

Whenever you're communicating in a downward direction about an issue that a subordinate needs to address, consider the possibility that the person will react defensively. After all, because you're in a position of power, you can negatively impact them in some way — through finances, status, or their ability to succeed. They may come up with excuses, point the finger of blame, or complain about something they think (or want you to think) is getting in their way.

As a leader, you need to be prepared to encounter some degree of defensiveness and to communicate around it. You want to give people an opportunity to be heard, but you need to steer the conversation in a direction that leads to a productive course of action. Your approach depends on the nature of the excuse or complaint the person presents, whether it's legitimate or chronic:

>> **Legitimate complaint:** A legitimate complaint is about anything that's preventing the person from achieving their objective and can be corrected; for example, the person lacks the funding, technology, or personnel to implement the proposed plan.

   Never ignore or dismiss a legitimate complaint. Doing so makes the person less likely to share anything with you in the future.

>> **Chronic complaint:** Chronic complaints are more akin to whining. Whining can be a cry for attention, in which case you would benefit from exploring the root cause — why the person is seeking attention in this way. A chronic complaint may also be a subtle attempt to shift accountability, in which case you can try to pivot by asking the person what their solution would be. For example, you may say something like, "I'm asking you to increase your sales by 20 percent in the next quarter. I hear that you think that's impossible. What would make it possible?"

When communicating in a downward direction, you may have a greater need to check for mutual understanding. Paraphrase the issue back to the person, listing all the obstacles the person mentioned (and adding any they may have missed) so that you mutually agree on the definition of the problem before you start exploring potential solutions. If you don't have all the information to clearly describe the problem, continue to ask questions to get to the bottom of it. At the end of your summary, ask, "Can you think of anything I missed?"

Lateral communication: Navigating peer-to-peer interactions

Lateral communication consists of communicating with people who are on the same level as you are — friends, colleagues, peers, or counterparts. In an organizational chart, these are the people who are in the same row as you. In business, lateral communication occurs in groups and teams. Beyond the confines of an organization, it occurs among networking partners and colleagues who may be in the same field, industry, or position but at different organizations. Outside of business, consider this communication with your friends and neighbors (not the ones on the board of your homeowners' association — those egos likely require upward communication!).

In some ways, lateral communication can be the easiest, especially when you're interacting with someone you click with. However, it can also be the most challenging because you're on a level playing field, where no one is in charge or acting as the point person. Making a decision involves reaching a consensus.

With lateral communication, relationship building is often at the forefront. Navigating lateral communication relies heavily on understanding the nature of your relationship with the person or people involved in the conversation or presentation.

In the following sections, I share several tips for engaging in effective lateral communication.

Seek mutually beneficial solutions

When communicating laterally, strive to create exchanges of equal value, and look for opportunities to create value that's mutually beneficial. All parties bring something to the table — time, money, knowledge, skills, talents, and so on. Recognize what everyone has to offer, and look for ways to negotiate and collaborate. Sometimes, negotiation results in a quid pro quo (this for that) exchange. In other cases, those involved can combine their resources to come up with a solution that benefits everyone.

Acknowledge and respect your communication history

Think about the relationship over time and take inventory of what you exchanged with your peer(s) in the past. If you've given more than you've gotten over time, referencing that in conversation can be an advantage. I'm not saying to hold this over somebody's head, but sometimes reminding them of the relationship equity you've built is necessary.

If you're trying to persuade peers who've done a lot for you already, express your appreciation for their support before requesting their additional aid. For example, you may say something like this: "I realize that this new project has taken up a lot of your time, and I've been calling in a lot of favors. I'm so grateful to all of you for your willingness to step forward and help me with this endeavor. To bring this thing to life, I need your help with one final step. . . ."

Lateral communication has a lot to do with investing in strategic relationships that grow each party involved and can also contribute to the growth of the organization.

Balance competition with cooperation

One challenge with lateral communication is that in some situations you may be competing against your peers. When you're trying to persuade peers to do something that may give you a strategic advantage over them, look for opportunities to provide something of value that benefits them equally in some other way. For example, if you're both CEOs at your respective companies, you may offer your expertise in process design in exchange for the other CEO's help in dealing with a tricky compliance issue.

Anticipating Possible Objections

An important part of knowing your audience is recognizing the reasons they may object to whatever you're proposing. Remember, persuasion involves changing the audience's status quo — their existing thoughts, behaviors, and feelings. Knowing what those thoughts, behaviors, and feelings are make you better able to anticipate any potential objections they may have.

Suppose you're planning to enjoy a rare relaxing evening at home. You open your favorite bottle of wine, pour a glass, settle into your couch, and curl up in a cozy blanket, preparing to binge-watch your favorite series. Then it happens. Your phone chimes to notify you of an incoming text from a valued team member asking, "Are you busy?"

You stare at your phone, debating how to respond or even whether to respond. The internal battle you're facing in this situation, even if it's only momentary, gives you a small glimpse into the battle that wages inside the mind or your audience anytime you're asking them to make a change. And when you're trying to persuade somebody to change or to act, they're capable of coming up with all sorts of objections: they don't have the time, they're too tired, they already tried that solution, and so on.

In this section, I offer tips and techniques for anticipating possible objections more effectively so that you're better prepared to counter them in your presentation.

Researching possible objections: Conducting surveys

One of the best ways to identify possible objections is to ask people what they think of a proposal. You can survey a more general audience or, for more accurate feedback, survey actual audience members, as explained in the following sections.

Conducting an indirect survey

An *indirect* survey asks people who are like those in your audience or who know your audience personally how they think your audience will respond to what you're proposing. It's useful for situations in which you have no direct access to your audience before your presentation, you've never met them, and you have only some basic demographic and psychographic information at your disposal.

Suppose your organization is part of the textile industry and you're planning to deliver a presentation at the next big industry event to persuade executives to implement various sustainability measures. You know a number of people in the industry but none of the executives, so you send the people you know a survey asking them how they think the leadership at their various companies would likely respond to various sustainability initiatives, such as using more sustainable materials, implementing cleaner manufacturing processes, committing to ethical labor practices, and promoting circular fashion (designing products for longevity, encouraging repair and reuse, and promoting recycling).

Surveying actual audience members

If you have good relationships, or even a semblance of a relationship, with those who will be in your audience, you can go straight to the source! Suppose you're planning to petition management to hold an annual volunteer day where they allow employees work time to volunteer in the community. You know that managers from multiple departments will be attending the meeting during which you'll be delivering your presentation. Indirectly, you could go to your peers in those respective departments and ask them where they believe their boss stands on the idea. Or, you could go directly to each of the managers and say, "I'm gathering information for the next company meeting on different perspectives on an annual volunteer day. Are you willing to share your thoughts on this as it pertains both to members of your team and to the company as a whole?" Notice that you're not disclosing whether you're pro or con. You're simply gathering information. This information may be quite valuable in helping you understand possible objections to your proposal.

Preparing your responses to objections

After conducting research, as explained in the previous section, you're ready to prepare your responses to objections and questions you're likely to receive. Make a list of questions and objections and brainstorm your responses, alone or with the assistance of your team or others. In some cases, you can proactively answer questions and counter objections through the information and insights you include in your presentation. In other cases, you can keep your responses "in your back pocket" so that you're ready to deliver them if someone in your audience challenges you.

Generally, the most effective approach is to answer questions and address objections before they're raised. For example, if your research shows that most department heads aren't against using work time for an annual volunteer day but are worried about having their full team out of the office, you could phrase a portion of your presentation like this: "I understand that having your entire team out of the office at the same time can present challenges. However, having your team participate together in something bigger can also benefit team morale and increase productivity. We can work on lessening the duration of project shifts so that a full day is not used."

Remaining objective and demonstrating it

When you're passionate about something you're proposing and well prepared to address possible questions and objections, you may struggle to remain objective or demonstrate that you heard and carefully considered an audience member's concern. Because you're well prepared, you can immediately fire back your response. However, the audience may perceive such a response as an indication that you have a strong bias and have failed to give the concern its due consideration. You don't want that to happen when you've worked so hard to get this far!

To avoid coming across as biased, use the technique of summarize, expand, and respond:

1. Summarize or, in some cases, repeat the objection or question back to the person who posed it. Summarizing buys you some time to collect your thoughts and prepare your response. It also ensures that everyone in the audience is on the same page.

2. Expand on the question or objection by bringing in any other relevant information that's likely to help the audience understand your response. Expanding enables you to build credibility by demonstrating that you understand the audience member's concern and can take it one step further.

3. Respond. Answer the question or address the concern.

After your stellar presentation on having a company-wide flexible work policy, wherein any employee can make a case to their department head for up to three days of remote work per week, one manager stands up and says, "Though this policy may work in many departments, I don't think it will in all of them." This isn't exactly a question, but it's definitely an objection!

Because you've done your due diligence and know your audience well, you're excited to respond. You take a quick breath and use the summarize, expand, respond framework by saying something like this:

> **Summarize:** "I definitely understand that not every department has the same work responsibilities, and that some roles are much more physical and hands-on than others, requiring more in-office time."

> **Expand:** "This was evident to me when I talked to eight of the ten department heads before giving this presentation . . ."

> **Respond:** ". . . . and is one of the main reasons the policy can be tailored to give each department ownership over the decision. I believe it is beneficial to everyone if employees are encouraged to make strong cases for their desired working environments that also align with commitments to productivity."

Summarizing, expanding, and responding enables you to maximize the impact of all the research and preparation you invested in your presentation. It shows your audience that you're not only well-prepared but also that you care enough about their concerns to respond in an empathetic and thoughtful way.

Chapter **13**

Engaging in Persuasion That Drives Results

Before GPS-enabled vehicles and phones were a thing, people had to plan road trips using awkwardly folded pieces of paper called *maps*. (I can't be the only one who could never manage to fold up the map properly, right?!) I'd plot my course from point A to point B and start the adventure. If I took a wrong turn, it wasn't as simple as recalculating a route. I had to stop, check the map, find road markers, and somehow manage to get back on track. Really, it's a miracle that anyone in my generation survived!

But that level of planning and detail was necessary then, and it's necessary now when it comes to crafting persuasive presentations (any presentation, really, but the focus in this chapter is on persuasion). If you plan to "wing it," then your internal GPS had better be up and running and able to course-correct in a split second — which is all the time it takes to lose your audience for good. And you know what happens when you rely on that GPS when you're on a road trip — you always need it most when you can't get a signal.

This chapter is all about preparing you with the correct map for your persuasive presentation — whether you're trying to persuade an individual or an entire room full of people. Here, I provide you with a roadmap for preparing and delivering a presentation that drives results and spurs action while steering clear of common presentation pitfalls. But first, I provide some guidance on laying the groundwork — identifying your stakeholders and envisioning the goal you hope to achieve (your final destination).

Sizing Up the Stakeholders

Persuasion is ultimately about getting your audience to take action on whatever you're proposing. It isn't entirely about what you're proposing or how you're proposing it. You can deliver the perfect presentation and still have someone adamantly opposed to your proposal. Stakeholders can carry a lot of baggage into a presentation in the form of biases, insecurities, conflicting interests, and more.

In this section, I explain how to identify stakeholders and what could be holding them back from saying yes and then reveal an approach that's often effective in getting them onboard. See Chapter 12 for more about the importance of knowing your audience *before* you even consider your approach to persuading them.

Identifying stakeholders and their interests

Every idea in an organization has an impact beyond the person who's championing the proposal and even beyond the people ultimately responsible for deciding for or against it. It may impact the person's role, compensation, or workload. It may even make a stakeholder feel threatened. If a stakeholder backs your proposal and it fails, their position or job may be at stake. Or, if what you propose becomes a phenomenal success, they may be afraid that you'll steal their thunder or score the promotion or raise they were seeking.

Determine who your stakeholders are and what they stand to gain and to lose by accepting or backing your proposal. Use the following questions to guide your thinking and research:

Identifying stakeholders

>> Who is/are the decision maker(s)?

>> Whose backing can I count on?

Having someone on the leadership team sponsor your proposal can significantly improve your ability to persuade others.

TIP

>> Whose help do I need to implement what I'm proposing? What personnel or departments need to be involved?

>> Who stands to shoulder the heaviest burden if my proposal is implemented?

Identifying stakeholder interests

>> What resources do I need to implement my plan?

>> How much will what I'm proposing cost?

>> How will my organization benefit and at what cost (financial, time, resource reallocation, and so on)?

>> How will the customer benefit and at what cost?

>> How will my team benefit and at what cost?

Answering these questions enables you to identify the stakeholders and what each stakeholder stands to gain or lose. The knowledge you gain from the process of answering these questions provides you with valuable insight into how to tailor your presentation to audience members with varying interests, and it prepares you to respond more effectively to questions and concerns that arise during your presentation.

Sharing the credit to give stakeholders a sense of ownership

TIP

You may be able to sway a reluctant stakeholder by sharing the credit with them or even going so far as to plant the notion in their head that what you're proposing was their idea all along. As the old saying goes, "People support what they help create." When stakeholders feel as though they came up with the proposal or played a crucial role in its acceptance and implementation, they're more likely to back it enthusiastically.

EXAMPLE

At my first full-time job, I served as communications manager for a new small but growing law association. My responsibilities included managing trade communication to our members and developing a web and media presence. (This was the early 2000s — before Instagram — so it wasn't as simple as it is today.) My boss had never turned on a computer a day in his life. His assistant printed out his emails for him. Truly — you can't make this up. One day I walked into his office to ask for funding to buy multiple domain names. He challenged my understanding of what a domain name and URL are! (Never mind that he had never turned on a computer — the employee 30 years his junior couldn't possibly know what she was talking about.)

I was furious. I left his office defeated and feeling unfairly devalued. The previous day he had told me that he was upset that our brand identity wasn't strong enough and that people often confused the association name — how did he not understand that I was trying to get multiple domains so that regardless of the name they typed they'd be redirected to our site?

Then it hit me: If I could make him believe it was *his* idea, I'd likely get approval. Later that same day I went back to his office and told him that I couldn't understand why he didn't approve the budget to purchase multiple domain names since it was his idea. I cited our previous conversation during which he voiced his concern over brand confusion. I said, "I know you're frustrated that people don't remember the association name, but as you mentioned, they remember part of it. I asked to buy domains to capture all the different parts so that they can find us even if they don't get the brand correct and when they type in the wrong name, it will redirect them to the right name." (I also drew a diagram to help him understand the whole redirect concept.) The result? My proposal was a resounding success. My boss even gave me more domain names to purchase!

Did that story hit a little too close to home for you? It wasn't the first time I needed to make someone think they came up with an idea to have it approved, and it probably won't be the last. Trust me, I know it doesn't always feel good, but it does illustrate the point — in an extreme way — that people are more likely to support what they have a hand in creating.

I'm not saying that this approach is effective for every situation, but it's certainly worth considering. We all like to receive credit for our work (some, with big egos, more than others). But if getting your proposal accepted is important, sometimes giving someone else the credit can go a long way.

Clarifying Your Goal and Aligning It with Your Audience

Before you start to plan your presentation, clarify in your own mind what you hope to achieve and then align your goal with your audience:

1. **Define your goal.**

   Are you trying to sell a product or service, persuade audience members to change their minds or behaviors, or motivate them to take action? You may have a goal related to your self-interests as well, such as meeting a sales target or earning a promotion. I take a deeper dive into goals later in this section.

2. **Align your goal with your audience.**

   Consider their demographics, interests, beliefs, and concerns. You may want to perform a formal or informal survey before you start drafting your presentation to understand their perspective and what they already know (or think they know) about the topic or issue. (See Chapter 12 for guidance on how to get to know your audience.)

WARNING

Two of the most common mistakes I see businesspeople make in their persuasive presentations is lacking a clear idea of what they hope to achieve and failing to ensure that their goal aligns with the sensibilities, concerns, and interests of the audience.

Putting your goals and the needs of your audience in perspective

You wouldn't make a business presentation if it didn't benefit you in some way. You have certain expectations regarding your self-interests. At the very least, a successful presentation can boost your ego and your reputation. If you're in sales, your compensation may be directly tied to your ability to deliver successful sales presentations. If you're in management, your ability to persuade team members can increase your opportunities for raises and promotions. Those are good reasons to want to become more persuasive; however, your personal reasons aren't likely sufficient to persuade an audience to do something.

I'm not saying that your goals are unimportant. What I'm suggesting is that the best way to achieve those goals is to put the needs of your audience front and center. By aligning your goal with your audience, you have a much higher chance of success. Find out what matters to your audience. Understand what's going to motivate them. Investigate their pain points and what solution(s) you can offer to alleviate that pain.

To put it a different way, your presentation isn't about you — it's about your audience.

Setting realistic goals and objectives

Persuasion doesn't always happen in the desired timeframe or to the desired degree. In fact, one of the healthiest and most realistic approaches to persuasion is to give yourself some latitude in progressing toward a goal without fully achieving it in one fell swoop. Communication researchers often reference latitudes of commitment — the fact that people feel various degrees of dedication to a project. I've modified this to make a research-based theory a bit more palatable. Hear me out.

Imagine your audience seated according to how open they're likely to be to the solution you're about to propose. On the far left are those who are likely to resist your idea. On the far right are those who are likely to support it. In the middle are those who are "on the fence." (See Figure 13-1.)

Not Likely	On the Fence	Likely

FIGURE 13-1:
Gauge your progress by movement toward your goal.

1 2 | 3 4 5 6 7 8 | 9 10

Often, speakers gauge their success based on the number of audience members they can move to full acceptance and support, but I think such a goal is short-sighted. Success might mean having people move one or two places to the right along the continuum, or it might mean getting someone in the unlikely zone to even stand up and look toward a chair in the on-the-fence zone. Any movement toward agreement is progress. You may not meet your ultimate goal in a single conversation or presentation, but you may meet lesser objectives that indicate progress toward that goal. But don't forget the likely zone by focusing too much on the others — the supporters need reinforcement to remind them why they're in the right spot!

REMEMBER

Progress is persuasive success. If you enter into any persuasive situation having a goal without objectives on the way to achieving that goal, you're setting yourself up for failure.

Set a realistic goal and then set objectives to meeting that goal. For example, your goal may be to have a prospective customer subscribe to your customer management software. Objectives along the way may include having the prospective customer download a white paper from your website or contact your sales team to discuss challenges they're facing with their current customer management software or register for a webinar on customer management software. All are actions that would position them "out of a chair" and looking forward with possibility.

TIP

Getting little yeses is easier than getting big yeses. The more little yeses you can get an audience to commit to, the closer and closer you move them toward the big yes you want.

Using Monroe's Motivated Sequence to Structure Your Persuasive Presentation

One of the most well-constructed organizational structures for persuasive communication comes from a psychologist back in the 1930s. Alan H. Monroe, a professor of communication at Purdue University, wanted to determine the best process for persuading an audience to take action. After much testing and work, Monroe developed a progressive method that helps a speaker structure a presentation, anticipate and overcome objections, and deliver results. This method has become known as Monroe's Motivated Sequence, and the structure is still one of the most commonly used and adapted nearly 100 years later.

Monroe's Motivated Sequence is a five-step process:

1. **Attention: Engage the audience with a compelling opening statement, a shocking statistic, a relevant anecdote, a rhetorical question, or other relevant information that focuses their attention.**

2. **Need: Make the audience aware of a problem or need.**

   Present evidence and arguments to make the case that the problem or need is relevant and significant or urgent enough to require action.

WARNING

   Avoid the common mistake of assuming that the audience knows or agrees on the need for the possible solution and skipping to presenting the solution. Presenting the solution without first ensuring that your audience is in agreement on the need puts your success at risk. (See Chapter 2 about the importance of establishing mutual understanding — that's what you're doing in this step.)

3. **Satisfaction**: Present a solution or propose a course of action to address the problem or need that has been established.

   The solution should be practical, feasible, and capable of effectively addressing the audience's concerns.

4. **Visualization: Describe the positive outcome that will result from the proposed solution.**

   Enable the audience to visualize how much better life will be after the desired outcome is achieved.

5. **Action: Issue a clear and specific call to action (CTA), urging the audience to implement the proposed solution or course of action (or buy into whatever you're proposing).**

   The CTA must be actionable, achievable, and aligned with the desired outcome. It also needs to be specific.

Monroe's Motivated Sequence is quite effective for sales presentations, whether you're delivering the presentation face-to-face, via videoconference, or as an advertisement in print, online, or video. It's also effective in any situation in which your goal is to persuade one or more people to accept or implement change, including changing their behavior.

In the following sections, I explain each of the five steps in greater detail and provide insight into how to use each step to your advantage in crafting persuasive presentations and conversations.

Step 1: Grab your audience's attention

Before you can persuade an audience, you need to get their undivided attention. Over the course of history, speakers have employed all sorts of techniques to wake up the audience and command their attention, ranging from the conventional to the cheesy — from telling an interesting story or citing a compelling statistic to making a theatrical entrance, with music blaring and flags waving. What's important is that your opening accomplishes the following three goals:

>> Grabs the audience's attention

>> Is at least somewhat relevant to the topic you're about to introduce

>> Breaks the ice (makes you relatable to the audience)

Here are some types of presentation openings to consider:

>> **Start with a provocative rhetorical question.** For example, at the beginning of a presentation to a group of small-business owners, you may ask, "Do you know the number-one reason some businesses thrive while so many others struggle to stay afloat?" This question gets the audience thinking about the topic before you even touch on the need you're about to introduce.

>> **Open with a surprising or shocking statistic.** For example, if you're promoting a business-to-business (B2B) marketing opportunity, you may want to start by pointing out that small businesses employ nearly half of all workers in the United States.

>> **Pose a hypothetical scenario.** Encourage the audience to imagine themselves in a situation in which they face a challenge related to the need you're about to introduce. For example, you may start with something like, "Imagine you're the CEO of a retail chain that's struggling to stay afloat in an era dominated by e-commerce."

>> **Challenge the status quo.** Introduce a perspective that's radically different from conventional thinking on the topic. For example, you may start by saying something like, "Conventional wisdom tells us that working hard and putting in long hours are the secrets to success, but efficiency and effectiveness are the true secrets. I'm going show you how to be more productive in half the time with half the effort."

>> **Stimulate the audience's curiosity.** Say something that makes the audience curious, such as, "What would you think if I told you that a simple shift in perspective could double your company's profits?"

>> **Engage the audience in an activity.** Ask a question, take a poll, or have the audience participate in a brief exercise. For example, if you're presenting on the importance of teamwork, ask the audience to participate in a small-group activity that demonstrates the effectiveness of collaboration.

>> **Share a compelling image or video that's relevant to the topic you're about to introduce.** For example, if you're recruiting volunteers to help with your organization's efforts to bring clean drinking water to disadvantaged communities, you can start with a brief video from a major news outlet calling attention to the issue.

>> **Have audience members share their experiences, thoughts, or opinions beforehand, or create a shared experience live, in the moment.** For example, if you're presenting on a common compliance issue that many companies in your industry face, you can ask the audience to share their experiences and insights. You score bonus points by tying points you make later in your presentation back to what the audience shared or experienced early on.

>> **Tell a relevant, compelling story that transitions into your main topic.** A story that has a hero (never you!) fighting the good fight and overcoming adversity to further the cause can be especially effective. In this case, you score bonus points for delivering the dramatic climax at the same time you reveal your solution during the satisfaction and visualization stages of your presentation. You earn more bonus points when you deliver your CTA by showing how everyone in the audience can be that hero.

These presentation openings can all be effective for grabbing your audience's attention when you're speaking to a group, but they're not always appropriate when you're trying to persuade only one or two people. In situations with a small audience, you can usually grab their attention simply by asking whether they have some time to discuss an issue or by moving to a more private space where you can talk more freely. Monroe's Motivated Sequence can be effective with small groups; adapt your opening be a little less dramatic.

You have an opportunity to attract your audience's attention as soon as they see you through your appearance, posture, and body language — nonverbal communication, covered in Chapter 3. Be sure your audience is paying attention to something positive. Dress appropriately and assume a posture that projects confidence and approachability.

Step 2: Highlight the need

Highlighting the need is all about alignment — making the audience aware of the problem or need that exists and the importance or urgency of addressing it. This is where your confidence, preparation, and knowledge are all on display, as you present the evidence and reasoning to recognize the need and, when appropriate, show how it impacts them. To establish the need and the importance and/or urgency to address it, do the following:

>> **Identify the need or problem.** Clearly articulate the problem or need. Use facts, statistics, anecdotes, expert opinions, or real-life examples to support your claim that the problem or need does in fact exist and that it's serious enough that the audience should be concerned about it.

>> **Highlight the potential negative consequences of failing to address the need or problem.** Discuss how the problem affects individuals, your organization, your community, or the world. Calling the audience's attention to the potential fallout helps to create a sense of concern and urgency. Paint a vivid picture, using words and visuals, of what the future could look like if the problem isn't addressed.

When possible, focus specifically on consequences that are likely to impact audience members directly. Make it clear how they're personally affected or why they should care about the issue. This helps to engage your audience and make the case for your later CTA.

Don't assume that everyone's on the same page. Even if the problem or need is obvious (or you think it is), some members of your audience may not agree with you on the importance or urgency. I've seen far too many presenters open with something like, "We all know why we're here today . . ." and then immediately introduce their solution. You're probably well aware of what you're setting yourself up for when you "ass-u-me."

Step 3: Propose a viable solution that satisfies the need

At this stage in your presentation, you deliver the goods — your solution to the problem or your proposal to address the need. This is the part that's fun to prepare for and deliver, but it can also be the most challenging because you need to anticipate and address any possible objections. To propose your solution most effectively, do the following:

>> **Clearly define your solution.** Summarize your solution and delve into the details of how it works, how it will address the problem or need, and why it's the most effective and efficient option. What's most important is to show how the proposed solution solves the problem or successfully addresses the need.

>> **Highlight key benefits of your solution.** Benefits may include increased efficiency, cost savings, improved safety, increased sustainability, better working conditions, or other advantages your audience values. Use data, reasoning, or case studies to support your claims and quantify the benefits.

>> **Anticipate and address possible objections or concerns and other possible solutions.** Consider anything that could possibly undermine the validity of your claim that your solution is viable and the best choice.

REMEMBER

Do your research before you step in front of an audience. The worst case scenario when you're delivering a persuasive presentation is to have someone in the audience ask a question, introduce an objection, or state a solution proving that what you're proposing isn't viable or isn't the best approach. Comprehensive research can help protect you from any surprises that could derail your success.

WARNING

Don't fall in love with your solution to the point of becoming biased. Consider other options, including the option of not taking action to address the problem or need as you see it. Engage your critical thinking skills to analyze what you're proposing from an objective third-party perspective. This approach helps you anticipate possible objections so that you're prepared to address them in your presentation.

Step 4: Empower your audience to visualize the ideal outcome

In this stage of your presentation, you paint a vivid picture of how much better life will be when the audience accepts and implements your proposed solution. Here you're showing what's in it for your audience, how their situation will be improved, and the benefits they can expect. To empower your audience to visualize the ideal outcome, consider using one or more of the following techniques:

>> **Present a narrative that describes the outcome.** Use descriptive language and storytelling to enable your audience to visualize the future upon the successful implementation of your solution. Suppose that you just proposed

your patented formula for biodegradable packaging to replace plastics. You could describe the differences in landfill situations in your local area and then expand that description to nationwide.

>> **Support your claims with concrete data and examples.** Use real-world examples, case studies, success stories, and data to support the effectiveness of your solution. For example, point out that when a certain coastal community was able to use your product to reduce their reliance on plastics, they achieved a 50 percent reduction in plastic waste, marine ecosystems rebounded, and ecotourism revenues increased by 30 percent.

>> **Demonstrate that the benefits outweigh any potential costs.** Show your audience that you've done the math and considered the potential costs of your plan in money, time, effort, and other resources. They need to see that your solution is "worth it." For example, show your audience that although your nonplastic packaging costs 25 percent more than comparable plastic packaging, it saves 10 percent in recycling costs and results in a 20 percent increase in revenues among local fisheries.

>> **Incorporate visual aids to support your claims.** Use images, graphs, infographics, video clips, and other visuals to help paint a picture in the minds of audience members. Showing before-and-after pictures, especially when you have demonstrated results, is particularly impactful if they're realistic.

>> **Appeal to the audience's emotions.** Highlight the positive human impact that your solution will have. Share stories of people whose lives have been transformed by the solution and describe the hope and optimism your solution has inspired.

TIP

If you're proposing a physical change, show a rendering or model with the change contrasted to the present state. If you're proposing a change that has financial implications, use data, charts, or other tools to show the projections and results. If you're proposing a service change, use a case study to enable the audience to envision how your service will streamline their operations in contrast to what their current service provider is offering.

Step 5: Deliver your call to action

At the end of your presentation, deliver your CTA — the action thing you need your audience to take right now or in the near future. To compose an effective CTA, follow the guidelines:

>> **Make it clear and straightforward.** Clearly state what you want your audience to do.

>> **Use a verb in the imperative.** The *imperative* is what you use to issue a command. A call to action commands the audience to do something — buy, subscribe, donate, register, volunteer. Using action-oriented language creates a sense of urgency that compels your audience to act.

>> **Increase the sense of urgency.** The longer your audience waits to act, the more likely they are to forget your presentation. If you're selling a product or service, you can increase the sense of urgency by presenting a limited-time offer. In other cases, try to highlight the negative consequences of any delay in taking action.

>> **Provide clear and simple instructions on how to take action.** Make the process as easy and clear as possible, whether it's clicking a button, making a phone call, filling out a form, or placing an order.

>> **When appropriate, ask for public commitments.** When people make a claim in front of others, they're more likely to follow through with what they promise. In the right situations, you can use this tactic to your advantage. It can be even more effective if you're able to propose an immediate action that audience members can take before they leave the room. (Remember that small action is a small yes and can lead to more impact and bigger yeses).

Avoiding Mistakes That Plague Persuasive Presentations

Having a carefully structured presentation, as discussed in the previous section, enables you to steer clear of many of the most common and critical mistakes associated with persuasive presentations, but additional pitfalls can weaken a message's impact. In this section, I highlight the most common mistakes and provide guidance on how to avoid them.

"Vomiting" your passion

I know that "vomiting" your passion doesn't sound appealing — and it isn't — but it must be tempting, because it's a mistake I often see presenters make. In their attempt to persuade others, they often overshare their perspective or passion. Yes, your passion is important. And your perspective is valid. But your passion and perspective aren't the sole factors that sway someone to your side. You have to balance your enthusiasm with something that ties your idea directly to an audience need.

Being overly passionate can alienate an audience as quickly as not being passionate enough. Tailor your presentation style to the topic and your audience and keep the focus of your presentation on establishing the need and delivering a solution that satisfies the need. Balance professionalism with passion to avoid overwhelming your audience with a blast of emotion.

Making it all about you

One mistake speakers often make is putting themselves at the center of the presentation. Persuasion isn't about you, and it isn't about winning an argument. It's about delivering the information and insight your audience needs in order to make a well-informed decision about doing what's best for themselves, their team, their organization, or others.

The first person you need to persuade is yourself. If you go into a presentation uncertain that what you're about to propose is the best solution, the odds are good that your uncertainty will be apparent in your presentation. Besides, if you're not convinced that what you're proposing is best, you shouldn't be proposing it, yet — instead, you should still be gathering data. Likewise, if you go into a presentation with an "I need to win" attitude, you run the risk of alienating the people you're trying to persuade. The people who need to win are the people in your audience and the people your solution will positively impact.

Not being "needy" enough

Nobody wants to come across as needy, especially when they're pitching a product or service or trying to persuade someone to join their cause or shift their mindset. What I'm referring to when I say "not being needy enough" is the common mistake presenters make in rushing through presenting the need or problem so that they can reach the proposed solution faster.

If your audience doesn't agree with you that there's a problem or that it's serious enough or urgent enough to call for action, they won't agree with your proposed solution. For example, if you're trying to sell traffic calming devices, such as speed humps, to a property owner's association, you won't be successful unless they think speeding is a safety issue on their roads.

I've seen many speakers fail to illustrate and garner sufficient buy-in on the need for the solution. Speakers often breeze over this step, assuming that the need is obvious and everyone is on the same page. Be sure to spend sufficient time establishing the need. Otherwise, everything you do after that point is a waste of time and energy.

Failing to ask: Omitting the CTA

WARNING

Don't make the all-too-common mistake of omitting the CTA. I've often seen people deliver an amazing presentation through the first four stages of Monroe's Motivated Sequence and then fail to deliver the all-important CTA. They grabbed the audience's attention, introduced a compelling need, pitched the perfect solution, anticipated and masterfully responded to every possible objection, painted a picture of a rosy future, and then — no CTA. Their closing statement: "Thanks for coming today. I think we can make real change." Arghhh! What a disappointment! It's as though they built a raging fire and then let it simply fizzle out at the end. Results don't manifest out of nowhere. You have to ask, directly, for what you want *before* your audience exits the room. Get their buy-in. This is essential but often assumed. Don't assume. If you don't ask, they don't know how and when to act.

Delivering a CTA is often the hardest step in a presentation because you're asking the audience to do something — presumably, for you — and that's not always easy to do. Most people don't like having to inconvenience others to ask for help. In most cases, though, you're actually asking the audience to do something that's likely to benefit them or their team or organization, their community, or the world. Remind yourself that you're not asking for yourself. Then make the request. Make it specific. Make it with confidence.

REMEMBER

A persuasive presentation isn't about you. It's about the positive impacts that others will experience (yourself included) as a result of your successful presentation.

IN THIS CHAPTER

» **Understanding the importance of knowing what you want**

» **Laying the groundwork for effective negotiation**

» **Shaping perceptions and expectations through the use of anchors**

» **Negotiating outside the box — considering alternatives**

» **Improving your success in common workplace negotiations**

Chapter **14**

Negotiating for Strategic Outcomes

N egotiating for strategic outcomes involves striving for longer-term, broader objectives rather than merely immediate self-interests. It goes beyond playing a zero-sum game, in which one party can gain only if the other party loses something of value. It enables individuals and teams to reach agreements with leadership that not only meet their needs but also propel the organization forward, enhance its competitive edge, and foster sustainable relationships with partners, suppliers, and customers.

Those who are capable of negotiating for strategic outcomes have the ability to align diverse interests and expectations toward a common goal. Through negotiation, parties can resolve conflicts, allocate resources more effectively and sustainably, and create mutually advantageous synergies. For example, a well-negotiated contract can ensure favorable terms that support your personal and professional goals as well as your organization's mission, market share, and profitability.

REMEMBER

Negotiating is not just about winning but also about building and maintaining relationships that are vital for future collaborations. This aspect of negotiation emphasizes the importance of communication skills in understanding the other party's needs and crafting proposals that benefit all parties. As a result, successful negotiations can help you build a reputation of integrity and reliability, making you a valuable asset to any organization.

Knowing Your Desired Outcome

Entering a negotiation with a clear understanding of your desired outcome is essential for several reasons, revolving primarily around strategic preparation and psychological readiness:

>> **Enables you to set realistic goals and stick to them.** Having a clear outcome in mind is like having a safety net or guardrails going into a negotiation. If you're clear on your objective, you're less likely to make impulsive decisions that could compromise your long-term interests for short-term gains. For instance, if you enter a negotiation knowing that you need certain terms to maintain your current level of productivity, you can steer the negotiation to ensure that these critical needs are met without getting sidetracked by less relevant offers.

>> **Guides your preparation:** By knowing what you want, you're better equipped to research and gather pertinent data to support your position and your request. This preparation may include understanding market trends, knowing the competition, or anticipating the other party's needs and constraints. This level of preparedness not only enhances your argument's persuasiveness but also boosts your confidence, making you more effective and assertive during the negotiation. (See Chapter 13 for tips on organizing persuasive messages.)

>> **Improves your ability to plan possible concessions:** Negotiations often involve give-and-take, and knowing your end goal enables you to determine in advance what you're willing and unwilling to compromise. This approach ensures that you conduct the negotiation with strategic flexibility rather than a hardline position or making reactive adjustments, which can lead to suboptimal outcomes.

>> **Facilitates effective communication and efficiency during the negotiation process:** Knowing your desired outcome helps prevent unnecessary digressions and focuses the discussion on achieving mutually acceptable solutions, saving both time and resources. It also helps build your reputation as a decisive and credible negotiator, strengthening your hand in current and future negotiations.

To form a clear idea of the outcome you desire, take the following steps:

1. **List your must-haves and nice-to-haves.** In other words, determine what you absolutely need to achieve from the negotiation and additional benefits that aren't strictly necessary. In this step, you're distinguishing between negotiables and nonnegotiables. This is important so that you have clarity going into any negotiation and are able to delineate quickly.

2. **Define your short-term and long-term goals.** Specify the immediate benefits you seek from the negotiation and what you hope to gain in terms of your broader, longer-term strategic objectives. Knowing your short-term and long-term goals helps you avoid making long-term concessions for short-term gains or vice versa. Though it's tempting to take a short-term win, always weigh that against long-term gains.

REMEMBER

When you enter a negotiation with a clear understanding of your desired outcome — knowing what you're willing to give to get and what you're not willing to compromise — you put yourself at an advantage.

Preparing for a Successful Negotiation

Successful negotiation involves more than mastering effective negotiating techniques: It requires careful preparation. Often, the party who's better prepared — the one who knows more about what's being negotiated — is the party that gains the most from the negotiation. It pays to be prepared by taking the following steps:

1. **Conduct a self-assessment.**

   Identify your needs, interests, and goals (both short-term and long-term), as explained in the previous section. Know your priorities and identify what you're willing and unwilling to compromise. Note that what you want can change through this preparation process as you increase your understanding.

2. **Gather relevant information.**

   Identify and analyze factors that are likely to influence your negotiating partner's thinking about what you're proposing. Understand the background, context, and all relevant data that could influence the negotiation outcomes. Your research may include market trends, industry standards or conventions, competitor analysis, and historical data within your organization.

TIP

As you conduct your research, document anything that supports your position. Documentation can strengthen your negotiating position significantly.

3. **Analyze your negotiating partner.**

Find out as much about your negotiating partner as possible, including the following:

- *Interests and priorities:* Look into your negotiating partner's responsibilities and goals, and try to identify what you bring to the table that can help this person achieve success in their position.

- *Constraints:* Identify any factors that may limit this person's ability to help you achieve your desired outcome, such as budget restrictions, corporate policies, laws, and regulations.

- *Negotiation history and style:* Consider how your partner negotiated in the past and the outcomes of those negotiations. You may need to talk with colleagues to gain the insight you're looking for.

  Essentially, understanding your partner in negotiation is similar to understanding your audience — see Chapter 12 for more about getting to know your audience.

4. **Explore mutual benefits.**

In this step, you're looking for win-win opportunities, which you can identify or create:

- Identify common interests.

- Look for opportunities to create additional value for both parties.

5. **Prepare your initial proposal.**

Put your proposal in writing, complete with any data and documentation you've gathered to support it.

6. **Anticipate objections and counteroffers.**

Put yourself in the shoes of your negotiating partner and imagine possible ways the person can respond to what you're proposing and how you can respond to any objections or counteroffers they may present.

7. **Seek input from others, if possible, and revise your proposal accordingly.**

Discuss your proposal/request with others, including trusted internal stakeholders and any advisors or experts who can shed light on what you're proposing and how your negotiating partner is likely to respond. In some cases, you may need to discuss your proposal with lawyers or other experts to ensure that it's legal and feasible.

8. **Prepare yourself mentally for the negotiation.**

Be ready to listen, stay patient, and remain composed under pressure.

TIP

Consider role-playing with trusted colleagues, mentors, and advisors, having one or more of them play the role of your negotiating partner. Practice can shed light on possible weaknesses in your proposal and build confidence.

9. **Arrange a suitable environment for the negotiation.**

You may need a small, quiet office, a conference room, or a digital device and videoconferencing platform for a virtual meeting.

10. **Prepare for post-negotiation steps.**

Formulate a plan for confirming any agreements you reached and holding responsible parties, including yourself, accountable. Having a clear plan can help ensure the implementation of negotiated agreements.

Sampling Common Negotiation Tactics

Negotiation tactics are methods that people often use to acquire more of what they want as they bargain. In this section, I focus on anchoring and introduce you to other common negotiation tactics.

Using the principle of anchoring to your advantage

The principle of *anchoring* in negotiations refers to the use of an initial piece of information or an offer that sets the tone and establishes a reference point for all subsequent discussions and agreements. This initial figure or proposal is called the *anchor*, and it can significantly influence the perceptions and expectations of all parties. Like the process of anchoring a ship, anchoring a negotiation establishes a center point beyond which the negotiation is not allowed to "drift."

Anchoring works because people tend to rely heavily on the first piece of information they receive when making decisions. After an anchor is set, all following counteroffers tend to revolve around it, even if the initial anchor is arbitrary or skewed. You can think of it as an initial reference point. If you're entering a conversation in which you have no initial frame of reference, whatever point of information is given first becomes the reference point.

People often use anchoring to their advantage in a negotiation by starting with an offer that's more extreme than what they expect to achieve. For example, if you want to sell a product for at least $100 and are hoping to sell it for $120, you might set the price at $150. Potential buyers may think $150 is high, but they're willing to pay a more reasonable price of $120 even though that's higher than your minimum. Conversely, a buyer may set the anchor by offering a much lower price than they're actually willing to pay, pulling the negotiation downward.

Why is anchoring effective? Because it has a psychological impact! An anchor can strongly impact a negotiation's trajectory because counteroffers and adjustments are typically made in relation to this anchor rather than on any objective evaluation. The initial reference point or piece of information biases or colors the rest of the conversation.

However, using an anchor to your advantage doesn't necessarily mean you should be the one "dropping anchor." You may benefit by allowing your negotiating partner to drop anchor so that you can gauge what they're willing to give to get. In the following sections, I present the potential advantages of dropping anchor versus the advantages of letting your negotiating partner drop anchor so that you can decide for yourself which approach is likely to be in your best interest in any given situation.

MY FIRST "SPEAKING FEE" NEGOTIATION

In 2012, I was asked to be the keynote speaker at a conference on higher education and technology. Because I worked at a university at the time, I was used to getting asked to speak at conferences, on stages, and in workshops. And, as a university employee, I was accustomed to not getting paid to speak. So imagine my surprise when this group called me, asked whether I was available to be their keynote speaker, and then, when I said yes, asked me what my fee was.

Fee?

I was a fish out of water.

I had no idea of what to ask for.

So I tossed out "$1,000."

"Great!" The caller instantly replied.

And then I realized I had left money on the table. I set the anchor, and because it was well within their speaker budget, they agreed immediately. I later learned that the budget for the keynote speaker was $2,500 that year. I negotiated myself out of a possible additional $1,500! *Ouch!*

Now, when I negotiate speaking rates, I ask for their event budget. I want to see *their* anchor first. Or, if they haven't set one, I will set the anchor at a higher price so that we can begin negotiations with me in a better position to compromise and still be profitable.

Anchors aweigh! Recognizing the benefits of dropping anchor

Setting the anchor at the beginning of a negotiation offers the following potential benefits:

>> **Controls the range:** Setting the anchor gives you initial control over the negotiation, allowing you to frame the discussion in terms that are beneficial to you. Anchoring can be particularly beneficial if you have a strong understanding of the value of what you're negotiating and are confident in setting a realistic yet advantageous starting point.

>> **Makes you the purveyor of value:** Anchoring can influence how your negotiating partner perceives the value of what you're proposing. By setting the anchor, you can potentially influence the other party's perceptions and expectations of value, making them react to your proposal rather than proactively setting their terms.

>> **Improves negotiating efficiency:** Because it establishes a starting point, setting an anchor can reduce the time and the back-and-forth required to reach a middle ground, especially if the other party is inclined to negotiate toward the anchor rather than redefine the terms.

REMEMBER

Successful anchoring requires a delicate balance. Set an anchor that's ambitious yet within a plausible range to encourage serious consideration. If you set an anchor that's ridiculously excessive, you risk losing its positive psychological impact.

Wait and see: Considering the benefits of letting the other party drop anchor first

Being first to set the anchor isn't always the best approach. Here are some potential advantages to letting your negotiating partner set the anchor:

>> **Keeps your negotiating partner at the table:** If you set an anchor that your negotiating partner deems overly aggressive, they're likely to leave the table. "Thank you. Next!" And that's not just a song (but without punctuation) by Ariana Grande; it's what will happen if you set the anchor too high or too low, depending on the context. When you do that, you run the risk of having your offer rejected outright, which closes down negotiation opportunities before they fully open, and it potentially harms business relationships.

>> **Gives you an opportunity to hunt for and gather information:** By letting your negotiating partner go first, you can glean useful insights into their expectations and limits. The information and insights can be especially

beneficial if you lack complete information about the other party's position or the market context.

If the other party sets anchor far from what you're willing to accept, you may have to hunt to find a reasonable middle ground to present an effective counteroffer.

Making the call: To drop or not to drop anchor?

The decision of whether to set the anchor or let the other party set it depends largely on the context, your understanding of the situation, your preparedness, and the amount of leverage you have:

Ultimately, the most strategic approach often involves a balance between assertiveness and adaptability. Being ready to set an anchor when you have the advantage, while also being prepared to let the other party reveal their hand when you're uncertain, can provide a flexible framework that adapts to the dynamics of different negotiation scenarios.

Misjudge at your own peril. The success of anchoring depends heavily on your ability to set an appropriate anchor. If you set an anchor that's too aggressive, you run the risk of ending the negotiation. If you're not aggressive enough, you stand to leave money (or whatever you're negotiating for) on the table. Letting your negotiating partner set the anchor can backfire as well. Whatever you decide, you always face some risk.

Adding other negotiation strategies to your toolbox

In addition to anchoring, you can employ other negotiation strategies (regardless of whether you set the anchor) to achieve favorable outcomes. Here's a look at some additional strategies I've found to be effective:

>> **Focus more on interests and less on positions.** Understand and address the underlying interests and needs of both parties rather than their stated positions. This approach, often referred to as *principled negotiation,* encourages collaborative problem-solving and seeks win-win solutions, which can lead to more sustainable and satisfactory outcomes for all involved.

>> **Know your limits.** Knowing your lowest acceptable offer and your best alternative if the negotiation fails gives you more power and confidence to walk away if the proposed terms are unfavorable.

>> **Hit the range.** Rather than set a single anchor point, set a range of possible agreements or options. You can use this technique to gauge the flexibility of the

other party without committing to a specific outcome. It allows both sides to explore options within a spectrum, which can help you find common ground.

>> **Graduate the give.** If you're going to give, make small concessions gradually rather than all at once. This strategy can make the other party feel as though they're making progress in negotiations, which can keep them engaged and more willing to make concessions in return. Strive to exchange concessions of equal value.

>> **Just one more bite.** Add small requests at the end of a negotiation that don't necessarily affect the main negotiation points but add value to the overall package. For example, consider asking for free delivery or an extended warranty after agreeing on the purchase price of equipment. Additionally, rather than negotiate item by item, bundle several items together and negotiate them as a package. This can often lead to better deals and can satisfy both parties' interests more comprehensively.

>> **Make comparisons attractive.** Introduce options in your proposal that you know are less attractive but serve to make the option you really want seem more appealing in comparison. This technique can be particularly effective in complex negotiations involving multiple issues or items.

No matter what strategy (or strategies) you use, I strongly recommend that you base your negotiation terms on objective criteria such as market value, expert opinions, or legal precedent. Using objective criteria can help ensure fairness and maintain professionalism, reducing the personal biases that can sometimes derail negotiations.

By diversifying your negotiation strategies, you can adapt to various situations and counterparties more effectively. Each strategy has its strengths and can be particularly effective, depending on the context and dynamics of the negotiation. What's important is that you assess the situation and choose the appropriate techniques that align with your goals and the nature of the relationship you want to maintain with the other party. This approach not only enhances the likelihood of achieving favorable outcomes but also helps in building and maintaining healthy long-term business relationships.

Navigating Common Workplace Negotiations

In the workplace, numerous situations present opportunities to negotiate, including agreeing on price and other terms of a sale with customers and vendors, discussing compensation and promotions with superiors or subordinates, and bargaining with stakeholders over budget allocations. In this section, I call attention to a number of the most common workplace negotiation scenarios and offer guidance for each scenario that can improve your ability to get more of what you want.

Effective negotiation can improve job satisfaction, productivity, and career advancement, making it a vital skill in professional development.

Negotiating salary, title, responsibilities, and more

Every job begins with a negotiation over compensation, title, responsibilities, and more, and similar negotiations occur over the course of a person's tenure with the organization. To ensure that your compensation and other benefits meet your needs and are commensurate with everything you bring to the table, you must be able to negotiate effectively. In this section, I offer the guidance you need.

The tips and techniques I share in this section are equally relevant whether you're negotiating the terms of a new job offer, a pay raise for your current position, or salary and other terms related to a possible promotion.

Consider the whole package

When most people negotiate with a current or prospective employer over compensation, their primary focus is on salary, and that's reasonable. However, focusing solely on salary can limit your ability to expand the pie during a negotiation. *Expanding the pie* involves increasing the overall value of what's at stake in a negotiation so that the negotiating partners aren't fighting over limited resources. Try to look beyond salary to other benefits that can sweeten the pot for you, and consider the following factors:

>> Job title

>> Responsibilities

>> Remote work options and flexible working hours

>> Bonuses and/or profit-sharing

>> Paid/personal time off (PTO)

>> Health and life insurance

>> Retirement plans

>> Childcare reimbursement

>> Professional development funds

>> Relocation assistance

>> Expense allowance

>> Severance package

REMEMBER

When negotiating a job offer, focusing beyond the salary can lead to enhanced job satisfaction and work-life balance. Enter the negotiation with a clear but flexible mindset, ready to consider alternative compensation options like benefits or bonuses if salary flexibility is limited.

Do your research

Every negotiation requires research. In the case of a salary negotiation, I encourage you to research the following:

>> **Job title and responsibilities:** Examine the job posting carefully to gain insight into the position and the responsibilities and workload it's likely to entail. In other words, find out what you're getting yourself into so that you can decide what to ask for that will make the offer of value.

>> **Market rates:** Research typical salary rates for your position and responsibilities within your industry. You can use websites such as Glassdoor, PayScale, and LinkedIn Salary Insights to find this data.

>> **Geographic considerations:** Consider the cost of living and typical salary ranges in your location.

>> **Organization-specific information:** Find out as much as you can about the organization: its mission statement, vision, values, financial health, and typical compensation packages. You may be able to locate this information on the organization's website, on sites like Glassdoor or LinkedIn, or by networking with current or former employees.

Align your goals with the organization's objectives

As you research the organization, you gain clarity into how the role you'll be playing in the organization contributes to its broader goals. This insight helps frame your negotiation points in ways that resonate with decision-makers. Additionally, clearly define your career objectives and identify the resources, support, and adjustments you'll need to achieve these goals within the context of your request. This approach helps you establish a mindset of seeking a mutually beneficial arrangement.

Aim for win-win outcomes. Approach the negotiation as an opportunity for collaboration, not confrontation. Propose solutions that advance both your interests and those of the organization. This collaborative mindset fosters positive relationships and can lead to more successful negotiations, making it a cornerstone of effective strategic negotiation.

Know your value

Research can provide insight into your market value based on the position and your education, skills, and experience. However, also factor in other qualities you bring to the table, including soft skills, such as your ability to communicate, solve problems, negotiate (yes, that's a marketable skill!), collaborate, lead, manage time, innovate, resolve conflict, think critically and creatively, and more. Soft skills also include character traits, such as dependability, flexibility, empathy, and integrity.

Practice

Practice your salary negotiation in advance. Rehearse your key points and potential responses to likely questions in advance to reduce anxiety and enhance your articulation during the negotiation. Spending time visualizing a positive negotiation outcome, which can help alleviate stress and increase your psychological readiness, is also a useful strategy.

Project confidence

Project confidence through your verbal and nonverbal communication. Shake hands firmly (but not too firmly), stand or sit with good posture, make eye contact, and smile appropriately for the situation because these cues can influence how assertively you present your case. See Chapter 3 for additional information and guidance on nonverbal communication.

Listen carefully

Active listening, as discussed in Chapter 5, is crucial. Pay attention to the feedback and priorities your superiors or negotiation counterparts express. This information can guide you in adjusting your proposal to better align with organizational priorities and individual values or motives, thereby increasing the likelihood of success.

Attracting the project assignments you desire and the resources you need to succeed

Project assignments present plenty of opportunities for negotiation. Initially, you may need to negotiate to attract the project assignments you want — promoting yourself or your team as the best qualified to complete the project. Then you can focus on negotiating the details, including the following:

>> The project's scope

>> The deliverables

>> Deadlines and milestones

>> Resources provided by your organization

The key to negotiating these details is to start with the goal in mind and then determine everything you need to reach that goal. Then present your proposal with confidence, knowing that if your organization provides you with what you or your team needs, you can deliver on your promise. Don't let anyone set you up for failure by leading you into making unrealistic concessions.

TIP

If your team's or department's resources are limited, you may be able to expand the pie by exploring what other teams or departments in your organization have to offer. Sharing or shuffling around resources such as budget allocations, technologies, and support staff within your organization may enable you to access additional resources.

REMEMBER

Negotiating with superiors, equals, or team members all require a different approach. See Chapter 12 for more about adjusting your communication style based on the communication direction — upward, downward, or laterally.

Negotiating an attractive yet productive work arrangement

With the increasing demand for work-life balance, negotiations about flexible working hours or the ability to work from home are becoming more common and, in many organizations, expected.

If you can do your job remotely (and you want to), negotiate for a remote work arrangement, which can range from working at home a few days a week to full-time. If you can't do your job remotely, you may be able to negotiate for a flexible schedule that gives you more control over *when* you work and not so much *where* you work. In either case, to negotiate effectively, you need to do your research to gather the following information:

>> Productivity data and statistics, especially anything you can find related specifically to your position. Search the web for relevant data and statistics.

>> Information about work-at-home or flex-schedule arrangements at your organization specifically. Consider interviewing employees and management for their input.

>> A list of tools and technologies the organization has to facilitate remote work and any additional resources you need.

Requesting time off

Though not always seen as a negotiation, requesting time off, especially during popular holiday periods, can require negotiating the timing and duration of leave to ensure that it doesn't disrupt business operations. If you're requesting time off at a particularly busy time, make sure your negotiation and request come complete with a plan for how you'll avoid or minimize any disruption; for example, by delegating your job duties to an assistant or associate.

Securing a more favorable and advantageous performance review

Performance reviews are part of an ongoing conversation between managers and employees that regularly evaluate the employee's effectiveness and identify areas for improvement and opportunities for personal and professional development. (I cover these reviews in much greater detail in Chapter 15.) Your performance reviews provide valuable opportunities for you to negotiate for raises or promotions, reassignments, flexible work arrangements, and more. As you prepare for your next performance review, keep the following important points in mind:

>> **Share your goals and objectives.** Your supervisor is likely to set goals or objectives for you, but these are often negotiable, especially if you have something better in mind.

>> **Be prepared to demonstrate your success.** If you receive a review you disagree with, be prepared to correct inaccuracies and highlight anything positive that was omitted.

>> **Be ready to propose changes in pay, position, responsibilities, tasks, and workload.** Changes like these are part of the natural evolution process in business, especially if you're on your way up the corporate ladder. Prepare to negotiate these changes by understanding what your capabilities are, given the resources available to you. If you get pushed to take on more responsibility with no additional compensation, benefits, or support, be prepared to negotiate.

Something's gotta give: Negotiating workload demands

I don't know any business owner (or management team) who doesn't want to get the most out of every member of their workforce. But with the narrow scope of profit and return on investment (ROI), sometimes people can go too far, placing unrealistic demands on individuals, teams, departments, or divisions. Unrealistic demands not only carry the potential of harming employees but can also harm the organization by driving away talent and diminishing productivity. As a member of an organization, one of your responsibilities — to yourself and your organization — is to negotiate reasonable workload demands. Here are some tips that can help:

>> **Do your research.** Data is your friend. Before entering negotiations, gather concrete data about your current workload, deadlines, and time spent on various tasks. Use this information to build a case for requesting the additional resources or the adjustments you need to meet the increased workload demands.

>> **Be clear about your capacity.** Explain how much work you can handle without compromising quality, and be specific about the impact of overloading on your performance and well-being.

Communicate using I+verb statements to express how the workload impacts you personally. These statements can prevent the conversation from becoming confrontational and keep the focus on finding solutions. See Chapter 8 for more about the power of using I+verb statements.

>> **Know your priorities.** Identify which tasks are most critical to your role and the organization's goals. Discuss these priorities during negotiations to reach a mutual understanding about what's most important. If additional resources or support can help lighten your workload, be specific about what you need — whether it's software, additional team members, or access to external vendors.

>> **Don't be a whiner; be a solution provider.** Focus on providing solutions, not on complaining about situations. For example, if your workload is too heavy, suggest delegating specific tasks, adjusting deadlines, or prioritizing projects differently instead of complaining that you have too much on your plate.

This approach ensures ongoing communication and flexibility to adapt to changes in the organization or project scope.

>> **Be prepared to exchange value.** Show your flexibility by being open to new work arrangements. For instance, you may agree to take on extra tasks in exchange for an extended deadline on another project. And, don't wait for your next performance review to discuss workload management; bring up concerns as they arise, and propose timely solutions to prevent burnout and maintain productivity.

By using these techniques, you can effectively communicate and negotiate your workload, leading to a more manageable and productive professional life. These approaches help you maintain your well-being and build a reputation as a proactive and solution-oriented professional.

5

Navigating Difficult Workplace Conversations

Navigate challenging workplace conversations with greater confidence and less stress.

Uncover the real issues underlying a perceived problem or challenge, and clarify what's really happening before you address what you believe is going on.

Follow three crucial rules to improve the results of performance reviews and other conversations in which you're giving or receiving feedback.

Recognize the difference between formal and informal feedback and the benefits of both.

Resolve interpersonal conflicts — from recognizing the potential benefits of conflict to adopting effective conflict-resolution strategies to understanding communication strategies people commonly use to deal with conflict.

Discover how to communicate effectively in a crisis, buy time so that you can think more clearly, and implement an effective framework for responding to a crisis — recognize, empathize, and respond (RER).

Chapter **15**

Giving Feedback and Discussing Performance

F *eedback* comprises everything from scheduled, formal performance reviews to casual daily interactions celebrating successes, correcting mistakes, and calling attention to areas for improvement. It's the lubricant that keeps the organizational machine running smoothly.

Unfortunately, in many organizations, feedback is one-directional, primarily corrective, and often relegated to annual or semiannual performance reviews. For optimal results, feedback should be frequent, corrective, constructive, and flowing in both directions. If feedback isn't interactive, it's merely instructive, and the people involved in the process miss valuable opportunities to improve themselves, one another, and the organization.

When people participate in crafting constructive feedback sessions, they become more committed. By encouraging others to share their needs and ideas, you enable participants to tap into a wealth of insights and innovations.

In this chapter, I provide guidance on feedback best practices and share ways to make your feedback more dynamic and actionable.

Don't reserve feedback sessions solely for addressing performance issues. Make them regular and balanced, celebrating successes as well as discussing areas for improvement and opportunities for personal and professional development. Research consistently shows that regular feedback boosts productivity, motivation, and engagement among everyone. Regular feedback discussions involve everyone in the growth process, reducing uncertainty, and enhancing understanding of each individual's role and contributions.

Following Six Rules for Effective Feedback Conversations

Engaging in constructive feedback conversations doesn't need to be a complex or stressful ordeal. In fact, you can significantly improve the tone and the outcome of your performance reviews and more casual feedback conversations by following the six rules I cover in this section.

Nurture a receptive state of mind

People tend to perceive unsolicited feedback as criticism, and when that happens, they can quickly go on the defensive, at which point they're not listening to or processing anything you're saying; their brain is too busy rejecting it. When you're giving feedback, you're aiming for lasting, positive change, and the only way to achieve that objective is to offer feedback in a setting and in a way that makes the other person feel safe.

Here are a few ways to make others more receptive to your feedback:

>> **Build rapport over time.** Nurture trust and respect, take a genuine interest in the other person's well-being, and provide feedback casually, frequently, and constructively so that you're not approaching the person only to point out problems.

>> **Choose the right time.** The right time is when the person is mentally and emotionally ready to receive feedback, not when they're overwhelmed, upset, or distracted.

>> **Select the right place.** Meet in a setting that's private and comfortable to ensure confidentiality and avoid embarrassment. Create a setting that

positions you equally — for example, sit beside the person at a conference table instead of sitting behind your desk.

>> **Set a positive, constructive tone.** Frame your feedback as an opportunity for growth and improvement.

>> **Encourage and facilitate two-way communication.** Invite the other person to share their perspective and then listen in a way that makes them feel heard. See Chapter 5 for more about developing active listening skills.

>> **Be mindful of your body language.** Maintain an open posture and appropriate, respectful eye contact. Don't stand too close or over the person, which can be perceived as threatening. See Chapter 3 for more about nonverbal communication.

The five rules covered in the following sections also help to nurture a receptive state of mind.

WARNING

Don't place someone in a situation in which they feel cornered or under attack; otherwise, they'll be in a reactive rather than receptive state.

Own your message

Many people who offer feedback fall into the trap of starting the conversation with the word *you*. Avoid this approach! Opening with *you* is akin to verbal finger-pointing and immediately puts the other person on the defensive. Using *you* in this way doesn't facilitate open dialogue or constructive feedback; rather, it comes across as a direct accusation.

Instead, initiate feedback discussions with *I* to take ownership of your thoughts. Start with phrases such as "I want to discuss," "I need to see," or "I notice." Although you can still use *you* in your statements, beginning with *I* asserts ownership right from the start, which is crucial for setting a strong tone. (See Chapter 8 for more about the power of using I+verb construction.)

Another common error is to preface remarks with qualifiers such as "It might just be me, but . . ." which undermines your position and dilutes the impact of your statements. Owning your message is what sets you apart. It's what distinguishes leaders who are unafraid to embrace their emotions, responsibilities, and actions. If you aspire to be a strong, confident leader and an exemplary manager, firmly owning your message is essential.

Stop apologizing and generalizing

I've encountered numerous managers and leaders who initiate feedback discussions with an apology, such as saying, "I'm sorry we need to have this conversation today, but . . . ." Although this statement isn't inherently incorrect, it suggests reluctance and discomfort from the speaker's side. Starting a conversation this way can imply a lack of interest or commitment to the discussion, potentially confusing or disengaging the employee.

WARNING

Don't apologize for your feelings, observations, or the needs of the organization. Apologizing can undermine the message you're trying to convey and may diminish the urgency of the action required. Effective feedback, particularly when it involves areas of improvement, needs to be direct and unapologetic to ensure clarity and prompt a constructive response.

Instead, approach feedback with confidence and assertiveness. Be clear about the purpose of the conversation without diminishing its importance. Emphasize the value of the feedback for the employee's growth and the betterment of the team or company. By communicating directly and respectfully, you reinforce the seriousness of the discussion and encourage a more engaged and proactive response, which is essential for driving meaningful change and achieving desired outcomes.

Focus on behaviors, not character

When conducting feedback discussions, concentrate on behaviors rather than on personal traits or generalizations about the person's character, which can come across as judgmental. For example, rather than describe someone as careless (a character judgment), you may point out that the person overlooked three items on the maintenance schedule or forgot to lock the doors after closing two days last week (specific behaviors).

Another problem with generalizing about a person's character is that it does little to no good. For example, if someone makes a statement that seems arrogant, labeling them as such implies that arrogance is baked into the person's character and nothing can be done to fix it. However, if you focus on the behavior, you're implying that the person can change that behavior.

REMEMBER

Focus on specific behaviors rather than on attributing a character flaw. This approach prevents you from unfairly labeling your employees or teammates, avoids putting them on the defensive, and provides them with an opportunity to correct the behavior.

Seek the underlying cause

People usually have a reason for their behaviors. Understanding their reason can shed light on other issues that need to be addressed and can lead to possible solutions. The natural tendency is to correct the behavior, but that's not always the most effective approach. When someone's saying or doing (or not doing) something and it's causing a problem in the workplace, engage in a conversation with the purpose of identifying and understanding the underlying cause. When you know the cause, you have a clear idea of how to address the situation. You shift the focus from the perceived problem to the real problem — the root cause.

WARNING

If you catch someone in a lie or counterproductive gossip, seek to understand the reason behind it. Investigating the underlying cause is far more beneficial to you and your business than reacting with anger and making a point in the moment. Although scolding an individual may be the natural reaction, it won't uncover the truth. Behind every counterproductive behavior is a reason for it. By identifying the root cause of the dishonesty or disruptive behavior, you can rectify the situation and realign your team. Addressing the core issue leads to a more honest, open, and productive work environment.

Be specific

When giving feedback, specificity is the key. Interestingly, research indicates that feedback based on character traits rather than on specific behaviors or actions can backfire, even if the feedback is positive. For example, if a manager frequently tells an employee, "Tay, you are so awesome," or "Tay, you're amazing," they might think they're providing positive reinforcement. However, Tay might feel good though they're still unclear about what exactly they did to earn such praise. They lack concrete feedback on what actions to continue or improve.

Although general compliments are well-meaning, they don't help employees understand what's specifically valued in their work. Nor do they clarify what behaviors or contributions they should focus on repeating. In fact, such vague praise over time can actually have the opposite impact.

Instead, aim for specific and behavior-oriented feedback. For instance, you could say, "Tay, you did an outstanding job on this project, particularly with how you managed the progress reports." This specific compliment not only acknowledges Tay's overall performance but also highlights a specific area of their contribution, giving them a clear reference point for what to maintain or enhance in future tasks. This approach makes it easier for Tay to understand what made their performance commendable and how they can continue to excel and grow in other aspects of their work.

Being specific also requires backing up feedback with data or specific examples. Focus on the behavior and its outcomes or results. Frame your feedback in the context of cause-and-effect by linking the behavior to a specific outcome; for example, you may say, "Because of X behavior, we couldn't achieve Y result." This method of feedback is usually more effective because you're pointing out why the disruptive behavior matters.

EXAMPLE

Suppose that you have an employee, Brady, who's been showing up late on Mondays. You ask him to meet you in the conference room as soon as he's had a chance to grab a cup of coffee. You sit next to him at the table and say something like this: "Brady, I've observed that you've arrived late on three of the past four Mondays. This seems out of the norm. Is something happening to cause these delays, or do we explore some potential solutions together?"

Here, you're meeting with Brady in a neutral environment that's quiet, comfortable, and confidential. You're sitting next to him, not across from him. Each of you has a cup of coffee. You're having a casual conversation, and you clearly state your observations without any apologies. You specify the instances of lateness without making personal judgments, focusing solely on the behavior and seeking to understand the underlying reason(s). You give Brady the opportunity to explain the possible causes and offer solutions.

Such an approach facilitates open communication, which can lead to a deeper understanding of the issue and collaboration to resolve it. For instance, you may discover that Brady's partner recently started a new job, and they're adjusting to sharing one car, which is impacting his morning routine. By addressing the situation directly and without making assumptions, you not only resolve the immediate problem but also gain insight into Brady's personal circumstances, strengthening your relationship and fostering a supportive work environment. This is more effective than vague feedback that lacks direct relevance to specific behaviors or situations.

Balancing Formal and Informal Feedback

In a business context, you can generally divide feedback into the following two categories:

>> **Formal feedback:** Structured, documented performance reviews that occur at regular intervals, such as annually or semiannually. These reviews provide a comprehensive assessment of an employee's performance, influence major decisions like salary adjustments and promotions, and involve discussions on long-term career growth.

>> **Informal feedback:** Spontaneous, casual conversations that focus on specific behaviors, incidents, or issues and are not documented. Though informal feedback addresses specific issues, identifies areas for improvement, and reinforces positive behaviors, it generally doesn't directly impact the employee's permanent record.

The difference between formal and informal feedback is like the difference between a final exam and a quiz. In high school and college, quizzes are no big deal. A final exam, on the other hand, can generate considerable anxiety because it can have a tremendous impact on the student's final grade, their grade point average (GPA), and possibly even their future career and living standard. Similarly, regular, casual feedback sessions enable employees to make small corrections to stay on track, but formal performance reviews can impact their pay, job status, and opportunities for advancement.

Together, formal and informal feedback create a balanced approach to guiding employee performance and development. Both are critical components of a company's performance management strategy. Formal reviews provide the structure and long-term planning needed for organizational and employee growth, and informal feedback ensures ongoing adjustments and fosters a communicative, responsive work culture.

In the following sections, I provide guidance on how to give formal and informal feedback.

Leading a formal performance review

If you're a supervisor or team leader, you may be responsible for giving formal performance reviews. One key to success is to structure your reviews carefully to balance past performance and future goals, strengths and areas for improvement, and talking and listening. Here's one effective way to structure an effective formal performance review:

1. **Greet your employee and briefly summarize the structure of the review.** Follow the first rule of giving feedback (covered previously in this chapter): "Nurture a receptive state of mind."

TIP

Take notes during the review. Taking notes demonstrates that you're listening actively and provides a written record of topics you discussed. This strategy comes in handy at the end of the review when you summarize points and discuss next steps. Or, if you want to leverage technology for expediency and accuracy, record the review (if doing so is legal in your state and/or country) so that precise records are available to all parties involved.

2. **Invite the employee to share their thoughts and insights.** Give the employee an opportunity to weigh in with their own observations and insights about their performance.

3. **Review the employee's performance.** Cover strengths, achievements, and areas for improvement. Be specific and provide examples.

TIP

Consider combining Steps 2 and 3. As you cover each point, invite the employee to comment on it. This approach creates a less formal atmosphere in which you're engaging in a more casual two-way conversation, listening as much (or more) than you're speaking. It can put both of you at ease and make the employee more receptive to your input and guidance.

4. **Discuss goals for the next review period.** Cover performance goals, professional development, and potential opportunities for promotion. Strive to make this stage of the performance review a collaboration. Although you may have some ideas, invite the employee to share their thoughts. Make sure goals are specific, measurable, achievable, relevant, and time-bound (SMART), as discussed in Chapter 7.

REMEMBER

One key challenge during this stage of the review is to ensure that the employee's goals align with those of your organization. Don't discourage the employee from discussing goals that don't align, but try to gently steer the conversation toward goals that do align.

5. **Summarize key points and discuss next steps.** Review the points you discussed, what you both agreed to do, and any deadlines or milestones. Again, documentation is important.

You may need to revise your written performance review before having the employee sign it, at which point it becomes a part of the employee's permanent record. Do this as soon as possible after the review and provide the employee an opportunity to review the revised document. This step shows that you listened, and it reinforces the conversation and subsequent actions.

Giving informal feedback

Giving informal feedback is generally easier than leading a formal performance review, but you still need to be careful about what you say, how you say it, and the location and timing. Here are some tips to provide more casual feedback in a way that has the most positive impact:

>> **Provide feedback as soon as possible after the event or behavior.** Memories fade as time passes and more stimuli get introduced. Act swiftly for optimal accuracy.

>> **Be specific.** Mention the event or behavior and provide clear, actionable guidance, if guidance is called for.

>> **Be constructive when providing corrective feedback.** Focus on improvement instead of just pointing out what's wrong. Even better, collaborate to find the solution.

>> **Make feedback a casual routine.** Incorporate feedback into your daily interactions to normalize the process so that it feels less intimidating. This approach can also help foster the proverbial open-door environment that many leaders want to have.

>> **Choose the right place and time, as explained in the earlier section "Nurture a receptive state of mind."** Know how your employee or team member communicates and provide feedback in that format if processing time is necessary.

Improving Performance Through Workplace Equity

Workplace equity involves treating everyone fairly and providing equal opportunities for all employees with regard to training, professional development, and promotions. Not only is this concept ethical, but it also benefits the organization with respect to performance and productivity. People are more productive when they feel they're being treated fairly and they have equitable opportunities for advancement. I cover the topic here, in a chapter about providing feedback, because equity plays a key role in ensuring that the feedback you're providing isn't biased in favor of or against anyone, or is based on anything but their performance.

To test your impartiality, ask yourself the following questions:

>> Are we (or am I) providing equal resources to everyone?

>> Are we (or am I) allocating a fair share of attention to each person?

>> Are we (or am I) expressing gratitude evenly?

>> Are we (or am I) offering everyone an equal chance to succeed?

If you answered no or if you're unsure of your answers to any of those questions, put self-reflection and improvement in your plans. The first step is to adjust your mindset, which is what this section is all about. To become an employee who is respected, a manager who is admired, or a leader who is followed, you must grasp the four principles of workplace equity covered in the following sections. As these tenets sink in, they can begin to influence your behaviors in a positive direction toward building a more equitable workplace. More specifically, they can influence the way you provide feedback (formal and informal), ensuring that you treat everyone fairly.

REMEMBER

Desiring fair treatment extends beyond just your internal team to other stakeholders, including leadership, clients, and shareholders. They too seek equity. If they sense that the value exchange for their investment isn't equitable, they're unlikely to remain loyal to your organization.

LEARNING ABOUT EQUITY ON THE PLAYGROUND

Rewind to your elementary school days. It's recess, and you've brought a shiny new ball to play foursquare with a friend. As you're happily passing the ball across the squares, suddenly, your friend snatches the ball and walks off with it. Imagine your shock and anger!

You're likely furious. What's your next move? Perhaps you confront your friend to snatch the ball back, deciding never to share anything with them again. Maybe you report the incident to the teacher to retrieve your ball, risking being labeled a snitch. You might even let your friend keep the ball but end the friendship altogether. Or you could throw a tantrum, crying and complaining.

As adults, people tend to think that they've grown out of these playground spats, but they really haven't. Adults still react emotionally when they feel they've been treated unfairly, and they still have the same initial impulses — to get even, tell the boss, or choose to be uncooperative with the supervisor or team member they feel treated them unfairly. These bad feelings can fester and negatively impact the workplace environment.

When you grasp the four tenets of workplace equity covered in this section, you'll be better equipped to engage in dynamic communication to uncover the root cause of the problem, manage the situation effectively, and ensure a fair resolution for everyone involved.

REMEMBER

Nobody would say, "Please, treat me unfairly." Humans desire equitable treatment. Everybody wants assurance that their contributions are valued, that their work is impactful, and that their efforts are fairly compensated.

Tenet 1: People exchange work for rewards

People work for rewards; it's that simple. I've yet to meet anyone who goes to work without expecting something in return. However, merely offering a salary, an hourly wage, or a contract rate is often insufficient. Many managers believe that monetary compensation alone is enough, but they're mistaken. In fact, poor management, not inadequate wages, is the top reason people leave their jobs. All your employees, contractors, vendors, and other workplace connections need to feel appreciated.

As a manager, seek to understand what motivates your employees. Money isn't always a top priority. Consider these other forms of rewards:

>> Additional responsibilities

>> Additional resources

>> Opportunities for collaboration

>> Regular positive and constructive feedback

>> Education, training, and professional development

>> Time off

>> Public acknowledgment (for example, calling out an achievement in the organization's newsletter)

Ultimately, employees want to feel that they're being compensated and rewarded commensurate with their contributions to the team or the organization and that their efforts are having a meaningful impact.

WARNING

Equity doesn't mean treating everyone exactly the same. For instance, though a $100 restaurant gift card may delight Jaime, Dylan may prefer the same amount to spend at a bookstore. Generic gestures of appreciation can often be ineffective because they fail to recognize individual preferences and levels of contribution (see Figure 15-1). Astute managers tailor rewards to whatever each employee values most.

FIGURE 15-1: Generic gestures of appreciation can backfire.

This principle applies to your clients as well. Rather than send a generic gift or thank-you note, personalize your gestures to resonate with each client. Avoid blanket solutions, like sending everyone the same box of chocolates, which could inadvertently disappoint someone who is lactose intolerant, for example. Treat people as individuals and watch the positive outcomes unfold.

Tenet 2: People actively search for empowering environments

People yearn to work in environments where they're treated equitably and they can make significant contributions. If employees feel valued, they typically take greater pride and responsibility in their work, and they often respond by working harder and producing more to reciprocate. To make employees feel valued in a way that also supports your organization's success, empower them and equip them with the resources they need to thrive in their respective positions.

REMEMBER

A notable reason for job turnover is the absence of opportunities for professional development. Creating an environment that promotes growth and development is a key to recruiting new hires and top talent and retaining existing employees. That also includes allowing for innovation and intrapreneuership to empower employees to have more ownership.

Tenet 3: People feel stressed when they're treated unfairly

Inequity leads to disappointment and frustration, which results in stress and decreased productivity. Employees who perceive they're being treated unfairly tend to be less effective and may even become counterproductive. For example, if an employee finds out that a colleague earns more for the same work, or if a manager appears to favor one individual or encourages one person's ideas disproportionately, it discourages everyone else who feels they've contributed the same — if not more. The disaffected employee's focus shifts from work to the unfair treatment.

If you sense that an employee is unhappy or dissatisfied, ask them directly (at an appropriate time and place) and be ready to address their concerns. Frustrated employees run the risk of creating a self-fulfilling prophecy, turning perception into reality. For example, the employee feels slighted, so they stop caring, which hurts their productivity and results in them being treated as less than other members of the team who are more motivated.

WARNING

Don't solicit feedback and then dismiss someone's ideas without giving them careful consideration. Consider all ideas and follow up with the person even if you choose not to implement the idea. You can follow up in writing or via a brief conversation, but explain your reasoning. If a suggestion is feasible, take steps to implement it and express your appreciation. If it's not immediately actionable but could be later, explain why and discuss interim solutions. If the idea is completely unfeasible, clarify why and encourage alternative ideas to keep the dialogue productive.

EXAMPLE

Here's an example of what *not* to do:

> Manager: "What's one thing you'd like to change about your current job responsibilities?"
>
> Employee: "I enjoy my role, but I'd like to explore other operations within the company."
>
> Manager: "Okay. Great."

The conversation ends there. The manager notes it down but takes no further action. The employee, feeling neglected, seeks to restore fairness (as explained in the next section), potentially leading to larger issues.

Tenet 4: People who feel they're treated unfairly will seek to balance the scales

Imagine this scenario: You've been in your current role for a year, and the time has come for your first annual review. You've not only met but also exceeded your million-dollar sales target and you're eagerly anticipating a bonus. You receive your check and initially feel quite satisfied, until you discover that a colleague, who has been with the company for five years and met, but didn't exceed, the same sales goal, is receiving double your bonus.

This situation does occur. Sometimes, bonuses are calculated based on factors like company tenure in addition to performance goals. However, as a newer employee who surpassed your sales targets, you may find yourself thinking, "What? I sold more than that person did! How is this fair?"

Even if the bonus structure is stipulated in your contract, it still feels like a slap in the face if you're the high-achieving newcomer. You may start to question, "Why am I not receiving more? Does this mean I'm not valued here? Should I start looking for another job, where my contributions are appreciated?" Given that perception often becomes reality, this feeling of inequity may lead you to reduce your effort. You think, "Maybe I should just aim for $750,000 in sales and adjust my efforts accordingly," or it can result in disruptive behavior, including sharing your frustrations with colleagues.

To prevent scenarios such as these, be proactive. Review your organization's policies and seek to change any policies that are unfair or could be perceived as unfair. If you can't change a policy, be transparent about the fact that it could result in unfair treatment and then explain the reasoning behind the policy and look for ways to "even things up." For example, though you may be unable to double the disappointed salesperson's bonus, you may be able to provide them with additional vacation time to enjoy the bonus they received.

Managing Yourself During Performance Reviews and Conversations

When you're on the receiving end of a performance review, be professional, open, and self-reflective. Approach the situation with a positive attitude, viewing it as an opportunity for growth and development rather than just a critique. Be prepared to discuss your accomplishments, challenges, and areas for improvement by bringing specific examples and data to support your points. Listen actively to the feedback provided, ask clarifying questions if needed, and avoid becoming defensive. Show a willingness to learn and adapt, demonstrating your commitment to your professional development. Additionally, set clear goals for the future and ask for specific guidance on how to achieve them. By managing yourself with composure and a proactive mindset, you can turn performance reviews into valuable experiences that drive your career forward.

In this section, I offer additional advice on how to prepare for and act during performance reviews and conversations. Take the advice in this section into consideration as you prepare for your next review. By following my suggestions, you can enhance clarity, foster better communication, and ensure that feedback leads to the desired outcomes. You'll not only strengthen understanding but also build trust and accountability.

REMEMBER

Actions speak louder than words. Maintain consistency in your verbal and nonverbal communication. You don't want to smile while delivering an unsettling message or look down while giving praise. The secret, which is not so secret, is to maintain your composure. If you're frustrated, angry, or disappointed, those emotions will show through in your posture, facial expressions, and gestures. Your demeanor will shut down the dialogue and put the recipient on the defensive, leading to fear-based reactions, which aren't conducive to productive discussion. See Chapter 3 for additional guidance on nonverbal communication.

Come prepared with challenges, strengths, and watchouts

Before your next performance review, prepare to discuss your strengths, challenges, and watchouts (shortcomings you know about and are working on improving about yourself). Here's an effective step-by-step approach to prepare for a performance review:

1. **Find out what the performance review will cover.**

   You can talk to your supervisor or to colleagues who've been through the process or obtain a copy of your organization's or team's performance review form, which is often the best approach.

TIP

   I suggest filling out the form yourself as you proceed through the following steps. This way, you're able to compare apples to apples when discussing your performance and goals.

   If you haven't had an evaluation or a formal performance review in your current role and you aren't familiar with the form and evaluation criteria that will be used, speak with your supervisor immediately to obtain this information.

2. **Reflect on your accomplishments over the review period.**

   Identify key strengths that have contributed to your success, and back them up with specific examples and data. For instance, if you excel in project management, highlight a recent project during which your leadership was responsible for meeting the goal ahead of schedule and under budget. This demonstrates your value clearly and tangibly. See Chapter 10 for more about self-promotion.

3. **Consider the challenges you faced.**

   Identify areas where you encountered difficulties and discuss what you learned from these experiences. For example, if you struggled with time management, explain the steps you took to improve, such as adopting new productivity tools or adjusting your workflow. This shows that you're proactive and committed to self-improvement.

4. **Identify and elaborate on watchouts.**

   Focus on challenges or shortcomings that require vigilance to avoid future issues. These could be potential pitfalls or ongoing areas of development. For example, if you tend to take on too much work, acknowledge this tendency and discuss how you plan to balance your workload more effectively moving forward. And if you need support, don't be afraid to ask for it! This demonstrates self-awareness and a commitment to maintaining and improving performance.

5. **(Optional) Gather feedback from colleagues, supervisors, and any self-assessment tools your organization provides.**

   This external input can provide a well-rounded view of your performance and help you identify areas you're unaware of before you walk into a formally documented situation. Additionally, review your job description and previous performance reviews to ensure that your discussion aligns with your role's expectations and any previously set goals.

6. **Rehearse your discussion points to present them confidently and clearly during the evaluation.**

   Practicing with a trusted colleague or mentor can help refine your delivery.

By preparing thoroughly, you can engage in a constructive and insightful performance review that highlights your contributions, acknowledges your growth areas, and sets the stage for continued development.

TIP

Don't hesitate to promote yourself by educating your supervisor(s) about the work you're doing! (See more about this in Chapter 10.)

Know what you need and want and don't be afraid to ask for it

If you don't ask, you don't get. After reminding yourself about your stellar performance since your previous review and patting yourself on the back for all you've achieved since then, make a list of what you need and desire from your employer to improve yourself and advance your career. Here are some tips for communicating with confidence what you need and want:

>> **Boost your confidence with thorough preparation.** Preparation breeds confidence! Before the performance review, clearly define what you'll ask for and gather evidence to support why you deserve it. Whether you're asking for a raise, promotion, additional resources, or professional development opportunities, be ready to explain the rationale for your request. Use specific examples, data, and accomplishments to make a compelling case.

>> **Make your requests matter, for both you and your organization.** Frame your request in a way that aligns with the organization's objectives and priorities. Show how granting your request will benefit the organization. For instance, if you're asking for additional training, explain how it will enhance your skills and contribute to higher productivity or better project outcomes.

>> **Rehearse your requests.** Practice what you're going to say to ensure you can articulate your request clearly and confidently. Role-playing with a friend or mentor or in front of a mirror can help you refine your message and reduce anxiety. Focus on maintaining a level and positive tone.

>> **Choose the right time to deliver your request.** Timing is everything! Wait for an appropriate moment in the conversation to bring up your request — ideally, after discussing your achievements and contributions. With the right timing, you reinforce your value to the organization before asking to be rewarded for it.

>> **Justify your request.** Clearly state what you're asking for and why. Avoid vague language and be precise about your needs and the rationale behind them. For example, rather than say, "I want more responsibilities," specify the type of projects or roles you're interested in and how they fit your career goals.

>> **Show off your negotiation skills!** Be open to discussion and compromise. Your manager may not be able to grant your request exactly as you envisioned it, but showing flexibility and a willingness to find a mutually beneficial solution demonstrates professionalism and adaptability. See Chapter 14 for guidance on perfecting your negotiation skills.

Confirm your understanding and next steps

As you come to the close of your performance review, confirm your understanding of key points and next steps. If you contested anything included in your supervisor's written review, and your supervisor agreed to make changes, wait until you've received the revised version and had time to review it before signing it.

WARNING

Even if a conversation appears to go well, never assume that you share the same understanding of what transpired. Assuming a shared understanding is a common and potentially critical mistake. To avoid misunderstandings, always include a summary at the end of any feedback conversation. For example, ask, "Can you summarize the specific support I'll receive to achieve my performance goal for the next period?" This ensures that both parties are aligned on the next steps.

REMEMBER

Just because you articulate a point clearly doesn't guarantee that the other party interpreted its intended meaning. People process feedback differently, and a successful conversation doesn't necessarily mean mutual understanding has been achieved.

A helpful strategy to reinforce understanding is to follow up with a summary email. Documenting the conversation ensures that both parties have a written record of the discussed points, responsibilities, and accountabilities. This written summary serves as a reference, reducing the risk of miscommunication and ensuring that everyone is on the same page.

Chapter **16**

Navigating Interpersonal Conflicts

onflict isn't a dirty word. It's a neutral term; it simply denotes a difference in opinions, interests, or values between individuals or groups. Inherently, it's neither positive nor negative; it can be either, depending on how it's managed and resolved. It's a natural part of human interaction, and it can occur in any setting, from personal to professional relationships.

When managed effectively, conflict can lead to positive outcomes such as improved understanding, enhanced relationships, and creative problem-solving. It can stimulate discussion, encourage diverse perspectives, and foster innovation by challenging the status quo. For example, in a workplace setting, a disagreement over project strategies can lead to a more thorough evaluation of options, ultimately resulting in a better solution.

Conversely, poorly managed conflict can lead to negative outcomes such as tension, decreased productivity, and damaged relationships. It can create a hostile environment and hinder collaboration. For instance, unresolved conflicts among team members can lead to resentment and disengagement, negatively impacting overall performance.

Conflict is neutral because its impact depends on its context, how it's managed, how it affects the individuals involved, and its outcome. In this chapter, I encourage and empower you to approach conflict as a neutral occurrence with the goal of achieving a positive outcome and seizing opportunities for growth, both personally and interpersonally.

Exploring the Pros and Cons and Potential Outcomes of Conflicts

Although conflict can lead to tension and discomfort, it also serves as a catalyst for positive change. It can enhance personal growth, drive innovation, and strengthen relationships. In this section, I examine the benefits and drawbacks of conflict and its potential outcomes to shed light on the power that you and others have in determining whether conflict leads to positive or negative outcomes.

REMEMBER

Just as the mind can make a heaven of hell and a hell of heaven (to paraphrase John Milton), you and your colleagues have the power to make the outcomes of conflict positive or negative depending on how you approach it. Conflict is not negative unless you and others make it so.

Considering the pros and cons of conflict

Conflict provides numerous opportunities for personal and professional growth, collaboration, innovation, and relationship-building. It can help build confidence and camaraderie and strengthen an organization's culture. It also provides opportunities to destroy relationships, morale, and productivity and can lead to individuals being frustrated, angry, bitter, and resentful. In this section, I call your attention to the potential benefits and drawbacks of conflict so that you can approach it with a more neutral mindset and with a clearer understanding of, and deeper appreciation for, what you and your organization have to gain by adopting a more constructive approach to resolving conflict — and what you stand to lose if you don't.

The benefits of conflict

Increasing your awareness of the benefits of conflict can help you approach it with a more neutral mindset, which increases the chances that any conflict you're involved in will have a positive outcome. You'll be less likely to approach a potential conflict sporting an attitude of fear or apprehension or other negative emotions that are often counterproductive. So, the next time someone warns you of a potential conflict (or red flags start waving in your own mind), you can say, "Hold on, not so fast — this can be a good thing!" To develop a more positive mindset about conflict, or at least a more neutral one, consider the following potential benefits:

>> **Results in a deeper, clearer, understanding:** Conflict uncovers underlying issues and provides a forum for sharing different perspectives. For example, during a team meeting, a disagreement about the project timeline can reveal that some members are upset about what they deem to be unrealistic deadlines and demands, leading to a discussion that results in a more realistic schedule and better planning.

>> **Improves problem-solving and collaboration:** Conflict is often the impetus that drives people to work together to explore and invent solutions. It can bring diverse viewpoints to the surface, leading to more informed and balanced decision-making. For example, a conflict between departments about budget priorities is coming to a head. You start asking questions, which leads to a brainstorming session that generates innovative ideas for significantly reducing costs — something that wouldn't have happened if the conflict hadn't arisen in the first place!

>> **Increases engagement and improves morale:** Properly managed, conflict can make people feel more involved in the decision-making process, which makes them feel valued and feeds their desire to contribute. As I often remind my clients, "People support what they help create!" Employees who feel their voices are heard tend to feel more deeply invested in the outcome.

>> **Drives innovation:** Conflict encourages the exploration of new ideas and approaches that otherwise may not have been considered. It can act as a catalyst for innovation by challenging the status quo and compelling people to think outside the box. For example, a heated debate over marketing strategies can spark the creation of a unique campaign that sets the company apart from competitors. Those who embrace conflict as a driver of innovation can stay ahead of competitors by continuously improving and adapting.

>> **Enhances relationships:** The process of resolving a conflict can strengthen relationships by building trust. Conflict resolution is a foundation of couples' therapy; it not only improves the couple's ability to communicate and solve problems together but also strengthens their respect and appreciation of one another. The same is true for coworkers: Resolving conflict through discussion leads to mutual respect, better communication and problem-solving, and closer collaboration.

>> **Highlights opportunities for improvement:** Conflict is like a symptom of a physical illness — it's a sign of an underlying issue. For example, a conflict over project priorities can lead to a reevaluation and clearer definition of the company's strategic goals, ensuring that your organization has the right people in the right roles and effective policies and procedures in place to ensure alignment.

By harnessing these benefits, you can turn conflicts into opportunities for growth and development, collaboration, and innovation.

The cons of conflict

The negative connotations that apply to the word *conflict* are mostly related to unresolved or poorly resolved conflict (often the result of compromise — yes, you read that correctly), which leads to the following:

>> **Festering issues:** Underlying issues aren't addressed, which leads to ongoing tension and dissatisfaction.

>> **Decreased morale and productivity:** Frustrated, disappointed, or disgruntled employees lack the motivation and commitment required to build and maintain a positive work environment.

>> **Damaged relationships:** Strong relationships are built on mutual understanding, trust, and respect. All of that suffers when conflicts result in disappointment and real or perceived inequities.

>> **Increased stress and anxiety:** Although conflict isn't inherently bad, it's often inherently stressful. Stress itself can harm people physically and psychologically if it's allowed to persist.

>> **A toxic culture:** Poor conflict management can result in a culture of distrust, disrespect, and conflict avoidance, all of which can negatively impact communication, collaboration, and innovation.

>> **Impaired talent recruitment and retention:** Nobody wants to work in a dysfunctional or toxic environment. Further, workplace tension can increase illness and drive employees to take days off to avoid the toxic environment — increasing absenteeism in the organization.

>> **Legal issues:** Certain unresolved issues can increase harassment or discrimination claims.

Conflict can also lead to changes and to shifts in the power dynamics within a team or the organization, which can be positive or negative.

Examining the possible outcomes of conflict and why compromise isn't the best

Conflict, on the surface, has three possible outcomes: win-win, win-lose, or lose-lose. Some people consider compromise a win-win outcome, but they're wrong. I place it in a class of its own — an outcome that straddles the gray area between win-win and lose-lose. In this section, I examine all four possible outcomes and explain why compromise, contrary to popular belief, is not the best outcome.

Win-win

A *win-win* result involves all parties working together to find a solution that satisfies everyone's needs and interests. Rather than one side winning at the expense of the others, all parties achieve favorable outcomes. This method emphasizes open communication, mutual respect, and creative problem-solving to address the underlying issues. Win-win resolutions foster a positive, cooperative atmosphere, enhance relationships, and ensure lasting agreements. For example, in a business context, team members might negotiate roles and responsibilities to ensure that everyone feels valued and empowered, leading to improved teamwork and productivity.

To achieve a win-win outcome, start by having everyone involved answer the following questions:

>> **What outcome would make this situation turn out the best for you and the organization?** Answers to this question reveal everyone's interests and concerns — what everyone seeks to gain for themselves, their team, and the organization.

>> **What are the negative consequences if that outcome doesn't occur?** Answers to this question reveal the stakes — what everyone stands to lose with respect to themselves, their team(s), and/or the organization.

>> **Why is this outcome important to you and to the organization?** Answers to this question provide insight into the priority of achieving a positive resolution.

>> **What's the root cause of this conflict, as you see it?** This is perhaps the most important question because it encourages participants to look past whatever they're disagreeing over to the underlying cause, which is what they really need to address.

REMEMBER

When exploring the root cause of the conflict, stick to facts and specific behaviors; don't attack perceived character traits (see Chapter 15 for more guidance).

Honest, open answers to these questions set the foundation for constructive conflict resolution. See the later section "Navigating Conflict More Effectively: Four Tactics" for guidance on how to reach a win-win resolution.

Win-lose

A *win-lose* conflict resolution occurs when one party achieves their goals at the expense of the other party's interests. This approach often involves competitive or confrontational tactics that involve one side imposing its will. Though the winning party may feel satisfied, the losing party often feels frustrated, discouraged, bitter, and resentful. In a business context, a win-lose outcome can manifest as one department securing the majority of resources while another is left underfunded, potentially harming overall organizational effectiveness and collaboration. Win-lose resolutions can create ongoing tension and are generally unsustainable in the long term.

If you're in a conflict and you sense that another party is hell-bent on winning at any cost, ask questions such as the following to steer the conversation in a more mutually favorable direction:

>> I'm curious why this outcome is essential — can you explain it to me?

>> For you to feel satisfied with the outcome, what needs to happen? Follow up each item the person mentions by asking, "What goal will it achieve that benefits you and the team/organization?"

Note that all these questions take the person's mind from the idea of winning and being right to a place where that's no longer important. The person now needs to explain what good will come of what they're proposing — how it will benefit the organization and the people who hold a stake in how the conflict is resolved.

Lose-lose

A *lose-lose* conflict resolution occurs when neither party achieves their desired outcomes, often resulting in mutual dissatisfaction. This outcome typically arises from rigid stances, poor communication, or destructive conflict tactics in which both sides focus more on defeating each other than finding a solution. In a business context, this can happen when two departments engage in prolonged disputes over resources, leading to a compromise in which both end up with insufficient support. Lose-lose resolutions can create ongoing animosity and hinder future cooperation, making it a particularly undesirable approach to conflict management.

The key to avoiding lose-lose outcomes is to commit to an outcome that satisfies everyone's needs and successfully addresses all concerns. After you've achieved what you consider the best outcome possible, check in with everyone involved to find out whether anyone is frustrated or disappointed in any way. Keep the conversation open until everyone's satisfied.

Compromise

Although compromise is often hailed as a fair and balanced approach to conflict resolution, it often falls short, for the following reasons:

>> **Delivers mediocre solutions:** By aiming to satisfy both parties partially, the resulting solution is often suboptimal for either side. For example, if two departments settle on a compromise regarding budget allocation, neither may receive the necessary resources to perform optimally, leading to subpar performance and unmet goals. Instead of a rising tide lifting all ships, a storm will take down both ships!

>> **Stifles creativity and innovation:** By avoiding deeper discussion and the exploration of ideas, opportunities for breakthrough innovations might be missed. In a conflict about product features, a compromise can produce a bland product that fails to stand out in the market, whereas a more thorough conflict resolution could have sparked innovative solutions. In an effort to avoid conflict, many people are often quick to compromise, and in the long run, this causes much more harm to individuals and the organization than it does good because frequent reliance on compromise can hinder assertiveness and confidence.

>> **Leads to resentment:** Parties may feel they've conceded too much, resulting in lingering dissatisfaction. For instance, an employee may agree to a compromise on their project role but feel undervalued and disengaged, affecting their long-term motivation and productivity.

See Chapter 15 for more insights into the tenets of creating and maintaining an equitable workplace.

REMEMBER

Conflict avoiders are often quick to compromise but become highly resentful over time as their frustration and bitterness build up. (See the later section "Dealing with Different Conflict Management and Communication Styles" for more about differences in how people approach conflict.)

>> **Fails to uncover and resolve underlying problems, leading to recurring conflicts:** A huge benefit of conflict is that it addresses underlying issues. Compromise often short-circuits the process. For example, compromising on a team's work schedule may temporarily appease everyone but fall short of tackling the root cause of workload imbalances, leading to ongoing scheduling issues.

>> **Promotes avoidance behavior:** To avoid having to compromise, individuals may avoid conflict altogether, limiting communication and growth. A team that continually compromises may stop addressing real issues, leading to a lack of critical feedback and the persistence of ineffective practices.

REMEMBER

Compromise is a shortcut that often routes people around what could be much better outcomes.

Navigating Conflict More Effectively: Four Tactics

I gauge the effectiveness of conflict management by answering the following two questions:

>> **Is it bringing out the best in people?** Good conflict management encourages and facilitates the best qualities in people, such as empathy, honesty, integrity, generosity, responsibility, and respect. Poor conflict management brings out the worst in people, including anger, envy, greed, resentment, dishonesty, and selfishness.

>> **Is it achieving outcomes that satisfy the best interests of all the stakeholders (including the organization as a whole)?** If an approach to conflict management leaves any stakeholders dissatisfied with the outcome, it's not serving everyone's interests.

If your approach to conflict management is falling short in either of those two areas, you have some work to do. In this section, I share four ways you can improve how you manage conflict.

Finding common ground

Common ground isn't just a good name for a coffee shop! It's a useful approach to starting a productive conflict-resolution session. Finding common ground involves finding something relevant — anything that everyone can agree on. That something could be a shared interest or goal or simply the fact that something's not working well or as effectively as it could be. (It may be something that's working great for someone else but not for you.)

One way to find common ground is to listen. Take turns. Let others go first, which demonstrates that you value their thoughts and allows you to model the listening and respect you expect everyone to practice. Ask questions until you fully understand your communication partner(s) and share your summary of what they said to confirm your mutual understanding. Then take your turn sharing and answering questions. See Chapter 5 for more about listening.

Another way to find common ground is to shift the focus from positions to interests or from issues to underlying causes. Naturally, your positions and perspectives on the situation will differ from those of others. By shifting to interests or underlying causes, you're more likely to find something you can agree on. You can change the direction and tone of the conversation to make it less adversarial and more collaborative. For example, if you disagree with a colleague over the best way to achieve a desired outcome, you may say something like, "Rather than focus on whether we use your method or mine, let's talk about what each method offers and how we can combine the best elements of both to meet our goal." Highlighting shared objectives can pave the way to more constructive dialogue and cooperation. And, when things get heated or frustrating, you can always call back to this common goal to give everyone a proverbial north star.

TIP

Be willing to explore alternative solutions that accommodate both parties' needs. Encourage open communication by asking clarifying questions and summarizing what the other person has said to ensure understanding. By maintaining a positive attitude and focusing on finding solutions instead of pointing fingers, you can create an environment conducive to finding common ground and resolving the conflict.

REMEMBER

Focus more on finding and creating solutions and less on assigning blame. If an individual's performance, behaviors, or actions are responsible for causing a problem, that certainly needs to be addressed at the proper time and in a proper way, as discussed in Chapter 15. And sometimes, the solution requires a change in roles or personnel. However, blame doesn't solve problems. Blame focuses on the past. Solutions need to be future-focused. Having said that, accepting blame you deserve can work in your favor; it demonstrates honesty and integrity and can often move blame out of the way so that the discussion can proceed to solutions. It's like saying, "Okay, I screwed up. Now, what do we need to do to fix it (or prevent it from happening again)?"

Agreeing on the facts and the desired outcome

When the flames of conflict are raging, emotions are the fuel that feeds them, and facts are the water that calms them. You must separate facts from feelings. I'm not saying that feelings are invalid. What I'm saying is that they can escalate the conflict to a point at which discussion becomes irrational. Shifting the focus to facts helps deescalate an emotionally charged conflict and reorients both parties to facts and reason.

When you sense that one or more parties are becoming excessively emotional, you can bring them back to the present moment by saying something like, "I understand neither of us is happy right now and we both want change. Before we discuss possible solutions, let's agree on the facts of the situation and the outcome we're trying to achieve." Then review the facts and the desired outcome before continuing an attempt at a resolution.

Setting aside emotionally charged moments

Conflict is inherently challenging to navigate because it often touches on personal values, beliefs, and emotions. Emotions are deeply intertwined with people's sense of identity and self-worth, making it difficult (if not impossible — we all have bias!) to remain objective during conflicts. When someone feels threatened, misunderstood, or undervalued, emotional responses such as defensiveness, disappointment, frustration, and anger naturally arise. And, when that happens, your reptilian brain (the nickname for the *amygdala*, the part of the brain responsible for the fight-or-flight response) takes over as rational thought goes on vacation.

Though emotions complicate conflict resolution, they also provide valuable insights into the core issues at hand. Effective conflict management involves acknowledging and addressing these emotions constructively rather than attempting to suppress them entirely. This approach can lead to more meaningful and lasting resolutions. But how do you do it? With calm, constructive communication. And how do you achieve that? In this section, I offer some suggestions.

IT'S COMPLICATED

One reason that separating emotions from conflict is so challenging is that emotions serve as a valuable form of communication, signaling an individual's needs and boundaries. For instance, anger may indicate that someone feels wronged, whereas anxiety can signal fear of the consequences. These emotional signals are crucial for understanding the underlying issues in a conflict, but they can also cloud judgment and impede rational decision-making.

Additionally, physiological responses to conflict — such as increased heart rate and adrenaline — can amplify emotions, impairing a person's ability to remain calm and think clearly. This fight-or-flight response is a survival mechanism, but it can be counterproductive in resolving modern-day conflicts that require thoughtful dialogue and compromise.

Past experiences can also intensify emotions during conflicts. Individuals may react more strongly if a current conflict triggers memories of previous disputes or personal grievances.

In short, don't be so quick to judge people (or yourself) for getting emotional during a conflict. Emotions are an integral part of being human, and they're tough to manage when people disagree over something they truly care about.

Take a break — and a breath

When emotions run high, pausing the conversation and taking a break enables all parties to calm down and reengage their rational minds. One way to encourage everyone to do this together is to request a break. Owning your request is even better. You could say something like, "I know that I could benefit from a short break to process all the information we've just taken in. Let's take a 10-minute break, gather our thoughts, and come back to approach this from a different perspective."

Listen actively (yes, I'll keep reminding you)

Active listening is crucial to success in every area of communication in business and beyond. Focus on truly listening to the other person's perspective without interrupting or thinking about what you're going to say when they stop talking. Listening is difficult when emotions are high, but focus, focus, focus and make that happen.

One way to improve your focus is to listen with the goal of being able to understand and summarize the other person's perspective and the information they shared. Ask questions until you fully understand. For example, you may say something like, "I understand that you're frustrated with the project timeline. Can you explain more about your concerns?" This response shows that you recognize the person's concern, you validate their emotions, and you're sincerely committed to understanding them.

Opt for "I" over "you"

In Chapter 8, I explain the power of using the I+verb framework instead of starting sentences with the word *you*, to avoid causing people to take a defensive posture. That technique is especially effective in the context of conflict resolution and can deescalate an emotional exchange. For example, rather than say, "You never listen to my ideas," try saying, "I feel unrecognized when my ideas aren't considered."

REMEMBER

You're probably getting the idea by now that the most effective communication strategies apply to a broad variety of situations. They're darn good strategies for a reason! And that's why I keep repeating them.

Don't make it personal

Do your best to separate the person from the problem and keep the discussion objective. For example, if a team member misses a deadline, focus on the impact rather than on the individual. Say, "The missed deadline has affected our project timeline. How can we prevent this in the future?" instead of saying something like, "You always mess up." (See Chapter 15 for more about keeping the focus on specific behaviors and not on character traits.)

Bringing in a moderator

Sometimes, despite your best efforts, you may not reach an agreement that satisfies everyone's interests, including those of your team or organization. And that's okay. To admit that help is needed is not a sign of weakness. In fact, seeking help is often a sign of strength, and in such cases, the help you seek is often available in the form of an objective, third-party moderator or mediator, especially someone who has received formal training in the art of mediation. Skilled mediators can help resolve conflicts in the following ways:

>> Bring a structured approach to conflict resolution. They set ground rules, guide the conversation, and ensure that each party is heard.

>> Facilitate constructive communication.

>> Provide a neutral, objective perspective.

>> Focus discussions on issues instead of on personal differences.

>> Create a safe space in which all parties feel heard and respected, which is essential for productive conflict resolution.

>> Manage emotions and diffuse tensions.

>> Identify underlying issues and root causes and address them effectively.

>> Expand the pie by identifying resources beyond what the participants in the conflict have brought to the table.

>> Accelerate conflict resolution by drawing on the learned experience of other clients they've helped through similar conflicts.

A mediator's expertise in conflict resolution can lead to more sustainable and satisfactory outcomes for all involved.

Dealing with Different Conflict Management and Communication Styles

Everyone has their own way of managing conflict. Some people try to accommodate everyone else's needs and preferences at the expense of their own and usually get trampled on and end up being resentful as a result. At the other extreme are those who put their own needs and desires ahead of everyone else's, including those of the organization. Somewhere in the middle are those who strive for something fair and are willing to compromise to achieve that goal (often at the expense of everyone involved).

In this section, I cover five distinct conflict-management styles along with a few different communication styles so that you can have a clear understanding of how different people embroiled in a conflict (including yourself) may behave and how you can adjust to engage with them more effectively and improve the outcome.

Recognizing the five conflict-management styles

People generally respond to conflict by accommodating, avoiding, collaborating, competing, or compromising. Understanding these styles can provide insight into the way you and others behave and communicate during the conflict-resolution process, and it can help you choose the most appropriate approach for resolving conflicts in various situations.

Accommodate

When someone wants to steer clear of conflict, they often yield to other people's demands or concerns, often at the expense of their own self-interests. In business, accommodation may involve taking on additional work to help the team meet a tight deadline, even if it means sacrificing your own work-life balance. Although accommodating can help maintain harmony and preserve relationships, it may result in resentment and an imbalance in a relationship if it's relied on too often.

In some situations, accommodation can benefit you, especially if you communicate clearly that you're accepting the additional responsibility in this particular situation only for a certain reason. However, if you don't provide a good reason and establish firm boundaries, be prepared for others to expect more accommodations from you in the future.

Avoid

People who find conflict psychologically painful or uncomfortable often avoid conflict at all costs. Some may fear rejection or loss or damage to a relationship. They ignore or sidestep conflict, hoping issues resolve themselves or differences dissipate over time.

Avoidance can lead to unresolved issues and increased tension as problems become more serious and frustration and disappointment build up. In this sense, it's one of the more dangerous conflict-management styles. It stifles the growth of everyone involved and threatens the health, vitality, and even survival of their relationships with one another.

If you tend to avoid conflict, try working on reframing the conflict into a conversation. Remind yourself of all the potential benefits of conflict and the fallout from unresolved conflict. In most cases, you have far more to gain than to lose by confronting an issue.

Collaborate

Of the five conflict-management styles, I think that collaboration is the best — and most experts readily agree! Collaborating to find or create a win-win solution is definitely the way to go. It's really through collaboration that people are able to come up with solutions that are truly beneficial and meet the needs of all stakeholders. And, when you approach a conflict collaboratively, you're more likely to be open to listening carefully to the concerns of others and better able to separate wants from needs.

Collaboration encourages open communication, creative problem-solving, and mutual respect, leading to more sustainable and effective resolutions. Though some people — <ahem> the competition-minded, which I cover next — may approach a project together with a win-lose mentality, as collaborators, these colleagues with different ideas for a project will brainstorm together to integrate their ideas into a comprehensive plan that leverages their combined strengths and resources.

Compete

A competing conflict-management style is characterized by a high degree of aggressiveness. It's "my way or the highway," or "win at all costs." Someone practicing this style is firmly entrenched in their position and unwilling to budge. They may even resort to bullying tactics to get their way. A competitive disposition is often a great asset in business, and being highly assertive can be useful when time is limited and urgent action is needed, but it's not so great for constructive conflict resolution.

This style can be detrimental to business and team outcomes, and especially relationships and morale. Steamrolling over others to get one's way may be effective, but it damages relationships and breeds hostility if it's done routinely. For example, when a manager insists on a certain approach to a project without considering the team's input, the team members are unlikely to feel as motivated and committed to the project as they otherwise would be.

If you're highly assertive, that's not necessarily a bad thing, but you may need to be more mindful in situations in which you perceive that your colleagues' or your organization's interests clash with your own and when collaboration would likely deliver better outcomes.

Compromise

Compromise isn't all bad and may be the best approach when you need a quick resolution, but it runs the risk of closing the doors to opportunities and better outcomes. Compromise often becomes the default approach to conflict resolution when people lack the imagination and creativity to come up with better solutions or when they think they're dealing with limited resources.

REMEMBER

Compromise can accelerate conflict resolution, but go into it with your eyes wide open. Be sure you have a good reason for compromising and that everyone involved knows the reason so that you can manage expectations more effectively.

Understanding and adapting to different communication styles

Within the context of conflict management are different *communication styles* — how people express themselves in conversations and interactions. A person's communication style encompasses not only the substance of what they convey but also how they convey it — through their tone, language choice, behaviors, and overall approach to interacting with others. It includes the use of humor, sarcasm, body language, and actions.

In this section, I cover common communication styles in business and provide guidance on the pros and cons of each style and how to engage effectively with others who are using each style.

Passive/submissive

Passive/submissive communicators often avoid conflict or seek to accommodate the needs of others at the expense of having their own needs met. (See the earlier section on different conflict-management styles.) They speak softly, apologize excessively, avoid eye contact, assume a submissive or protective posture, and often qualify their statements, using phrases such as "It might just be me, but . . ." or "I'm not sure if this is the best idea, but . . ."

Passive/submissive communication can help deescalate a highly emotional situation, but you need to use it sparingly or else you risk becoming the proverbial punching bag or doormat. In other words, if you're routinely passive, people will take advantage of you. Passive communication can also result in workload imbalances — passive communicators taking on more of the workload — which can damage long-term productivity.

When interacting with a passive communicator, provide plenty of reassurance and actively request their input. Let them know the value of different perspectives and ideas in solving problems and driving innovation. Remind them that disagreeing is okay, and reward them for sharing their perspective and ideas. Be careful not to dismiss or criticize what they say, especially in front of others. You don't want them to turn into a turtle on you (by retreating into their shells).

Assertive

Assertive communicators tackle issues head-on. It's a style that's an effective part of collaborative conflict management. Assertive communicators are confident and demand clarity. They value honesty and transparency, often using direct language to articulate their points. They're likely to initiate conversations about issues they perceive, seeking to address problems before they escalate. They're not afraid to confront an issue.

Of all the communication styles, assertive is generally the best in the context of conflict management as asking pointed questions and providing clear, specific feedback is par for the course. They prioritize open dialogue and may challenge others' viewpoints to reach a deeper understanding and find effective solutions. This approach can foster an environment in which issues are quickly identified and addressed, potentially leading to rapid problem-solving and innovation.

However, an assertive style can sometimes be perceived as aggressive or confrontational, potentially making others uncomfortable or defensive (especially if you come off as competitive and needing to win at all costs). If you're assertive, balance your assertiveness with empathy and active listening to ensure that your approach is constructive rather than combative. Though your proactive stance on conflict can drive positive change and prevent lingering issues, remain mindful of your delivery and the impact it may have on your colleagues' morale and engagement.

Aggressive

Aggressive communication is in-your-face and demanding, a style that's characteristic of a competition management style. Aggressive communicators are committed to getting what they want and having things done their way at the expense of anyone else's interests, including those of the organization. They may even resort to personal attacks and other bullying behavior to force submission. As a result, aggressive communication can harm relationships, stifle creativity, increase stress, and damage workplace morale.

REMEMBER

Aggressive communication isn't always bad. It can be useful when used tactfully when negotiating with a competitor, managing a crisis, addressing misconduct or noncompliance, or protecting your interests when they're being threatened — or whenever decisive leadership is needed and being assertive isn't quite getting people's attention.

If you're in a situation in which someone else is assuming an overly aggressive communication style, the best response is to adopt a calm, assertive demeanor. Don't fight fire with fire, which escalates tensions. And don't become passive or submissive in an attempt to deescalate, which results in your getting steamrolled. Be assertive, and bring the discussion back to issues, interests, and goals.

Passive-aggressive

Passive-aggressive communication combines the worst of both passive and aggressive communication styles. It involves submitting on the surface while responding aggressively at a deeper level — for example, agreeing to a proposal and then working behind the scenes to sabotage its success. These communicators use sarcasm and biting humor, backbiting, noncompliance, and other devious means to indirectly "assert" themselves. Passive-aggressive is one of the most destructive communication styles in the workplace. It destroys trust and creates tension, confusion, and additional conflict.

If you're in a situation with someone who's speaking or acting passive-aggressively, assume a direct, assertive demeanor to ensure that the communication shifts to a more productive style.

WARNING

Any style can use manipulative communication, which involves using tactics like flattery, guilt-tripping, gaslighting, and exaggeration to influence others. This tactic damages trust and leads to confusion and unhealthy relationships. Manipulators often believe they can outsmart others without being noticed. To counter this, it's crucial to stay calm and assertive when engaging with them. Work on refocusing the conversation on the real issue and work toward a productive, mutually beneficial solution.

Not Letting Complaints Turn Into Conflict

If you're in a leadership role, it's a solid move to have an open-door policy so that you can be aware of any issues that threaten the health, safety, and productivity of the workplace you manage. However, an open-door policy can make your office a clearinghouse for complaints, so you need to be able to manage complaints effectively and efficiently. Otherwise, you place yourself at the beck and call of chronic complainers, who are often merely seeking attention and approval or, in some cases, justice (also known as revenge).

Managing complaints requires an ability to differentiate between legitimate and chronic complaints, address each according to their validity, and move from complaint to solution. In the following sections, I provide the guidance you need to transform complainers into problem solvers.

Differentiating between legitimate and chronic complaints

People complain for various reasons. A solution-oriented team member who's frustrated or stressed may present a concern as a complaint rather than as a problem that needs a solution. On the other hand, someone may complain chronically because they feel that their contributions aren't appreciated. These two situations require vastly different approaches.

The first step is to determine whether a complaint is legitimate or simply the source of frustration or dissatisfaction. Here are a few factors to consider:

>> **Frequency:** Numerous complaints from the same person, especially over the same issue when no action has been taken to resolve it, often indicate that you're dealing with a chronic complainer. Unfortunately, like the boy who cried wolf, occasionally one of their complaints might be legitimate, so you have to evaluate every complaint on its merits.

>> **Specificity:** Legitimate complaints are usually specific and accompanied by supporting evidence, such as specific examples and documentation. Chronic complaints tend to be vague and lack new or concrete information.

>> **Confirmation:** If two or more people complain about the same issue, you're probably looking at a legitimate complaint.

>> **Constructiveness:** Legitimate complaints are typically in the form of constructive criticism seeking positive change. Chronic complaints, on the other hand, are often negative and can be whiny or confrontational.

>> **Acknowledgment of previous attempts to resolve an issue:** A legitimate complaint acknowledges any past efforts to resolve the issue and highlights what worked and what didn't. A chronic complaint often disregards past efforts; claims that nothing has changed, even if changes were made; and introduces new reasons to complain.

In the following sections, I present techniques and tips for addressing legitimate and chronic complaints, and I provide steps for complaining constructively — by turning a complaint into a problem-solving activity.

Addressing legitimate complaints

To deal effectively with legitimate complaints, do the following:

>> Acknowledge and paraphrase the complaint to demonstrate that you listened, heard, and understood the issue being brought to your attention.

>> Ask questions to clear up anything you require more clarity about.

>> Ask the person to share their thoughts about the following:

- The outcome they're seeking

- What has been tried before and the outcome of that attempt

- Possible solutions or actions they think need to be taken

This approach demonstrates that you're listening and hearing the other person, that you care, and that you value their input. It also sets the stage for collaborative negotiation and problem-solving.

Handling chronic complaints

Nobody likes a complainer — those who always have something negative to say. They find the one flaw in an otherwise perfect situation and never let it go. They go on and on about issues but never take action to fix or improve their situation. Fortunately, a couple of techniques are available for handling chronic complaints, which can also be helpful for correcting their behavior.

First, consider that chronic complaints may be cries for attention. If someone never seems satisfied, explore the roots of their dissatisfaction by doing the following:

>> **Ask open-ended questions.** For example, ask, "Can you tell me more about what's bothering you?" Open-ended questions can help uncover hidden concerns — for example, sources of stress inside or outside the workplace.

>> **Look for patterns in people, processes, and situations.** Patterns can help identify potential causes and triggers such as disruptive relationships or unhealthy group dynamics.

>> **Discuss the impact the chronic complaining is having on the team, the work environment, or a specific project.** This approach may initiate some self-reflection and openness to sharing the cause of the person's frustration.

>> **Explore possible unmet needs.** Ask questions to encourage the person to share their needs and expectations, such as "What would make your work more satisfying to you?"

Another approach for dealing with chronic complaints is to turn the complaint into a problem-solving exercise, placing the onus on the complainer to take responsibility for the situation. This helps them recognize their role in the issue or understand whether they simply want to vent or actually want to see issues resolved.

Complaining constructively

Let's shift gears from discussing how to handle legitimate and chronic complaints, to how you can complain effectively when you need to bring an issue to the surface. The key is to turn the complaint into a problem-solving activity. Take the following steps:

1. **Present the relevant facts — the essential information needed for someone to understand the situation.**

   Provide any necessary context. If you're sharing an opinion, clearly state that it's your own (own your message, as explained in Part 3).

   Keep opinions to a minimum unless they're directly pertinent to the problem or the situation you want to change.

2. **Describe the situation or problem and any actions you've taken to resolve the issue.**

   For example, if you're trying to determine the proper protocol for requesting professional development funds and you have already consulted the employee handbook without finding the answer, mention it. It shows that you've been proactive in seeking a solution on your own.

3. **Request assistance or propose a solution.**

   Ask for help with finding or creating a solution and be prepared to act on any recommendation. If you have a potential solution, present it for feedback and consideration.

Suppose that your supervisor, Luigi, assigned you to lead a team of four to complete a project. One of your team members, Mario, is working hard to overshadow you. You tried addressing it with Mario, but it didn't help.

You want fair treatment and feel like complaining, but you know that won't achieve the desired results. Running to your supervisor and saying, "Luigi, you told me to lead this project, but Mario took it away from me," won't be effective. Instead, you decide to frame your complaint as an opportunity to take on a different responsibility.

You go to your boss and say, "Luigi, I'm excited to be working on this new project. The whole team is energized. In fact, Mario has started taking the lead on the project reporting and seems to be enjoying it. Is that okay with you? And if so, what's something else I can take the lead on?" or "And if so, is it okay if I take over the creative side of the project?"

You're not complaining; you're stating the facts, presenting the problem, and then asking for help with figuring out a solution, or you're presenting a possible solution.

Chapter **17**

Communicating When Everything Is Falling Apart

O rganizations of all sizes are always at risk of bad public relations (PR), deserved and undeserved. The threats take many forms — natural disasters (earthquakes, floods, tornadoes); operational failures (product defects, service interruptions, supply chain disruptions); legal/ethical issues (fraud, corruption, unfair labor practices, harmful environmental practices); social/cultural threats (discrimination, insensitive comments, failure to support social responsibility initiatives); attacks from competitors; customer complaints and negative reviews; data breaches; and more. And given the popularity of social media, bad news goes viral at warp speed.

Many threats are unpredictable, so you need to be prepared to respond at a moment's notice. Addressing the underlying issue is only the first step. You also need to slow or stop the spread of bad news and explain what your organization is doing to fix the problem. Over the longer term, you may be facing an uphill battle to restore your organization's reputation and customer trust and loyalty.

In this chapter, I provide the information and guidance you need in order to prepare for and respond in a crisis. I don't talk about addressing the underlying issues in this chapter (that's on you), but I share some helpful strategies in Chapter 6 about asking questions and Chapter 7 about engaging in productive conversations. What I do cover can give your organization a little more breathing room, slow the tide of bad news, and help you deal more effectively with the resulting fallout.

Hoping It Won't Happen or It'll Blow Over: Not a Plan

For far too many organizations, the crisis communication plan is hope; they hope nothing bad happens, and then, when it does, they hope it just goes away. Hope is not a plan; it's a gamble. Chances are good that if anything bad can happen, it eventually will (Murphys' law, anyone?), and chances are bad that if it does happen, the organization will emerge without a scratch on its shiny reputation.

Won't it just go away?

As much as most of us would like to sweep negative news under the rug and pretend that it never happened, ignoring a crisis can have severe repercussions, including the following:

>> **Reputational damage:** Stakeholders expect transparency and accountability. Failure to address the crisis can lead to a perception of dishonesty or incompetence. A tarnished reputation can result in lost business opportunities, decreased market value, and difficulty attracting and keeping top talent. Rebuilding a damaged reputation requires significant time, effort, and resources.

>> **Lost trust:** Customers and other stakeholders may lose confidence in the organization's commitment to its stated mission, vision, and values or to delivering quality products and services. Lack of trust leads to decreased brand loyalty, negative word-of-mouth, and, ultimately, lost business. Trust can be lost in an instant and takes a very long time to restore.

>> **Low morale:** Employees look to leadership for guidance and reassurance during challenging times. When a crisis isn't addressed effectively, it creates uncertainty and anxiety within the workforce. This can lead to decreased productivity, increased absenteeism, and higher turnover rates. Ensuring that employees are informed and supported during a crisis helps maintain morale and fosters a positive, resilient work environment.

A crisis doesn't just go away. Nor do the repercussions of ignoring it or hoping it'll pass without causing much damage. Don't sacrifice short-term comfort for long-term negative repercussions.

Crisis in the age of digital communication

Crisis communication is even more crucial in today's business world, due to two factors: heightened expectations and social media. People expect organizations to not only deliver quality products and services at competitive prices but also to do so ethically and sustainably. And, if they don't, they'll be punished in the media, especially social media. In today's media environment, you're not just dealing with a handful of broadcast news outlets.

Users of social media platforms and news outlets can disseminate information in seconds, meaning companies must be prepared to issue statements and updates quickly to control the narrative and address concerns promptly. In part because of this expediency, the demand for immediacy and transparency has risen. Stakeholders expect immediate and clear information about the crisis, including the causes, the impact, and the steps being taken to resolve it.

Businesses must now manage crisis communication across multiple channels, including social media, email, websites, and mobile apps. Each platform has its own audience and communication style, requiring tailored messages to reach and engage stakeholders and everyone else who follows the story. Though maintaining active engagement can be a burden, it's also a gift to businesses: Digital tools enable businesses to monitor public sentiment and feedback in real time.

TIP

By analyzing data from digital platforms, companies can assess the effectiveness of their strategies, identify areas for improvement, and refine their approach for future crises. The ability to gather information is invaluable to a business at any time, but especially during a crisis. Digital platforms allow for swift adjustments to communication strategies and direct engagement with stakeholders, enabling organizations to address concerns and correct misinformation as it arises — rather than have to wait until the next news cycle.

The plethora of immediate transmission channels available also enables businesses to reach a global audience instantly. Though this increases the potential impact of a crisis, it also provides an opportunity to communicate directly with diverse stakeholder audiences, ensuring that messages are received and understood across different regions and cultures.

The digital era has emphasized the importance of preparedness. Businesses are investing in crisis communication plans, training, and simulations to ensure that they can respond effectively when a crisis occurs. This includes having drafted statements, designated spokespersons, and clear protocols for digital engagement.

TYLENOL 1982 VERSUS TODAY

In 1982, seven people died in the Chicago area after consuming Tylenol capsules laced with cyanide. Johnson & Johnson, the manufacturer, quickly recalled 31 million bottles of Tylenol, costing the company over $100 million. The company introduced tamper-evident packaging and offered refunds and replacements to restore public trust, and its transparent communication and decisive actions during the crisis became a model for effective crisis management. But in 1982, social media was nonexistent — news spread via television, radio, and print media. Though Johnson & Johnson reacted swiftly, company leaders had time to edit and control the narrative before the public became widely aware of the crisis.

If the Tylenol crisis of 1982 were to occur today, Johnson & Johnson's response would need significant adaptations to address the challenges posed by the digital communication landscape. In 1982, the response was lauded for its transparency and swiftness, but today's digital era demands even more immediacy and multichannel engagement.

If this situation were happening today, company leaders would need to issue real-time updates across various platforms — including X and other Twitter-like platforms, Facebook, TikTok, and Instagram — to reach a broad audience quickly. They'd still issue an immediate product recall across all stores, which is *easier* today than it was back then; now they can do it with a click of a button instead of having to make phone calls and send faxes. Leveraging digital platforms to manage the product recall would be critical. This could include a website for consumers to check whether their product is affected, instructional videos on what to do with recalled products, and coordination with e-commerce platforms to halt sales and alert customers.

Consistency of messaging across all channels would be paramount, and that would apply only to the messaging within the company's control. (Can you imagine the memes that would emerge from such a crisis?!) A dedicated crisis response website and regular video updates from company executives would be essential; and engaging with consumers directly via social media, responding to their concerns, and correcting misinformation would be crucial.

Real-time monitoring of social media and news outlets would be vital to gauge public sentiment and address emerging concerns promptly. Company leaders also have to monitor misinformation (unintentionally incorrect information) and disinformation (intentionally misleading information). Using digital tools to track the spread of information and sentiment analysis would help refine the communication strategy.

Overall, Johnson & Johnson's response today would need to be faster, more transparent, and more digitally integrated to effectively manage the crisis and maintain public trust. So, although faster, more transparent communication is, in most cases, a good thing, it can also be a major hurdle for organizations to navigate.

Formulating a Crisis Communication Strategy

The key to effective crisis communication is to have a solid *crisis communication plan* — a framework that prepares an organization to mitigate the reputational damage from disruptive events. A solid plan makes you proactive, so you're not as reactive when a crisis strikes. A plan empowers you to act immediately and decisively. With such a plan, you won't waste valuable time assembling a team and leading it through the various stages of team development, as explained in Chapter 19. Your team is trained and ready to jump into action. Likewise, you won't waste time identifying key communication channels and figuring out how to structure your messaging. Everything's already in place, which expedites effective communication and compresses your response time.

REMEMBER

Silence communicates. The greater the delay in your response, the more time misinformation and disinformation has to spread and the greater the public scrutiny and stakeholder anxiety.

Without an established plan, organizations lack clear guidelines and protocols for action, making them vulnerable to confusion, inefficiency, and critical errors during a crisis. Mixed messages and poorly worded statements can exacerbate the situation, causing more damage to the company's reputation, finances, and stakeholder relationships. Imagine various team members sending inconsistent or conflicting messages — that's the perfect recipe for disaster! You definitely don't want to make a bad situation worse.

Okay, you get it. You need a crisis communication plan. If you're an entrepreneur, this includes you! If you work for an organization, ask your supervisor what the plan is and where you can find out more about it. Even if you're not directly responsible for communication during a crisis, knowing the organization's strategy enables you to find the best ways to be useful. And, when you're useful in a crisis, your opportunities can expand quickly!

Every organization's crisis communication plan is unique. Plans and priorities vary according to several factors, including these:

>> **Industry:** The nature of the risks and the regulatory environment change based on industry. For example, a pharmaceutical company must consider issues that may arise regarding the safety of its products, whereas a bank may need to prepare more for potential data breaches and service interruptions. Some industries may have regulatory requirements that govern how they communicate during a crisis.

>> **Organization size and complexity:** Larger organizations tend to have broader and more complex vulnerabilities, but they also have more resources to invest in dedicated communication teams.

>> **Geographic reach:** Global organizations need to account for differences in languages, cultures, time zones, and local laws and regulations.

>> **Stakeholder diversity:** Large organizations may have diverse stakeholders, including customers, employees, investors, and regulators, all of whom have varying information needs and communication preferences, such as traditional media, social media, websites, and press releases.

>> **Degree of centralization:** A centralized organization may rely on senior leaders to craft more uniform and consistent messaging, whereas decentralized organizations may rely more on regional leaders to tailor messages to local audiences.

>> **Available resources:** Every organization's plan is limited to the resources it has in terms of personnel, communication tools, and monitoring capabilities.

As you begin to construct your crisis communication plan, you must account for the unique characteristics and needs of your organization. However, several essential components are common to all crisis communication plans. In the following sections, I focus on different areas of the plan, highlighting what each area needs to cover.

Defining what constitutes a crisis

Defining what constitutes a crisis involves conducting detailed risk analysis. Risk analysis is beyond the scope of this book, but generally, it needs to examine the following factors:

>> **Nature of the threat:** For example, natural disaster, cyberattack, product recall, executive scandal, financial crisis, regulatory noncompliance

>> **Impact type:** Operational disruption, financial loss, reputational damage

>> **Severity and scope:** Extent of damage, degree of impact, geographical reach

>> **Legal and regulatory implications:** Legal action, fines, investigations

>> **Stakeholder impact:** Customer safety, satisfaction, and trust; employee health, safety, and morale; investor relations

TIP

Start by brainstorming various scenarios that can happen to your organization and then consider the possible repercussions.

Designating a crisis communication response team

List members of the team who need to assemble as soon as a crisis is noticed. Start with corporate leadership — for example, chief operations officer, vice president of marketing, and director of legal. You may also want to designate a spokesperson and support staff — for example, marketing or public relations personnel. Other team members may play key roles on a case-by-case basis. For example, in the event of a cyberattack, you'll need the head of IT or cybersecurity. If the crisis is related to a product defect, you'll need to call on the head of engineering or that department's representative.

You need team members to fill the following key roles (in a small organization, one person may fill more than one role):

>> **Coordinator/leader** is in charge of implementing and overseeing the communication plan, must keep everyone aligned during a crisis, and serves as the liaison between the executive team and those who are executing the plan.

>> **Spokesperson** is the official voice of the organization during the crisis, responsible for delivering public statements, press releases, media interviews, and other communication.

>> **Media coordinator** is responsible for managing relationships and interactions with media outlets, including coordinating press time, distributing materials, and monitoring coverage. The media coordinator maintains a record of media contacts along with stories and angles they've already covered. (In small organizations, the media coordinator may also serve as the spokesperson.)

>> **Social media coordinator** focuses specifically on social media and may be responsible for monitoring and analytics; tracking crisis development; and public perception. (Your media coordinator or someone on your marketing or public relations team may fill this role.)

TIP

If your organization lacks the resources for a full-time social media coordinator, consider outsourcing the role on an as-needed basis to a third-party service provider. Establish a relationship with the provider before any crisis can occur so that they're on call and ready to spring into action when a crisis occurs.

>> **Internal communication coordinator** is responsible for ensuring that everyone in the organization is on the same page by keeping employees informed about the crisis and the company's response and reminding everyone about the importance of adhering to the organization's crisis

communication policies and procedures. This person may also monitor internal communications.

>> **Stakeholder relationship coordinator** keeps key stakeholders in the loop — including directors, investors, partners, regulators, customers, and shareholders — and tailors the messaging to each audience. (Some organizations designate a separate individual to be in charge of customer communication.)

>> **Legal advisor/compliance officer** reviews communications to identify anything that could expose the organization to any legal risks.

>> **Support staff** may be helpful for monitoring social media, drafting messages for review, and distributing and sharing approved messages.

By clearly defining roles and responsibilities, an organization can ensure a coordinated, efficient, and effective response to a crisis, thereby mitigating its impact. See Chapter 19 for more about effective team management.

Establishing communication policies and procedures

Communication policies and procedures are essential for controlling the flow of information from your organization. Communication policies must cover these guidelines:

>> **Confidentiality:** Which information can be shared, who's permitted to share it, and under what conditions

>> **Social media:** Social media posts and responses to other people's posts about any information related to the organization

>> **Internal communication:** Ensuring timely and accurate information flow within the organization, including approved communication channels and methods

>> **External communication:** Communicating with anyone outside the organization, along with approved channels and methods

>> **Spokesperson:** In addition to the name of the designated spokesperson, what the spokesperson can say, to whom, and how (for example, press releases, press conferences, social media)

Identifying stakeholders

Identify your key stakeholders and list detailed information about them that enables you to communicate most effectively with them during a crisis. Key stakeholders may include investors, directors, employees, customers, and industry leaders, which vary based on the organization and the specific crisis. For each stakeholder group, identify the most effective communication channels and include details that enable you to craft messages that target their specific needs and concerns.

You also need to communicate with the general public, but they're not the focus here. Even so, include in your crisis communication plan a list of media contacts so that you can leverage traditional media to spread the word.

Identifying and establishing communication channels

When a crisis strikes, you need to know how to reach your stakeholders and other parties and how they can reach you to access information and updates. Consider establishing a dedicated crisis hotline for customers and other stakeholders to call for information and assistance. A website and blog can also be effective during a crisis. Consider, too, the leading social media platforms — not necessarily the most popular ones overall, but the ones your stakeholders and brand advocates prefer to use.

As you identify and establish communication channels, also set timelines for communication to serve as guidelines for days and times to post messages and the frequency of posts.

Confirming key brand messages

Ensure that everyone on your crisis communication team has a clear understanding of your organization's MVVPs: mission, vision, values, and purpose. These concepts serve as a north star, or guiding light, for messaging strategy during a crisis. Your messaging should be clear and consistent throughout the crisis (and, really, all the time).

To kick-start the process of confirming key brand messages, follow these suggestions:

>> **Prepare a set of approved responses for common scenarios.** An example is a cybersecurity breach in which customer data may have been accessed or a product defect that places customer safety at risk. Focus on the most likely and serious scenarios.

>> **Create templates for the media replies, press releases, and official statements.** They contain essential information about your organization and brand(s) with spaces to fill in with more detailed information about the crisis.

Defining your overall crisis-communication strategy

The overall crisis-communication strategy is how you present the nature of the crisis and what your organization is doing to respond to it. The strategy needs to cover two options, which I like to refer to as the we're-all-in-this-together approach (for crises outside your organization's control) and the *mea culpa* approach (for crises that your organization is, to some degree, responsible for). Include both approaches as part of your strategy:

>> **We're all in this together:** If the crisis results from a catastrophic event, clearly explain how your company is managing operations, ensuring customer safety (both physically and digitally), and outlining the recovery path. Though your company may not control the event, customer frustrations remain and may become public. Emphasize that you're all in this together and that you're doing everything possible to address stakeholder concerns. See the nearby sidebar "Force majeure" for more about the legal liabilities of damage caused by forces outside an organization's or individual's control.

>> **Mea culpa ("my fault"):** If the crisis results from human error within your organization, the stakes are typically higher from a reputation and trust standpoint. Taking responsibility is usually the best course of action. Avoid the temptation to create a scapegoat. Even if one person's actions caused the crisis, people will scrutinize the system in which they operated and the hiring processes. Human error doesn't happen in a vacuum, and blaming one or several individuals won't get your organization off the hook.

FORCE MAJEURE

Unless you learned it in school, you've probably had to search online at some point for the term *force majeure*. In essence, it refers to events caused by a superior force. In contractual terms, it frees both parties from liability if an extraordinary event, such as a natural disaster or state of emergency, prevents them from fulfilling their contractual obligations. Often, the contract isn't completely canceled; instead, it's more commonly extended or temporarily suspended.

Exploring other considerations

Crisis communication plans take many forms. If your plan includes all the items I mention in the previous sections, you've covered all the essentials. But some organizations take it further. Here are some other areas to consider adding as you flesh out your strategy:

>> **Feedback:** Establish systems and tools to gather feedback from stakeholder audiences before, during, and after a crisis. For example, you may use surveys or analytic tools to evaluate stakeholder sentiment about your organization's response to the crisis, which can be quite helpful in guiding decisions and crafting more effective messaging.

>> **Training/capabilities:** Identify the capabilities your organization currently has and the capabilities it needs to execute its plan. Decide whether additional training is needed, and do your best to include simulations to evaluate and learn from simulated crises. If your organization lacks the resources to build a solid team, consider adding third-party service providers to complement your internal capabilities.

>> **Continuous improvement:** Establish a system for evaluating and improving your crisis communication strategy, identifying the good, the bad, and the areas you must improve. Create a debriefing process for post-crisis evaluation. Establish a timeline and process for updating or editing the crisis communication plan based on what you learn.

>> **Reporting:** Create post-crisis reporting forms and a system for gathering and summarizing relevant data and issuing updates. Decide who needs to sign off on reports before they're released and who receives the reports after they're approved.

Responding in a Crisis: Initial and Ongoing Communication

When a crisis hits, you need to buy time to formulate your response (especially if you have no crisis communication plan in place), but you must communicate immediately to your key stakeholders (and, depending on your company and the crisis, perhaps also to the general public). In this section, I explain how to respond quickly to buy yourself some time and then maintain communication until the issue is resolved.

Before I dig into the nitty-gritty of crafting messages in response to a crisis, here's my advice in a nutshell:

>> **Own your sh*t.** Take responsibility for mistakes and oversights and apologize sincerely.

>> **Cut the bull.** Focus on what truly matters. Address immediate questions and concerns.

>> **Feel the pain.** Share genuine empathy and demonstrate your understanding of what's at stake.

>> **Fix it.** Explain ongoing efforts to rectify the situation.

>> **Say you're sorry — and mean it.** Apologize again and thank those impacted as appropriate.

Respond to the human condition. Mistakes happen, and people are generally understanding as long as you handle the situation competently and are transparent.

Buying yourself time to get your head on straight

The first step is to acknowledge what's going on so that you don't appear clueless or come across as avoiding the situation. Remember, silence communicates. State what you know and then work on putting your plan into action.

Promptly acknowledge the crisis without delving into specifics. A brief statement can reassure stakeholders that you are aware of the issue and are addressing it. Here's the anatomy of an effective acknowledgment statement:

1. **Acknowledge the issue and share presently available facts.**

   Let people know you're aware of the exact (or as exact as possible) issue. Don't let people fill in the gaps on their own, which can be catastrophic for your organization.

   For example, if you have no details, you may say something like this: "We've uncovered a bug in our software, and we are working on determining the extent of the damage and the impact on our customers." That's okay if you're lacking details, but it leaves your customers wondering, "Is my data safe? Do I need to change my password? Are my customers safe?" If you have more details, share them. For example, say something like this: "We've uncovered a bug in our software service that is impacting your dashboards. This does not impact software security, your data, or your customers' data. We are working on determining the extent of the damage and the impact on our customers."

The extra detail gives your customers some comfort in knowing that this is a crisis of convenience and efficiency, not privacy or security, and that you're working to resolve the issue.

2. **Explain what you're doing to address the issue.**

Stakeholders need to see that you're not only aware of the issue but are also taking steps to resolve it. After acknowledging the issue and sharing details of what you know about it at this time, let your stakeholders know the steps you're taking to address it.

For example, you may say something like, "We are working on a patch to make the software operational while we make more substantial changes to prevent similar problems from occurring in the future."

3. **Provide an estimated timeline and a channel for updates.**

Clearly communicate a timeline for when and where stakeholders can find additional information and updates. This information helps manage stakeholder expectations and reduces the pressure for an immediate detailed response. It can reduce the number of calls coming in that expend time and resources that could be better allocated toward resolving the issue.

4. **Give your audience something to do.**

In a crisis, people need to know what they should do. In some cases, they may simply need to remain patient while your organization resolves the issue. In other cases, they may be able to help solve the problem or do something on their end to protect themselves or their customers. In any event, giving people something to do gives them a sense of control that can lessen their anxiety.

TIP

Set up a dedicated channel for inquiries, such as a web page, crisis hotline, specific email address, or single point of facts for information. A dedicated channel not only centralizes communication but also demonstrates your commitment to transparency and responsiveness. Inform stakeholders where they can direct their questions and assure them that their concerns are being taken seriously. For example, you can wrap up your acknowledgment statement with one like this: "If you have questions or comments or you notice another issue in your service, please communicate this information to <insert dedicated channel or person's name and contact info>." You can also point any social media post or comment to this same location for consistency.

By structuring your acknowledgment statement in this way, you can buy yourself the necessary time to develop a well-thought-out communication strategy while maintaining stakeholder trust.

Preparing your acknowledgment statements

Here are some common acknowledgment statements you can use as starting points (let me stress the term *starting points*) for your own, followed by my commentary about each one:

General audience

"We are aware of the current situation and are actively investigating the matter. Our team is working diligently to gather all the facts. We appreciate your patience and will provide a detailed update as soon as possible."

This statement acknowledges that a situation exists and lets people know that you're working to remedy it. But what exactly is "it"? This statement is okay, but take it one step further and add either a timeline for the next communication or an immediate step people can take if they're impacted. Giving people some course of action besides "sit and wait" is a good strategy.

Customers

"We understand that an issue is affecting our valued customers. Please know that we are looking into it with the utmost urgency. We are committed to resolving this issue as quickly as possible and will share more information shortly."

Admitting the existence of an issue impacting customers is important, but this message is short on detail and doesn't go far enough in expressing how much the organization values its customers. Additional details about how the issue is impacting customers and what you're doing to remedy the situation can improve it significantly.

Here's an example: "We understand that you rely on <product name> to efficiently run your business accounting, and this current bug is slowing down your operations. Right now, our team is busy uncovering the source of the error and is working on a temporary fix before we look into how it happened, to ensure that it doesn't happen again. Please report any issues you're having via <dedicated feedback channel>, and then we will post real-time updates of our progress on <dedicated channel for updates>. Getting everyone up and running safely is our top priority."

The information in this example buys you more time to get to the bottom of the issue, conveys how much you value your customers, and lets them know that you realize exactly what is going on and have a plan to resolve the issue.

Employees

"We recognize the ongoing issue that is impacting our operations. Our priority is to understand the full scope and address it effectively. We are working around the clock and will keep you updated with the latest information."

This is an actual statement. I'm not naming names of the organizations that have used it. If I were an employee on the receiving end of this post, I'd be upset. It's full of corporate-speak that says absolutely nothing of value. I've placed this one here as an example of what *not* to say, so that you can do it better.

Here's a more effective revision: "We realize that the issue impacting X is causing Y for people in Z. We all have the goal of <insert MVVP in some form here>. We are working on <the solution> and will keep you updated at/on <insert time interval/channel>. Thank you for all you do for <organization name>. If you have further information that can help our team remedy <the issue>, please contact <insert person's name>."

This statement starts by referencing the issue, the problem, and the group of employees most impacted. It proceeds to reinforce the organization's commitment to its MVVP (refer to the earlier section "Confirming key brand messages" for a refresher) and provides details about the solution and timeframe. It wraps up by thanking the employee and giving them an opportunity to become a part of the solution. Now we're talking!

Monitoring and managing ongoing communication

As a crisis unfolds and even as it nears its end, monitoring and updating all communication channels is crucial. Even if you have nothing new to report, err on the side of caution and post frequent updates. (Remember that silence communicates and time stamps matter.) In this age of digital communication, people expect on-demand access to information, and they can be quite demanding. The last thing you want is for important information to be buried when stakeholders need immediate answers.

TIP

Make it easy for people to find relevant information. Pin a post at the top of your social media feeds so that users don't have to scroll for updates. Create a pop-up box on your website that immediately highlights important details and actions to take. Add a temporary header on your website alerting visitors to the situation and providing clear steps to meet their needs. Clearly communicate response times and set expectations.

Provide factual updates on what has happened and which actions are being taken. Always apologize sincerely to your multiple audiences — not just a "Sorry you're impacted" message but, rather, a genuine acknowledgment of the situation and the frustrations they're experiencing.

SOUTHWEST AIRLINES

One exemplary crisis response occurred in July 2016 when Southwest Airlines experienced a system-wide outage affecting over 250,000 travelers. Here's a snapshot borrowed from a response from Southwest's chief operations officer, which will likely be highlighted in future textbooks as a model of effective crisis management:

> We realize that this situation is more than an inconvenience. It's keeping many of you from important life experiences that can't be re-created. You trusted us with your transportation needs. We let you down, and we let our employees down. Our employees are working around the clock to find solutions, and in turn are away from their families and lives. And while it can't make up for it right now, realize that we are sorry and are doing everything in our control to make it right for everyone involved.

Notice that this response includes nearly all the elements I recommend in my anatomy of an effective acknowledgment statement (refer to the earlier section "Buying yourself time to get your head on straight"), delivered authentically and empathetically. The only thing missing in this quote is actions the customers can take — other than realizing that the company is doing everything possible to solve the problem, though company reps provided it in subsequent messaging.

REMEMBER

Communication consists of more than just words. It's not only what you say and how you say it but also the combination of your message, delivery, and subsequent actions that shape the public's perception of your organization.

For instance, after the Southwest Airlines system outage in July 2016, angry customers voiced their frustrations on social media. However, empowered to act in the customers' best interest, Southwest employees at airports made efforts to provide comfort during the travel crisis. Alongside the angry tweets, positive images surfaced of employees serving pizza, communicating facts to stranded passengers, and doing everything possible to assist with travel plans.

If you use video (live-streamed or produced) during a crisis, be authentic. To see the impact of authenticity, compare the video-based responses of Southwest Airlines (www.facebook.com/watch/live/?ref=watch_permalink&v=101544946 69698949) and Delta (https://twitter.com/DeltaNewsHub/status/762707203 207761920?ref_src=twsrc%5Etfw) to their respective technical outages in July and August 2016. As much as I love Delta (longtime Diamond Medallion and Million Miler here), its response was inauthentic, lacked emotion or sincere recognition, and was clearly read from a script.

Taking Responsibility Within Your Power

Taking responsibility for what's within its power during a crisis is vital for a company's integrity and long-term success. When a company acknowledges its role and takes ownership of the situation, it demonstrates accountability and transparency, which are the key to maintaining trust with stakeholders. This honest approach reassures customers, employees, investors, and the public that the company is committed to doing the right thing.

REMEMBER

Doing what's right puts you in control. By taking responsibility, your organization can control the narrative, reducing speculation and misinformation that could exacerbate the crisis. This proactive stance enables your organization to implement effective solutions and communicate its actions clearly, showing that it's on top of the situation and actively working toward a resolution. Even more, taking responsibility can mitigate legal and regulatory fallout, as it often involves complying with laws and regulations that mandate transparency and corrective action.

When an organization's executives own up to the role the company played in causing the crisis or failing to prevent it, they reinforce a culture of responsibility within the organization, encouraging employees to uphold high standards of conduct and ethics — lead by example, right? Ultimately, demonstrating responsibility during a crisis helps preserve the company's reputation, builds stronger relationships with stakeholders, and enhances resilience, ensuring that the organization emerges from the crisis with its credibility intact and better prepared for future challenges.

Not convinced to own up yet? Here's the rundown of the benefits of taking responsibility for a crisis:

>> **Builds and strengthens trust:** Admitting fault takes courage and conveys confidence in finding a solution.

>> **Reduces uncertainty and anxiety:** Taking the lead prevents people from filling in the gaps with false assumptions. People usually assume the worst, unless they have good reason to believe otherwise.

>> **Demonstrates control and competence:** By owning the situation, you control the narrative and send a clear message that you have what it takes to solve the problem.

>> **Reduces exposure to legal or regulatory threats:** Transparency, carefully managed, demonstrates that your organization is operating in good faith. However, be sure that your legal team reviews any communications that can increase your organization's exposure to lawsuits and regulatory fines.

>> **Facilitates recovery:** Taking responsibility facilitates recovery in two ways. First, it's like lancing the boil — it uncovers root causes that need to be addressed. Second, it empowers stakeholders with the information and insight they need to become part of the solution.

>> **Enhances organizational learning:** Disclosure empowers leadership and employees with the truth, enabling them to evaluate and analyze what happened in order to prevent future crises. It drives the growth of the organization.

Being careful when admitting fault

WARNING

Admitting the role the organization played in creating or not preventing the crisis can be positive or negative, depending on the context and execution. It's often positive because of all the reasons I've shared. But you need to be careful. Doing so prematurely, without a full understanding of the facts, can lead to legal liabilities, financial repercussions, and damage to the company's reputation. Company reps *must* thoroughly investigate the situation and consult with legal and PR advisors before making any admissions. A hasty admission may expose the company to lawsuits or regulatory penalties, and stakeholders may perceive it as a sign of incompetence or instability.

Walking the talk and following through

Because this book focuses on business communication, this chapter on communicating in a crisis is limited mostly to messaging, but that strategy gets an organization only so far. Business leaders need to follow through on their promises and follow up with stakeholders to gain their respect and demonstrate their commitment to positive change. That task isn't easy, but it's the path that leads to restoring and strengthening relationships and growing as an organization. (They're called growing *pains* for a reason.)

Start by taking concrete steps to address the root cause of the immediate crisis (and communicating those steps and results to your stakeholders). Then implement long-term corrective measures, such as revising policies, improving processes, and enhancing oversight to prevent future issues. Publicly share the changes you're making to demonstrate your commitment to improvement, and then keep in touch with stakeholders. As customers and other stakeholders observe and experience these commitments being fulfilled, their loyalty is reinforced and they're more likely to support the business moving forward.

REMEMBER

Ever have one of those "friends" who's in constant contact during a crisis and disappears as soon as things settle down? Don't be *that* friend to your stakeholders. Remain engaged with them throughout the recovery process that follows the crisis. Provide regular updates, seek feedback, and actively listen to their concerns and suggestions. By involving stakeholders in the recovery, your organization's leaders show that they value their input and are committed to meeting their needs. Go beyond involvement to actively support affected parties, whether by way of compensation, support programs, or other means. Following up and following through can help repair relationships by demonstrating genuine concern for your stakeholders' well-being.

Casting a wider net never hurts, either. After you've been in the news for an unpleasant (or worse) event, investing in reputation-building activities — such as community engagement, corporate social responsibility initiatives, and transparent reporting — can help restore and even enhance the organization's image. Through these efforts, an organization can emerge from a crisis not only stronger but also more respected and trusted.

Embracing the Framework of Frameworks: RER

It's January 2020. I'm speaking at a conference for leaders in the travel industry. Then it happens — the first case of COVID-19 is confirmed in the United States. The CEO of the organization pulls me aside and asks me whether I can create some communication strategies for the community to help them manage client expectations when it comes to traveling in times of confusion. It wasn't a full-on crisis — yet — but there was looming uncertainty (and lots of questions). And, just like that, RER was born: RER — or *recognize, empathize,* and *respond* — is a three-step framework for communicating in the midst of a crisis.

Okay, it didn't really happen just like that — it was after more than 20 years of study, research, and practice that RER came together, but my version makes for a more dramatic story. See the nearby sidebar for more about the origins of my RER framework.

The RER framework enables you to take a breath and helps you avoid jumping to conclusions. It makes you a more active listener and more closely aligned with your stakeholder's needs and concerns (as explained in Chapter 9), and it leads from acknowledgment to action.

Recognize

When you're an expert and you already know the answer to a question, the tendency is to jump immediately to sharing the solution, which isn't necessarily bad. However, when someone is afraid, anxious, frustrated, or angry, their brain may be unable to fully register and process what you have to share. To paraphrase Colonel Nathan R. Jessup, played by Jack Nicholson in *A Few Good Men*, "They can't handle the truth!" At least not yet.

You need to recognize first what your audience is feeling and their perception of the situation so that their brains have the time and cognitive space to adjust and become more receptive. Back in 2020, when my travel industry clients were looking for guidance on what to say to their customers during the pandemic, I advised them to start with something like, "I understand that it's a difficult decision whether to go on this trip with your family right now, with a lot of uncertainty present on the safeness of travel." Simply recognizing and validating the person's emotional response is often enough to calm it.

EXAMPLE

Let me give you an example that many people have experienced: being blamed for something you didn't do. Suppose that you were blamed by some of your colleagues for inappropriately using the company's resources to fund leisure activities during a professional development trip (when, in fact, you had approved the expense through your supervisor beforehand and reimbursed the company). Such a rumor, if it caught fire, could definitely damage your professional credibility.

Your reputation is at stake. It's not a full-blown crisis, yet, and you want to keep it from becoming one. So, when you're confronted, your initial impulse is to deny the accusation by saying something like, "No. I didn't. I reimbursed the company." However, if your coworkers are already convinced that you're guilty of stealing, they wouldn't put it past you to lie about it, so your denials may simply be added to your growing list of suspected indiscriminate behaviors.

Fortunately, you know better than to deny the charges outright. Instead, you begin your response by recognizing what the person is probably thinking and feeling. As a result, you say something like, "I understand that it appears I used company funds for a personal activity while I was on the trip to the development conference." This is you recognizing what they believe is happening and putting it right in front of them, letting them know that you're not ignoring what's going on (and, calling them out on the rumors that they've been discussing). Now, before you tell them the full story, you need to proceed to Stage 2, described next.

Empathize

The second step in RER is to empathize, which involves relating to your audience in some meaningful way — not just giving it lip service. Empathy demonstrates to your audience that you not only see the facts of the situation but also genuinely understand that it's a problem and why they might be concerned about it. To continue with the earlier example of airline reps communicating with customers during the pandemic, they could express empathy by saying, "If I were making the decision on whether to travel with my family right now, I would also be conflicted."

Continuing the example from the blame game, you could add something like, "I would be pretty upset, too, if I thought one of you was using corporate funds to finance your personal activities."

Now you're ready to get to the solution part of the conversation — the response.

Respond

The final step in the RER framework is to respond. In this step, you present the facts. For the travel situation mentioned in the previous two sections, airlines could respond, "What I can tell you is that . . ." and then present their solution, such as trip insurance will cover X, the suppliers being used are practicing Y, and so on.

To build on the blame game example from the previous two sections, you say something like, "I got the approval from our supervisor before I left on the trip to charge the activity on the company card and then reimburse the budget with my per diem overages." Then be prepared to answer any questions, but stick to the facts. No denials. If anyone wants to check your story, they can talk to the supervisor.

That's it. The magic of the RER framework lies in its simplicity.

6
Communication for Collaboration

Land an interview for the position you desire, and then knock it out of the park by being prepared to answer and ask questions.

Master three simple techniques for becoming a better interviewer: putting the interviewee at ease, adapting to the conversation, and knowing when to dig deeper for details.

Collaborate more effectively with colleagues by managing team development, defining roles, and protecting and promoting your team and its individual members.

Understand and overcome the challenges of communicating across cultures — techniques for effective cross-cultural communication.

Chapter **18**

Communicating during the Recruitment and Hiring Process

The recruitment, application, and interview processes are often the first interactions between the people who lead organizations and those who carry out their daily operations. Whether you're playing the role of employer or prospective employee, you need to be able to communicate and interact in an engaging manner that appeals to the needs and desires of the other party and gets you the information you need to make a hiring or career decision. In this chapter, I explain how to do just that. The first part of this chapter is devoted to job seekers. The second, shorter part is for employers.

REMEMBER

The information and guidance I offer in nearly every other chapter in this book also applies to recruitment and hiring, especially Chapter 5 on listening, Chapter 6 on fine-tuning your questions, Chapter 7 on having meaningful conversations, Chapter 12 on knowing your audience, and Chapter 14 on negotiating. The purpose of this chapter is to explain how to put those skills and others into practice specifically in the context of job-seeking and recruiting processes.

Landing Your Dream-Job Interview

The process of getting hired is a lot like dating: You and your prospective employer are meeting for the first time and getting to know one another before either of you decides to commit to a long-term relationship. And, as with dating, nobody will ask you out (to that initial interview) unless they find you attractive. Nor should you apply for a job unless you find the opportunity and the organization attractive.

Scoring an interview is all about presenting yourself as someone an organization wants to hire. It's about putting your best foot forward — presenting your qualifications in a way that gets you through the door and into the interview room. In this section, I provide tips and techniques to improve your chances of getting that "first date" (the initial interview).

Covering all the bases

When you're applying for a position, you need to be thorough. If you let anything slip between the cracks, you lose your competitive edge against other candidates. So, before I dive into the higher-level topics of writing a killer cover letter and pursuing an inside track to the decision-makers, I want to be sure that you're solid on the fundamentals. Here, I provide essential steps you need to take, in no particular order (except for maybe the first and last ones).

Polishing your digital profile

Assuming that your application passes the prospective employer's initial AI or HR screening, the first thing many recruiters do is check you out via a search engine and various social media sites. They'll look at your digital footprint, your profile — anything they can find out about you online. They may even order a background check.

Be sure your digital profile is one that you're confident recruiters will find appealing to the organization and the position you're applying for. I'm not telling you that you need to delete all those photos of your partying and shenanigans or your posts promoting various conspiracy theories or political views, because I have no idea what you're into or the positions you're applying for. But I am telling you to be aware of what others can find by searching for you, and make sure that what can be found is the story you want to be telling. The point is to make sure your digital profile aligns with the organization and position you're pursuing.

Check all social media platforms you have accounts on, such as LinkedIn, Facebook, Instagram, YouTube, and TikTok.

TIP

"Google" yourself. Put quotation marks around your name for more accurate results (for example, "Jill Schiefelbein"). If you have a common name, you can add one or more relevant words to your search phrase (for example, "Jill Schiefelbein" AI expert) for more focused search results. Use words that prospective employers might use to search for you in the context of the position (for example, "engineering" or "graphic artist").

Networking your way to the interview seat

As the saying goes, "Your network is your net worth." It's one of the best "ins" you have to find out about openings, build connections, and get referrals. Leverage your professional network. Use job search websites and platforms such as LinkedIn, Indeed, and Glassdoor to find job postings and see whether you have any inside connections. Connect with current or former employees of the organization on LinkedIn, attend industry events, and join professional groups related to your field. Personal referrals can significantly increase your chances of getting an interview.

You can also work with recruitment agencies or headhunters who specialize in your industry. They can help match you with potential job opportunities and often have direct connections with hiring managers. See the later section "Getting others to introduce you" for more about requesting referrals.

Researching the organization and the position

Being a detective pays dividends in landing interviews. Avoid the temptation to instantly apply for that dream job that just caught your eye. Research the organization and the position first so that you have a better sense of the organization's culture and what type of person and qualifications they're looking for to fill the position.

Visit the organization's website and, if applicable, social media accounts. Check out their mission and vision statements, values, and statement of purpose. Look at the products and services it offers. Follow them on social media. Organizations often use their social media accounts to highlight company news, employee activities, and industry trends that can be useful for personalizing resumes and cover letters and preparing for interviews.

Additionally, review industry-related news and reports (often from professional or trade associations or competitor websites) to gain a broader understanding of the organization's position within its sector. Knowing the market dynamics and competitors can help you discuss industry challenges and opportunities, showcasing your strategic thinking.

REMEMBER

Research is all about getting to know your audience, as I explain in Chapter 12. Until you have a clear understanding of the organization and the position it needs to fill, you have no idea how to pitch yourself. Research is essential for enabling you to tailor your cover letter and resume to the organization's needs, and demonstrating relevant knowledge during interviews.

Following the application instructions

Don't rush through the application process in an attempt be first in line for the job. Rushing will do more harm than good. Carefully read and follow the application instructions. If the application consists of answering questions online, respond thoughtfully. Before submitting your answers, review them for typos and other errors. Tailor your responses to the organization and the position, and try to word your responses in a positive, enthusiastic tone.

REMEMBER

Keep a record of the jobs you've applied to along with any dates and required follow-up actions. Creating a spreadsheet is a good way to do this.

Following up

After submitting your application, follow up with a polite email or phone call to the hiring manager, the HR department, or your contact to ensure your materials were received and to reinforce your interest. Inquire about the next steps in the hiring process and ask whether you can do anything else to help move the conversation forward. A little initiative can go a long way!

Tweaking your resume and cover letter

Every resume and cover letter you submit should be unique. Each one should be tailored to the organization and the specific job. In this section, I explain how to tailor your resume and cover letters and how to streamline the process with the help of ChatGPT.

Personalizing your resume

Assuming that you have a basic resume detailing your education, experience, and skills — and you've carefully researched the organization and job description — you're ready to personalize your resume. Do the following:

1. **Revise details on your resume to include the keywords in the job description.**

   Using the keywords and phrases from the job description provides a clear link between what your prospective employer is looking for and what you have to offer. It also ensures that your resume clears any screening software.

2. **Rearrange your education, experience, and skills to reflect the priorities suggested in the job description.**

   For example, if the job description stresses that experience with a specific software package is essential, put that information toward the top.

3. **Adjust your previous job titles and roles to more closely align with the titles and roles suggested in the job description.**

   Don't misrepresent your job titles and roles; simply revise them slightly, if necessary, to reflect their alignment with what your prospective employer is looking for.

REMEMBER

4. **Quantify your achievements where possible.**

   Provide numbers, such as "Managed a software development team of seven" or "Increased customer retention by 12%."

5. **Add relevant certifications and education.**

   Include any relevant ongoing courses you're taking or training you're currently undertaking.

Tailoring your cover letter to the organization and position

A cover letter is your opportunity to make a distinctive first impression, and it may be the only chance you get, so make it outstanding. Here are some tips and techniques for personalizing your cover letter and making it stand out from the crowd — in a good way:

>> **Don't rehash your resume.** Think of your cover letter as a movie trailer. It needs to make anyone reading it want to find out more about you by reading your resume.

>> **Express your genuine interest and enthusiasm for the organization and the position.** Convey a) why you're passionate about the position b) how your values align with those of the organization, and c) how your professional goals are aligned with the organization's mission.

Don't be boring. Express your enthusiasm in the tone of your writing. If you read your cover letter and it sounds dull to you, it'll sound doubly dull to everyone else who reads it. I find that reading my responses out loud (rather than just in my head) helps me craft the tone I'm looking for more effectively.

>> **Explain how you're uniquely qualified for the position.** Make a compelling case for why you're the best candidate for the position. Elaborate on key accomplishments and how they directly relate to the position you're applying for.

>> **Address any concerns a recruiter may have (the proverbial elephant in the room).** These concerns may include gaps in your employment history and any skills you're lacking in the job description, such as a specific certification or experience with certain software. Be sure to provide explanations (when necessary), reasons for any gaps in your employment history, and explanations for how you plan to deal with any skills or experience you're missing, such as seeking additional education and training.

>> **Highlight any significant challenges you've overcome.** Focus mostly on challenges in the workplace, but you may also include challenges in your personal life if they're relevant. Briefly describe the challenge and what you did to overcome it, and how the experience has contributed to your growth and readiness for the role you're applying for.

>> **Tell your story in a way that will resonate with the organization and position.** Start with a strong opening that captures the recruiter's attention; introduce yourself; highlight relevant experiences, skills, and training; connect all that to the job and the organization; and end with a strong closing.

Don't forget to end with a call to action, something like, "I welcome the opportunity to find out more about this role, the organization, and how I may best contribute to its success. Please contact me to schedule an interview by calling or texting [phone number] or emailing me at [email address]."

A well-written cover letter highlights your attention to detail, command of language, and ability to convey key points succinctly and memorably. It reflects your professionalism and ability to structure information logically, making it easier for the hiring team to understand your qualifications and motivations. It truly can make the difference between you and another equally (or even better) qualified candidate.

Getting a little help from an AI friend

Generative AI tools, such as ChatGPT, can be helpful for drafting resumes and cover letters and tailoring them to specific organizations. The key to using ChatGPT effectively is in the *prompts* — the instructions and information you provide. For example, go to https://chatgpt.com and type **Write a professional** and enthusiastic cover letter for this job application followed by details such as these:

>> **Organization name and website address:** ChatGPT will gather information from the organization's website to tailor your cover letter to the organization.

>> **Details of the job opening:** Include the job title, description, and any other relevant details from the job posting (if the job ad has keywords, doubly make sure you include those).

>> **Key skills and experiences:** Highlight the skills and experiences from your resume that you want to emphasize in the cover letter.

>> **Personal introduction:** Provide a brief personal introduction that includes your career goals and why you're interested in this specific job and company.

>> **Tone and style:** Specify the tone and style you want the cover letter to have (for example, professional, enthusiastic, playful, formal).

EXAMPLE

Here's a sample prompt:

Please help me write a professional and enthusiastic cover letter for a marketing position at XYZ Corporation (xyz.com). Here are the details:

Job title: Marketing manager

Job description: The marketing manager will be responsible for developing and executing marketing strategies, managing a team of marketing professionals, and driving brand awareness and lead generation.

Key skills and experiences from my resume:

Over 5 years of experience in digital marketing and campaign management

Proven track record of increasing social media engagement by 40%

Experience managing a team of 10 marketing professionals

Excellent communication and project management skills

Proficient in using marketing software like HubSpot and Google Analytics

Personal introduction:

I am a dedicated marketing professional with a passion for creating impactful campaigns and driving business growth. I am particularly interested in XYZ Marketing Solutions because of your innovative approach to marketing and your commitment to client success.

That's it. After you click the icon to enter your prompt, ChatGPT generates the letter. You still have to revise it to include specific details and offer a more human touch (as shown in Figure 18-1), but editing a cover letter is a whole lot easier than writing one from scratch.

[Your Name]
[Your Address]
[City, State, ZIP Code]
[Email Address]
[Phone Number]
[Date]

Hiring Manager's Name
XYZ Corporation
[Company Address]
[City, State, ZIP Code]

Dear [Hiring Manager's Name],

I am excited to apply for the Marketing Manager position at XYZ Corporation, as advertised on xyz.com. With over five years of experience in digital marketing and campaign management, I am confident in my ability to contribute to your team and drive brand awareness and lead generation through innovative marketing strategies.

Throughout my career, I have demonstrated a passion for creating impactful marketing campaigns and achieving business growth. At my previous position with ABC Corp, I spearheaded digital campaigns that increased social media engagement by 40% within six months. This success was driven by my ability to analyze audience behavior, develop strategic content plans, and collaborate effectively with cross-functional teams.

In addition to my technical skills, I have extensive experience managing a team of 10 marketing professionals. At DEF Inc., I led my team to develop and execute a comprehensive marketing strategy that aligned with the company's vision, resulting in a 25% increase in annual revenue. My leadership style focuses on fostering a collaborative and creative environment, where team members feel empowered to contribute their best ideas.

I am particularly drawn to XYZ Corporation because of your innovative approach to marketing and your commitment to client success. Your recent campaign on sustainable marketing practices resonated with me, as I strongly believe in promoting sustainability in business. I am eager to bring my expertise in digital marketing, project management, and team leadership to your organization.

Furthermore, my proficiency in marketing software such as HubSpot and Google Analytics has enabled me to optimize campaigns and deliver measurable results. I am confident that my skills and experiences make me a strong candidate for the Marketing Manager role at XYZ Corporation.

I am enthusiastic about the opportunity to contribute to your team and help drive your marketing efforts to new heights. I look forward to the possibility of discussing how my background, skills, and passions align with the needs of XYZ Corporation. Thank you for considering my application.

Sincerely,
[Your Name]

FIGURE 18-1:
Cover letter for a marketing position generated by ChatGPT.

WARNING

With this technology and writing style readily available to everyone, you're able to use this tool to produce a perfectly lukewarm cover letter, as shown in Figure 18-1. It's basically a resume in letter form with a little bit of expansion. But with everyone able to use the same tool, that won't make you stand out! To make a positive impression and be memorable, you have to spend some time making the letter more human and including more narrative — stories sell!

REMEMBER

You can use ChatGPT to varying degrees. For example, you can simply direct it to analyze a job posting and extract key details to highlight on your resume. Or you can provide the job description along with a list of your qualifications and ask it to generate ten or so bullet points that showcase your skills and expertise relevant to the job description.

CHATGPT WRITES A COVER LETTER

"This is amazing — ChatGPT wrote my cover letter for me!"

I had a student tell me this and I cringed a little because, unless the student had written a prompt with details and specifics for customizing the letter, it likely wouldn't measure up to the task. So I asked, "What prompt did you use?"

I was impressed with his answer: "I uploaded my resume, the job advertisement, and the mission statement page of the company, based on what you told us in class, and asked for a 250-word cover letter for the position, emphasizing my previous experience in sales — and it gave me this."

He proceeded to show me the letter. I could tell that AI had generated most of it, but given the fact that with ChatGPT's help, he was able to write and revise the letter in about one-fifth the time it would've taken him to write it from scratch, it was a well-written and well-tailored cover letter. The framework was there. He edited it to match his personality and added anecdotes and stories that brought it to life and made it memorable.

I tell you this story to make the point that there's not a single excuse I can think of for not taking the time to tailor a cover letter. With technology's help, it's easier than ever. Now, you can spend more time focusing on crafting the narratives that give you a competitive edge. It's in that humanization — that personalization — of the generated AI output that you can set yourself apart from others.

Getting others to introduce you

Warm leads are better than cold handshakes. If you can persuade someone inside the industry or organization (or a former employee who maintains a positive relationship with the organization) to provide a reference, you have a much better chance of sneaking past the automated filters and human gatekeepers. Someone who knows you and who can vouch for your work ethic, integrity, and skills can curtail the vetting process and significantly improve your chances of landing the interview. In this section, I offer some guidance on how to find an inside track.

TIP

Even if you don't know anybody in the company where you're applying, doing some advance research can make you feel like you do! It's so much easier to walk into an environment where you feel like you have a little familiarity with what lies ahead.

Stalk the social

It's okay to creep! Check out the organization's social media sites to see whether you know anyone who is working there or is closely connected to someone on the inside.

TIP

If you have a dream of working for a certain organization and you're having trouble getting your foot in the door, follow the organization on social media platforms and actively engage with it — read, comment on, and share its posts. Become a *brand advocate* — someone who actively supports the brand via word-of-mouth marketing. Visibly promoting a brand can demonstrate your enthusiasm for the organization and your commitment to its success.

Check out what employees are saying

Two valuable resources for evaluating an organization through the eyes of its employees are Glassdoor and Indeed. On these sites, employees can post reviews, which often provide valuable insights into the organization's work environment, management style, and employee satisfaction.

Though you're wise to take individual reviews with a grain of salt, common themes can provide a more comprehensive picture of the workplace culture and inspire potential questions to ask during your interview. Be sure to check out the organization's page on LinkedIn and do a search for news about the organization (Google searches include a News tab you can select to focus your search). On the organization's Company page, check out the employees to determine whether you have any first- or second-degree connections you can follow up with, as explained in the following section.

Ask others to open doors

Having a warm lead into the company can be incredibly beneficial. A warm lead, such as a referral or a connection within the company, can provide inside information about the company culture, management's expectations, and the specific duties of the role. Warm leads can offer insights that aren't readily available from public research, helping you tailor your application and interview responses more effectively. Additionally, a referral can often increase your chances of landing the interview because recommendations from trusted sources tend to carry a lot of weight.

Preparing For and Performing Well in an Interview

I don't know how you feel about job interviews. Some people look forward to them with eager anticipation; some treat them as routine business conversations; many become highly anxious. Regardless of how you feel, being prepared to answer and ask questions and respond to the questions you're asked significantly improves your chances of success. In this section, I provide guidance on preparation, practice, and using proven methods to craft your responses, all of which will make you better prepared and more confident going into your next interview.

Prepping for an interview

Preparation pays off in spades. It provides you with the knowledge and practice to remain confident and focused and to formulate intelligent responses on the fly. To prepare for an interview, here's what you need to do:

>> **Review information you gathered about the organization and the position.** See the earlier section "Researching the organization and the position."

>> **Review your cover letter and resume.** Refresh your memory about what the interviewers already know about you. Be prepared to discuss anything you mentioned in those documents, including your experiences, achievements, and career progress.

>> **Pack essential documents.** Bring several copies of your resume and cover letter and any relevant documents. If applicable, bring a portfolio of your work to showcase your skills.

TIP

While you're at it, pack a blank thank-you card (or a handful of them). After the interview, you can compose a quick thank-you message and leave it with the receptionist to pass along to the team that interviewed you. Or, if you're in a rush, put stamps on them so that they're ready to put in the post later that day.

>> **Prepare answers to the most commonly asked interview questions.** See the later section "Crafting intelligent responses." Here are 15 commonly asked questions during a job interview, divided into two groups — general and behavior-based questions:

- *General questions:* Keep your answers short and sweet, tying them as closely as possible to the job description and requirements.

  Can you tell me a little about yourself?

  Why do you want to work here?

  What are your greatest strengths?

  What are your greatest weaknesses?

  Where do you see yourself in five years?

  Why are you leaving your current job?

  Why should we hire you?

  What do you know about our company?

  Can you explain a gap in your employment history?

  What are your salary expectations?

  Do you have any questions for us?

- *Behavior-based questions:* These questions are designed to assess how you handled situations in the past.

  Can you describe a challenging situation you faced at work and how you handled it?

  Can you give an example of a time you demonstrated leadership skills?

  How do you handle stress and pressure?

  Can you describe a time you made a mistake and how you handled it?

>> **Write a list of questions.** Focus your questions primarily on the organization and the job description, and on the requirements and the role and its responsibilities. Consider questions about the organization's culture, educational and training opportunities, and opportunities for advancement. See the later section "Preparing questions to ask."

Can't think of any questions to ask? You may want to reconsider. You may be judged harshly for not asking any questions, and you can improve your chances of standing out from the crowd by asking intelligent ones. See the "Preparing questions to ask" section, later in this chapter, for suggestions of questions you can ask an interviewer.

>> **Practice.** See the later section "Practicing for an interview."

Crafting intelligent responses

As part of your preparation, I encourage you to prepare answers to common questions. I also encourage you to engage in mock interviews with colleagues, friends, or family members who may ask questions you haven't considered. Coming up with intelligent answers may be the most challenging aspect of an interview. Fortunately, I know a strategy that can help.

A widely known technique for formulating solid responses to job interview questions is the STAR method. I can't take credit for it, but I can highly recommend it, especially for answering behavior-based interview questions. The STAR method goes like this:

>> **Situation:** Describe the context within which you performed a task or faced a challenge at work.

>> **Task:** Explain the actual task or challenge that was involved.

>> **Action:** Detail the specific actions you took to address the task or challenge.

>> **Result:** Share the outcomes or results of your actions, quantifying the impact if possible.

The STAR method has been popularized by the business and human resources community as an effective way to help candidates articulate their experiences in a clear, concise, and relevant manner during interviews. Though no single individual is credited with its creation, it has been widely adopted and promoted by HR professionals and career coaches to improve the interview process for both candidates and employers.

Wrap it up! When nerves hit, you may be prone to running on and on. Avoid rambling. Keep your answers concise and focused on the question. Provide enough detail to be informative but avoid long-winded explanations. Adhering to the STAR method can help. Prepare a range of examples and stories from your past experiences that you can draw on to answer various types of questions. These sample responses should illustrate your key skills and achievements and how you've handled various situations.

Take a moment to process each question, and if anything is unclear, don't hesitate to ask for clarification. If you don't know the answer to a question or haven't had a particular experience, admit it and discuss how you would approach the situation if you had experienced it or what you're doing to develop the knowledge or aptitude in question. You may say something like, "I don't have direct experience with X, but I did have a similar experience. . . ." Following this approach, you can tailor your answers to highlight your relevant skills and experiences.

Preparing questions to ask

Coming prepared with questions to ask your interviewer is essential. Asking thoughtful questions demonstrates your genuine interest in the role and the organization. It shows that you've done your homework and you're aware of the importance of finding a position that's the right fit. This can set you apart from other candidates who may not exhibit the same level of engagement.

REMEMBER

Interviews are not just opportunities for employers to evaluate you, but also for you to evaluate employers. By asking questions, you gain valuable insights into the company's culture, expectations, and growth opportunities, helping you determine whether the job aligns with your personal and professional goals and values. Questions about team dynamics, company vision, and professional development opportunities can provide a clear picture of what working at the organization would be like.

Additionally, asking questions can clarify any uncertainties about the role, such as specific responsibilities or performance metrics. This ensures that you have a comprehensive understanding of the job and can make an informed decision if you receive an offer. Overall, coming prepared with questions not only demonstrates your enthusiasm and preparedness but also empowers you to make a well-informed career choice.

Not sure what to ask? Don't worry! I have you covered. Here's a list of a dozen or so questions you can consider asking at the appropriate times during your next interview. You don't need to ask all of them, but coming prepared with a few that are important to you is a good strategy to employ so that you get employed! (See what I did there?)

>> What is your favorite part about working for the company?

>> Can you describe the company culture?

>> What are the main responsibilities and expectations for this role?

>> What would you like to see this role accomplish that it hasn't in the past?

- How is success measured in this role?
- Can you tell me more about the team I would be working with?
- What are the opportunities for professional development and career growth?
- What are the biggest challenges now facing the team or department?
- How does the company support work-life balance?
- What are the policies around flexible work?
- Can you tell me about the company's approach to diversity and inclusion?
- What are the next steps in the interview process?
- How does this role contribute to the company's overall goals and mission?

Practicing for an interview

Now, practice. I don't believe that practice makes perfect, but I do believe that practice can help you be more present in the moment. And that presence can pay off in spades with increased focus and confidence. Practice delivering your answers and asking questions. Consider conducting mock interviews with a friend or in front of a mirror or video-recording a mock interview to evaluate your performance and make improvements. Practice not only what you say but also how you say it, using nonverbal communication to reinforce your message and be more expressive overall. Practicing helps you articulate your thoughts clearly and reduces anxiety by making you more familiar with the interview process.

TIP

If the interview is to be conducted remotely via a videoconferencing platform, practice with a colleague, friend, or family member using that platform so that you can identify and address any technical glitches and become more accustomed to that interview format.

Attracting and Interviewing Candidates

Business communication is a two-way street, and when you're trying to find the right person to fill a position, it's a collaborative effort. It's not all about attracting as many candidates as possible and having them compete, elimination-style, for limited openings in your organization. It's about attracting the right people and vetting them in a way that ensures a quality placement and reflects positively on your organization.

In this section, I provide guidance on how to communicate clearly during the recruitment and interview processes to ensure that you attract and choose the best candidate for the job and enhance your organization's reputation in the process.

Communicating effectively during the recruiting process

Effective business communication is crucial in the context of recruiting and interviewing candidates. The following techniques can help ensure that the process is smooth and professional, and that all parties are well-informed:

» **Post detailed and accurate job descriptions.** Describe the role, responsibilities, qualifications, and skills required. This step attracts the right candidates, discourages the wrong ones, and provides applicants with the information they need to clearly communicate their qualifications in their cover letter and resume.

» **Maintain professional correspondence.** Provide timely responses to candidate applications, inquiries, and other correspondence. Personalize responses instead of (or in addition to) providing scripted replies.

» **Use technologies effectively.** Use technologies such as an applicant tracking system (ATS) to streamline the application process, track candidate progress, and ensure that no applications are overlooked. If you conduct virtual interviews, ensure that candidates are familiar with the videoconferencing platform.

» **Maintain consistent messaging.** If you have multiple people communicating with a candidate, ensure that the information they're sharing is consistent. Also ensure that all messaging reflects your organization's brand, mission, and values.

» **Conduct structured interviews.** Develop a set of standard questions to ask each candidate to ensure a fair and objective comparison. Include behavior-based questions to assess how candidates have handled situations in the past and to predict future performance.

» **Be honest and respectful.** Provide feedback to candidates, especially those who made it to the later stages of the interview process. Constructive feedback helps maintain a positive relationship and can improve the candidate's perception of your organization.

Being a good interviewer

As an interviewer, you're no longer in the proverbial hot seat. But you know how hot that seat can be, and you don't want to burn talented candidates. You need information and insight to make a well-informed hiring decision, but you want to acquire it in a compassionate way that's aligned with your organization's mission, vision, and values. You need to be a skilled job interviewer. Well, you've come to the right place. In this section, I share best practices for interviewing job applicants.

Putting interviewees at ease from the start

Interviews can be highly stressful, especially for the interviewee. After all, the person is in unfamiliar surroundings with unfamiliar people who have the power to decide their fate to some degree. So stay attuned to the interviewee's feelings and comfort during the process. Here are some ways to ratchet down the tension and set the tone for an honest, open conversation:

>> **Attend to the interviewee's creature comforts.** Arrange a comfortable physical space with appropriate seating arrangements and minimal distractions. Offer the candidate a moment to settle in.

>> **Begin the interview with a warm welcome and a brief introduction to set a friendly tone.** Explain the interview process and what to expect, which can help reduce anxiety.

>> **Practice active listening.** Show genuine interest in the candidate's responses during the interview by nodding, maintaining eye contact, and not interrupting. Active listening involves fully concentrating on the interviewee's words, body language, and tone of voice. Ask follow-up questions if a candidate's response is unclear to fully understand their experiences and skills. See Chapter 5 for more about active listening.

>> **Ask open-ended questions that encourage the interviewee to share their thoughts and experiences in their own words.** Follow up with clarifying questions to show that you're paying attention and interested in their detailed responses. Avoid interrupting them and allow them time to think and respond fully. For instance, if they pause to collect their thoughts, give them the space to do so without rushing them.

>> **Offer positive feedback and encouragement throughout the interview.** Acknowledging the interviewee's accomplishments and strengths can boost their confidence and make them feel more comfortable. You can start questions in a positive way, "We were impressed to see your experience with X. Tell us more about that. . . ."

>> **If the interview is lengthy, allow for short breaks.** Breaks enable everyone to remain focused.

By staying attuned to the interviewee's feelings and comfort, you can foster a more honest, open, and pleasant interview experience. This approach not only helps in getting the best out of the interviewee but also reflects well on the organization's culture and values.

REMEMBER

Not all interviews, roles, or positions are the same, but the general tips in the preceding list can apply to most interview situations. You can start with these basics and refine them as needed for the role you're trying to fill.

Adapt to the conversation

Have you ever had one of those telemarketing calls that make you believe the person isn't really listening to you but merely following a script? Well, you don't want your interviewee to feel like you're that telemarketer! Be flexible and adapt to create a conversation that flows more naturally, making the interaction more engaging and insightful. Sticking rigidly to a list of scripted questions can limit the depth and relevance of the information shared. By being open to deviating from planned questions (where allowed), you can explore topics that emerge organically, which may provide valuable insights into the candidate's experiences, skills, and personality. As a bonus, this adaptability also demonstrates to the candidate that you're genuinely interested in their unique experiences and perspectives, creating a more positive interview experience and helping to build rapport.

Actively listen to the candidate's responses and identify opportunities to delve deeper into relevant topics. If a candidate mentions a significant achievement or an interesting project that you hadn't planned to discuss (but is relevant to the role or company in some way), take the opportunity to explore it further. For example, if a candidate casually references their role in a major corporate turn-around, you might ask, "Can you tell me more about the strategies you implemented and the challenges you faced during that process?" This question shows attentiveness and enables you to assess skills and experiences that may not have been covered by the original questions.

TIP

Even if a candidate is talking about a topic that may not be directly related to the job description, consider finding out more. In some cases, you may find that the candidate is the ideal fit for a different position you need to fill. I've been in a situation where someone on the interview committee asked me to join their team instead because they felt it would be a better fit!

Digging deeper (when appropriate)

Though your hiring team may have prepared a list of questions for you, sometimes they aren't enough. Knowing when to dig deeper in a job interview is crucial to uncovering the candidate's true potential and ensuring a good fit for the role and organization.

If a candidate provides vague or generic answers, probe further. Ask for specific examples, details, or situations that clarify their experience and skills. For instance, if a candidate mentions that they have "extensive project management experience," you might ask, "Can you describe a challenging project you managed and how you handled it?" (Of course, if the candidate has read this chapter, they'll know to provide more detail than that!)

If you notice inconsistencies in the candidate's resume or gaps in their employment history, digging deeper is necessary. Politely ask them to explain these gaps or inconsistencies to understand their career path better. For example, "I see a two-year gap between these roles; can you tell me more about what you were doing during that time?" Having a gap isn't necessarily a bad thing — life happens and sometimes what happens in the gap is more valuable than if the candidate had been employed the entire time.

WARNING

Employers are prohibited by law from asking certain questions during an interview (for example, "Do you have children?"). Make sure you're up-to-date on regulations in your location and in your organization and industry to avoid crossing a line.

If a candidate's answers touch on critical skills or experiences relevant to the role, delve deeper to gauge their proficiency and relevance. For example, if the role requires strong leadership skills and the candidate mentions leading a team, ask, "Can you provide an example of a time when you had to resolve a conflict within your team?" This and other behavior-based questions can reveal much about a candidate's suitability. When a candidate provides a surface-level response, such as "I always meet deadlines," prompt them with, "Can you describe a time when you faced a tight deadline and how you ensured the project was completed on time?"

Finally, understanding the candidate's passion and fit for the company culture is vital. If their answers seem rehearsed or lack enthusiasm, ask follow-up questions such as, "What excites you most about this industry?" or "How do you see yourself contributing to our organization's culture?"

By paying attention to these cues and asking follow-up questions, you can gain deeper insights into a candidate's qualifications, experiences, and potential fit for your organization.

IN THIS CHAPTER

» Recognizing the difference between goals, objectives, and tasks

» Dealing effectively with evolving group dynamics

» Playing your part and letting others play theirs

» Adopting team management best practices

» Singing the praises of others — and reaping the benefits

Chapter **19**

Collaborating with Team Members

I n a business setting, you're part of a *team* — a group of individuals working toward a common goal. You may be working alone most of the time, onsite or remotely, but it doesn't matter: You're still part of a team. You may be a member of one or more teams. The teams you're on may be physical, virtual, or a mix of the two. You may be leading the team or serving in a different capacity. Whatever the situation, you need to know how to communicate and interact with others in a group setting toward a common goal.

In this chapter, I provide the information and guidance you need to be a more effective team player and improve your team's productivity regardless of the team's structure or the role you play.

Getting Up to Speed on Team Fundamentals

Working alone is far different from working on a team. When you're alone, you have total autonomy and control. You can focus entirely on a single task without interruptions. When the time comes to make a decision, you don't have to consult anyone. You're free to explore ideas without having to compromise or seek consensus. You're accountable only to yourself, and you don't have to attend meetings (well, at least not meetings with others).

When you're a member of a team, all of that changes and your simple life becomes far more complex — but also comes with the potential to be far more rewarding. Now you need to communicate, collaborate, and coordinate not only your work but also your schedules. You will inevitably have meetings, interruptions, and disagreements. But look on the bright side: On a team, you have access to diverse knowledge and skills, perspectives, and ideas. Your team members can become a constant source of motivation, support, learning, development, creativity, and innovation. And the more you know about how teams work, and specifically how *your* team works, the more you, your team, and your organization stand to benefit.

In this section, you build your understanding of teams and how they function in ways that enable you to contribute more to making any team you're on stronger and more productive.

Understanding the difference between a team and a group

In this chapter, the focus is on collaborating as a team, not merely on working with others as a group. The difference is important because it establishes the level of communication, collaboration, and coordination needed for success.

In business, a *team* is a unit of individuals working collaboratively toward a common goal or objective. Teams are characterized by shared responsibilities, interdependent tasks, and collective accountability. Team members typically have roles, knowledge, training, and skills that complement one another's, creating synergies and enhancing overall performance. Effective teams communicate openly, make joint decisions, and focus on achieving high levels of productivity and innovation.

In contrast, a *group* is a collection of individuals who may work together but don't necessarily share the same goals or levels of interdependence. Group members may work independently on their tasks with less emphasis on collaboration and collective accountability. Groups are often formed for administrative or logistical purposes, without the strong sense of unity and shared purpose that defines a team.

REMEMBER

The key difference between a team and a group lies in the level of collaboration and mutual accountability; teams work interdependently toward a common goal, whereas groups consist of individuals working more independently. For example, you can have a baseball team and a running group. The baseball team's goal is to win, and the only way they can do that is together, whereas with a running group, you may train together and help hold each other accountable, but at the end of the day your goal is your goal.

Getting it done: Goals, objectives, and tasks

To work effectively as a unit, teams need to agree on goals, set objectives, and assign tasks. Everyone on the team needs to have a clear understanding of the differences between those elements:

>> **Goals:** Broad, overarching outcomes that a team aims to achieve. They provide direction and serve as long-term targets that align with the organization's vision and mission. Goals are usually qualitative and aspirational, setting the stage for what the team wants to accomplish over an extended period. For example, a business team may set a goal to "become the market leader in customer satisfaction within three years." Goals inspire and motivate the team, offering a clear sense of purpose.

>> **Objectives:** Specific, measurable accomplishments on the way to achieving the broader goals. They're short to midrange targets that are concrete and quantifiable, making it easier to track progress and measure success. Objectives break down the goals into actionable components. For instance, to support the goal of becoming the market leader in customer satisfaction, an objective may be to "improve customer service response times by 20 percent within the next six months." Objectives provide clear milestones and ensure that efforts are focused and aligned with the overall goals.

>> **Tasks:** The individual actions or activities that need to be completed to achieve the objectives. Tasks are the smallest units of work, assigned to team members, and tasks have specific deadlines and deliverables. Tasks are highly detailed and actionable. For example, a task to meet the objective of improving customer service response times could be "implement new customer service software by the end of the month." Tasks are the building blocks of objectives and goals, ensuring that the necessary work is done systematically and efficiently.

To accomplish anything in a group, set a specific goal, break it down into the objectives you need to accomplish to meet that goal, and assign tasks to team members to meet the stated objectives.

REMEMBER

Goals provide the strategic vision, objectives offer measurable milestones, and tasks are the actionable steps that drive progress. Together, they form a structured approach to achieving success.

Surviving ever-evolving group dynamics

If you've ever been part of a team, you've observed and participated in *group dynamics* — the behaviors people exhibit and the patterns they follow when interacting in a group setting. By understanding group dynamics, you're better prepared to deal with how people behave and interact on a team. Understanding the different stages of team development, as proposed by Bruce Tuckman and later enhanced by Mary Ann Jensen (see Figure 19-1), can be especially helpful. According to Tuckman, groups, including teams, pass through four stages of development: forming, storming, norming, and performing. Jensen added a fifth stage — adjourning — to cover the separation that occurs when the group disbands. In the following sections, I describe each stage.

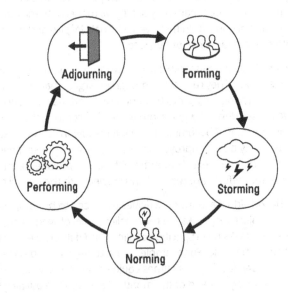

FIGURE 19-1:
The five stages of group development.

Forming

The forming stage is the initial phase in the development of a business team. During this stage, individuals are often polite and positive as they get to know each other. The atmosphere is a mix of excitement and anxiety as team members explore the team's purpose, their roles, and the boundaries within which they will operate. Communication tends to be cautious and formal as members establish trust and learn about each other's skills and personalities. This stage is characterized by a high dependence on the leader for direction and support.

Team members may engage in discussions about the team's goals and individual roles and expectations. However, they typically avoid deep or challenging conversations as they strive to present themselves favorably and avoid conflict. The primary focus is on building relationships and creating a foundation for future collaboration.

Effective leadership during the forming stage involves facilitating introductions, encouraging open communication, and clearly defining the team's goals and processes. By fostering an inclusive and supportive environment, leaders can help the team transition smoothly through the next stage of development, storming, which can be the most challenging of the five stages.

If you're leading the team, follow these tips to facilitate and accelerate team formation and cohesion (everyone on the team can contribute by following these suggestions):

TIP

>> **Encourage open dialogue.** Foster an environment in which team members feel comfortable sharing their thoughts, ideas, and concerns. Encourage everyone to participate in discussions, ask questions, and provide input.

   During initial meetings, set aside time for team members to introduce themselves and share their backgrounds and the skills they hope to contribute to the team. This helps build rapport and ensures that everyone's voice is heard from the outset.

>> **Set clear goals and expectations.** Clearly communicate the team's purpose/ goal, objectives, roles, and responsibilities. Ensure that all team members understand what's expected of them and the overall vision for the team's work. During the initial meeting, outline the project's goal, key milestones, and individual roles. Use visual aids such as charts or presentations to make expectations clear, if necessary, and provide written summaries that team members can refer to. Using project management software or a shared dashboard can also be an effective way to coordinate efforts.

>> **Practice active listening.** Active listening, as presented in Chapter 5, is especially useful when forming a team. Challenge team members to practice active listening by paying full attention to speakers, acknowledging their points, and responding thoughtfully. Active listening helps build mutual respect and understanding. During discussions, use techniques such as paraphrasing or summarizing what someone said before responding.

This approach demonstrates that you value their input and are engaged in the conversation. For instance, say, "What I hear you saying is . . ." followed by a summary of their points, and then proceed with your response or questions.

Storming

The storming stage is the second phase in the development of business teams, characterized by conflict and competition as individual personalities and working styles clash. During this stage, team members begin to push against the boundaries established in the forming stage, leading to power struggles and disagreements about goals, roles, and responsibilities.

Communication during the storming stage can be tense and confrontational as members express their differing opinions and sometimes vie for influence. This period of conflict is essential for team growth because it helps to bring underlying issues to the surface and encourages open dialogue about expectations and processes.

REMEMBER

Conflict isn't a bad thing unless it's handled poorly or not at all. See Chapter 16 for ways to approach conflict constructively.

Leaders play a critical role during the storming stage by demonstrating constructive conflict resolution and guiding the team through disagreements. They need to encourage open communication, actively listen to concerns, and mediate disputes to help the team move forward. Establishing clear channels for feedback and conflict resolution is vital.

Despite the challenges, the storming stage is crucial for the development of a strong, cohesive team. It provides an opportunity for members to address and overcome their differences, leading to better understanding and stronger relationships. Successful navigation through this stage sets the foundation for a more collaborative and high-performing team in the subsequent norming and performing stages.

If you're leading a team through this stage, let everyone know that this is a normal stage in team development and that conflict is part of it — acknowledge that conflict is not wrong or bad. You may say something like, "I realize that there's some disagreement in how we approach this next phase of the project — that's normal and expected. Let's all share one next step and why you feel it's the appropriate move so that we can better understand one another and decide on a path forward."

Norming

In the norming stage, the third phase in the development of business teams, members establish *norms* (standards for accepted behavior), build stronger relationships, and develop a sense of cohesion. During this stage, conflicts from the previous storming phase begin to subside as team members resolve their differences, understand each other's strengths and weaknesses, and appreciate their roles within the team.

Communication becomes more open, constructive, and collaborative. Team members feel more comfortable sharing their ideas and feedback, leading to increased trust and mutual respect. The norming stage is characterized by a greater focus on team unity and a shared commitment to achieving the team's goals.

Leaders play a less directive role during the norming stage, as the team begins to operate more autonomously. However, leaders remain available to provide guidance and support as needed. The emphasis shifts to establishing efficient processes, setting performance standards, and ensuring that everyone adheres to agreed-on practices and procedures. Let the team know that you recognize how it's maturing. For example, you may tell the team something like, "I've noticed that we've reached a point of collaboration and everyone is working well together. I'm impressed with how quickly we found a way to proceed."

Team members begin to work more effectively together, leveraging their diverse skills and perspectives to tackle challenges and make decisions. This stage is characterized by a sense of camaraderie and team spirit, which lays the foundation for high performance. Don't get complacent here! Make sure you're still practicing solid communication skills and proactively checking in with team members throughout the process.

Performing

In the performing stage, the fourth phase in the development of business teams, the team reaches its highest level of functionality and productivity. During this stage, team members are fully aligned with their roles and responsibilities, and they work together seamlessly toward achieving their goals. The team operates with a high degree of autonomy and confidence, making collaborative decisions efficiently and effectively. Communication is open, honest, and fluid. Team members trust each other and feel comfortable sharing ideas, feedback, and concerns, often in a less formal way. They develop a strong sense of camaraderie and mutual respect, which fosters a positive and supportive work environment. They're comfortable with conflict, and they deal with it collaboratively, with a focus on problem-solving and continuous improvement.

This stage is characterized by high levels of motivation, morale, and job satisfaction. The team is able to adapt quickly to changing circumstances and tackle complex challenges with confidence. It consistently delivers high-quality results and achieves its objectives efficiently.

REMEMBER

Remain vigilant and be careful not to get sloppy with communication as you settle into routines. Continue to follow best practices for communication, including listening actively and asking questions to check for mutual understanding, as explained in Part 2 of this book. Remember that conflict is natural, even during the performing stage, but team members need to resolve their differences constructively, as explained in Chapter 16.

As team leader, you may need to adopt a more hands-off approach, stepping in only when necessary to provide guidance or support. Teams work best when members are empowered to take ownership of their tasks and encourage innovation and initiative.

Adjourning

The adjourning (or mourning) stage is the point at which the team disbands and members prepare to move on to new projects and roles. Emotions can be a mixture of satisfaction, pride, relief, sadness, anxiety, uncertainty, gratitude, and disappointment (in the event that the team fell short of expectations).

To provide closure and disband the group in a constructive manner, conduct a final team meeting, during which you

>> **Review areas for improvement — mistakes made, opportunities missed, and tasks the team could have completed better.** This review is often referred to as a *post mortem,* which translates to "after death" but refers to the completion of any project. Give team members the opportunity to reflect on and share their experiences and the lessons they learned, which can be valuable for future team endeavors and personal growth.

>> **Recognize and celebrate the team's accomplishments and individual contributions.** Give each team member the chance to voice what others have achieved and contributed. (See the later section "Acknowledging Contributions and Achievements" for details.)

>> **Encourage team members to share what's next for them — their next project or role — and perhaps how their experience on this team has prepared them for it.** Looking forward enables team members to experience the adjournment as more of a transition than an end.

Defining Team Roles and How to Play Them

Just as a basketball or soccer team has multiple positions, each with unique responsibilities and a specific skill set, business teams have multiple roles. For the team to function as a unified whole and achieve its full potential, it must have the right people in the right roles — it definitely wouldn't work if every person were trying to be the leader! In this section, I focus on defining, assigning, and rotating roles and provide guidance on how to take the lead and step back (when appropriate) to let others lead.

Assigning and rotating roles

When you're building a business team, you need to fill multiple roles: leader, coordinator, facilitator, and subject matter expert, for example. Not all roles need to be filled on every team, some team members may perform multiple roles, and roles can shift over the course of a project or even the course of a single meeting. What's important is that you understand the roles, know which roles your team needs, and have the right person filling each role. Common roles include

REMEMBER

>> **Leader:** The leadership role is often a formal position, such as team leader or project manager. However, informal leadership roles can also emerge. This person oversees the project; coordinates team activities; sets deadlines; provides direction, motivation, and support; and ensures that the team meets its objectives and goals.

If you're serving as the team leader, you're responsible for communication and setting the tone. Establish clear communication parameters, including preferred communication channels, meeting frequency, and accountability tracking. Discuss these parameters and be sure everyone understands the expectations.

>> **Facilitator:** The facilitator guides discussions, keeps the team focused, maintains productive meetings, ensures balanced participation in sessions, and manages conflict. If you're the facilitator, setting guidelines upfront can be helpful; for example, ask permission upfront to interrupt any meeting that's heading off course or to call out any counterproductive behavior.

>> **Subject matter expert (SME):** The SME provides specialized knowledge and expertise critical to the project, advises on technical aspects, and ensures accuracy and quality. When questions or problems arise, the SME is often the go-to person. They may be a permanent member of the team or someone who's on call; for example, an IT specialist who makes software recommendations.

>> **Analyst:** The analyst gathers and interprets data, identifies trends, calls attention to potential issues, and provides insights to support decision-making. The analyst must remain impartial and report only on the available data and research. Any insights must be backed by facts and figures.

>> **Communicator:** The team's communicator manages internal and external communications, distributes information, maintains transparency, and manages public relations and stakeholder engagement, keeping everyone in the loop and on the same page.

>> **Scribe:** Also known as the recorder (and, in older generations, the secretary), the scribe documents meeting discussions, decisions, and action items and ensures that records are accurate and accessible for future reference. Often the scribe works closely with the communicator to ensure that the appropriate information is communicated to relevant parties. Depending on the scope of the team, these roles are often combined.

>> **Implementer:** The implementer (or implementers) puts the plan into action, performing all the tasks required to meet the team's stated objectives. This person checks the boxes, crosses the *t*'s, and dot the *i*'s.

>> **Evaluator:** Though every team member is involved in this role to some degree, the designated evaluator serves as an objective third party, evaluating the team's output and providing constructive feedback. You can think of the evaluator as a critic or devil's advocate, whose purpose is to identify and uncover issues and defects. The evaluator also serves an important role in the planning stage — picking apart the plan to identify areas of concern and ensuring that the team has considered all perspectives.

>> **Encourager:** The encourager is the team's cheerleader or mascot, boosting team morale, supporting colleagues, and fostering a positive working environment. The encourager provides emotional and motivational support, regularly recognizes and acknowledges achievements and contributions, and leads the team in celebrating progress. Note that encouragement isn't flattery — it's recognition of achievements, contributions, and progress.

>> **Coordinator:** The coordinator maintains the team's alignment with its goal and strategy, manages logistics, and ensures resources are available to keep the project moving smoothly. The coordinator knows what various team members need and ensures they have it.

Regardless of whether you're the team leader, strive to ensure that someone on the team is playing each of these roles. You can do this subtly and nonconfrontationally by asking questions during the initial team meeting, such as "Who's in charge of procuring resources?" and "Who's managing the schedule?" Some team members may fall into these roles naturally, but you still need to ensure that all the bases are covered.

Deciding whether to lead or let others lead

To paraphrase Shakespeare, some are born leaders, some develop into leaders, and some have leadership thrust upon them. In most cases, team leaders are chosen, either by a superior or the team; leadership is thrust upon them. In other cases, the person best suited to that position fills the role naturally; they're natural leaders. And, when a leadership vacuum exists, someone on the team needs to step up and fill that role, acquiring the necessary skills through on-the-job training — they develop into leaders.

If you're in a situation in which you need to decide whether to take the reins, you must consider whether you have the qualities, desire, and focus to lead the team effectively and then decide what's best for you and the team.

Conducting a self-assessment

Before agreeing to take on a leadership role, conduct a self-assessment to ensure that you have the right stuff, the bandwidth (mental and time capacity), and the desire. Consider the following factors:

>> **Your leadership skills, experience, and confidence:** Do you feel confident that you're the best choice for team leader based solely on ability?

>> **Desire/motivation:** Many exceptional leaders accept the responsibility reluctantly, but motivation to lead is a plus. Make sure it's not only ego-driven motivation!

>> **Time/focus:** Given your current workload and responsibilities at work and outside work, do you feel confident that you can commit the time and focus required to lead effectively? Balancing leadership duties with your regular responsibilities can be challenging, potentially leading to burnout or decreased productivity in other areas.

>> **Charisma:** Do you generally command respect and inspire hard work and collaboration? Can you rally the troops?

If you're asked to lead, or if you're considering stepping into that role, be honest with yourself and with your fellow team members. Have an open discussion about why you feel you're best suited for the role, or why someone else may be better suited to lead at this time. It's okay to accept a leadership role with boundaries in place. For example, "I'm honored to be asked to lead this time. In order to do it effectively, I will need someone else to step up to do the XYZ portion of this project."

Considering what's best for you

To decide whether taking on a certain leadership role is in your best interest, carefully consider the following pros and cons of assuming leadership (see Figure 19-2):

To Lead
- If you're ready to gain skills and experience
- If you want to enhance your career trajectory
- If you're prepared to fill a leadership vacuum
- If you want to have influence and ownership
- If you want to experience professional growth

Not To Lead
- If you can't handle increased workload and stress
- If you're unprepared to face potential criticism and blame
- If you know that someone else might be a better fit
- If you lack the necessary experience and skills
- If you have no way to balance existing responsibilities

FIGURE 19-2: Weigh the pros and cons of assuming a leadership position.

Pros

>> Provides an opportunity to showcase your knowledge, skills, and ability to lead and manage others. A leadership role can raise your profile and enhance your reputation in the organization.

>> Improves your career prospects, opening the doors to promotions and other opportunities.

>> Provides valuable experience that contributes to both your professional and personal growth and builds confidence. Specifically, it sharpens your skills in management, communication, collaboration, and problem-solving.

>> Gives you more influence over the project's direction and outcome and gives you a greater sense of ownership.

>> Expands your professional network and strengthens your reputation among colleagues.

Cons

» Increased workload, responsibilities, and stress. Leading a team often requires managing multiple responsibilities, resolving conflicts, and ensuring the project's success. This added pressure can impact your performance and well-being if not managed properly.

» Increased exposure to criticism or blame, which can negatively impact your reputation (and your personal confidence). As the leader, the buck stops with you, and if you're in a situation with an outcome you can't control, you may experience a great deal of frustration.

» May increase conflict and damage existing relationships if you need to make tough decisions that are unpopular with team members, such as having to terminate a team member or change the person's role.

» Potential negative impact on your reputation if you step into the leadership role unprepared.

Considering what's best for the team

Great leaders don't always take the lead. They have the integrity to recognize when other people are better suited for that role for whatever reason — knowledge, skill, personality, availability, and so on. As you deliberate over whether to assume the leadership role, weigh the following factors to consider what's best for the team:

» **Leadership vacuum:** If nobody else is capable or willing to lead the team, you may be the best candidate.

» **Ineffective leadership:** If the person currently leading the team seems unable to provide the motivation and guidance for the team to achieve its full potential or at least achieve the group's goals, you may be more inclined to step into that position.

» **Team dynamics:** Consider whether your team members are more likely to follow you or someone else on the team. If you're leading but everyone on the team is looking to the other person for information and guidance, you're going to clash with the other leader.

Ultimately, you need to decide whether you would serve best as team leader or in some other capacity on the team. You may be better suited to serve a more supporting role — for example, as SME or coordinator. Reflect on your motivations: Leading should be about contributing to the team's success. Remember: because you have expertise doesn't mean you're necessarily the best person to lead.

Keeping Your Team on Track

If you're team leader, communication is essential for keeping your team on track. Here are a few tips and techniques for communicating effectively:

>> **Maintain transparent and consistent communication.** Clearly outline expectations, objectives, and responsibilities to avoid misunderstandings. Recap important meetings and key decisions to clear up any misunderstandings and ensure alignment. Share relevant information appropriately. Cloud-based file-sharing and collaboration platforms simplify the process of sharing information and keeping everyone posted.

WARNING

Don't hoard information! Some leaders limit access to essential information out of a desire to maintain control or compete with team members perceived as threats to their status. Effective leaders act as information hubs, promoting free-flowing and transparent communication.

>> **Set up team members for success.** Invite team members to let you know what they need to be successful and encourage them to advocate for resources. (See Chapter 14 for more about negotiation.)

>> **Establish clear accountability.** Ensure that everyone knows their roles and holds themselves — and each other — responsible for their tasks.

>> **Insist on strict adherence to legal and ethical standards.** Part of keeping a team on track involves ensuring compliance to any laws and standards regarding their work or what they're producing. Consult with legal advisors when necessary to clarify any complex issues and communicate them to the team.

>> **Provide the necessary oversight.** Keep detailed records of the plan, including the agreed-on goal, objectives, tasks, deadlines, and each team member's role and responsibilities. Refer to your records over the course of the project to ensure that your team is on track and to correct course if it's not. Documentation can help identify potential problems early so that contingency plans can be developed if they become necessary.

REMEMBER

Detailed documentation also serves as a valuable resource for future projects, providing insights and lessons learned that can improve efficiency and effectiveness.

>> **Solicit feedback and provide feedback via performance reviews and casual conversations.** Address any issues that arise promptly and constructively to prevent them from escalating. See Chapter 15 for details about providing and receiving feedback constructively.

Acknowledging Contributions and Achievements

As a member of a team, especially if you're serving as team leader, your responsibilities extend beyond the performance of the team to ensuring the success of all team members — when they're actively serving on the team and beyond. Celebrating the team's accomplishments and individual contributions benefits you, your fellow team members, and your organization in numerous ways, including these:

» Opens the door for advancement and new opportunities for team members

» Increases motivation and individual and team morale

» Improves performance

» Fosters a positive work environment

» Improves employee retention and loyalty and enhances recruitment efforts

» Promotes communication, cooperation, and collaboration

» Encourages the sharing of information and ideas, which fuels creativity and innovation

» Builds a culture around recognition, which increases confidence and self-esteem

» Encourages personal and professional development

GIVING CREDIT WHERE CREDIT IS DUE

Who doesn't like to be recognized for doing something well? Nobody I know! Recognizing the achievements of others on your team, regardless of whether you're the team leader, is an outstanding communication strategy. And it doesn't take away from you to give credit to someone else. Giving credit where credit is due is a solid move to let others know that you not only see them and their efforts but you're also aware of their contributions and their impact on the team's success.

Aside from creating a positive and motivating environment, when team members — heck, when people in general — feel appreciated and valued, they're more likely to be engaged, productive, and committed. In essence, you get more work out of people

(continued)

(continued)

when they feel valued! Both morale and job satisfaction positively correlate with recognition. Recognition can even inspire others on the team to strive for a higher level of performance.

Nearly everyone wants to work in a culture or environment in which respect and collaboration are the rule, not the exception. When you receive credit and recognition regularly, it encourages a sense of unity and teamwork because people see their efforts contributing to the collective success. This sense of belonging can strengthen relationships and improve overall team dynamics.

Here are a few concrete ways to acknowledge contributions and achievements:

» **Sing their praises!** Publicly acknowledge someone's efforts during meetings or team gatherings, highlighting specific accomplishments. Remember that the best feedback is specific rather than general. For tips on giving effective feedback, see Chapter 15.

» **Make it personal.** Send a personalized email or a handwritten note expressing gratitude for their contributions. Again, making the feedback specific is important. Receiving feedback in such an intimate way makes it meaningful. In fact, I know people (myself included) who keep a file of the thank-you messages and the recognition they've received so that, on a bad day, they can pull it out and remember the contributions they've made. Small gifts or tokens also belong this category — little things that help celebrate milestones and accomplishments.

» **Award the winners!** And the trophy goes to . . . you get the idea — hand out awards for the best and the worst. Get everyone involved by requesting nominations and coming up with names for the awards. The awards don't have to be serious; they can be fun. For example, you can have a Best Idea That Fell Flat award or Holds the Best Poker Face in Meetings award. If you're being lighthearted, balance the humor with authentic examples of positive contributions.

» **Shine a press light.** If your organization has a monthly newsletter or weekly outreach communication or an all-hands meeting, submit your team members' accomplishments to be recognized at the broader organizational level.

Acknowledging others helps you, too! Consider the following benefits:

>> **Increases your visibility.** Promoting others is an excellent self-promotional strategy (see Chapter 10).

>> **Demonstrates that you're not threatened by the success of others.** Instead, you're confident enough to celebrate their contributions, knowing that it doesn't diminish your value or accomplishments.

>> **Demonstrates leadership qualities even if you're not in a formal leadership role.** What a win! It shows that you can see the bigger picture and prioritize the team's success over individual recognition, especially your own. This kind of behavior can inspire trust and respect from colleagues because they see you as a supportive and collaborative team member. As a result, they'll be more likely to return the favor later.

>> **Projects confidence in your ability to judge and appreciate quality work.** When you communicate positively about the stellar success of others, it shows that you have high standards and that you're unafraid to acknowledge excellence when you see it. What a wonderful situation to be in and an exceptional way to expand your collaborative abilities because who wouldn't want to be on a team with you when you're that bright and generous?

Chapter 20

Communicating across Cultures

'll never forget my international management class in college. Although I can't recall the professor's name for the life of me (sorry, whoever you were/are!), I can recall — with clarity — a story he told on the first day of class.

He was on a business trip to Japan and was visiting a seafood market. As he walked around, he observed a woman standing over a small pool of fish. Other than her head rotating to look around the pool, she was as still as a statue. Curious, he stood there watching her for a few minutes. Nothing changed. So he continued through the market. On his way out, a good 30 minutes later, the woman was still standing in the same spot, watching the same fish, in the same pool. All of a sudden, she started screaming something in Japanese and waving her arms and pointing. Turns out, she was watching and waiting for a fish to die, because a dead fish was a fraction of the price of a live fish and she wanted to get the freshest fish possible for the lowest price.

She clearly had patience, in spades.

But what does waiting for a fish to die have to do with business communication and cultural communication? Well, quite a bit.

All cultures — all people — deal with daily activities, events, interactions, and messages differently. Recognizing, understanding, and being able to communicate with, to, and in respect to these differences effectively requires an understanding of the complexities and nuances of communicating across cultures. It's what distinguishes a good communicator from a great communicator (or, as I like to say, a dynamic communicator).

In this chapter, I present information and guidance to increase your awareness to the way different individuals communicate and interact and to facilitate the process of adapting to one another to achieve a mutual understanding.

Understanding Intercultural Communication

Intercultural communication is the process of sharing information, ideas, and meaning between individuals with different cultural backgrounds. It encompasses verbal, nonverbal, and contextual elements that are influenced by the norms, values, and practices of the various cultures. Effective intercultural communication requires navigating these cultural differences to achieve mutual understanding, respect, and cooperation. This type of communication is essential in a globalized world where interactions between diverse cultural groups are increasingly common in business, education, and social settings.

Effective intercultural communication helps break down barriers, reduces prejudices, and promotes inclusivity. It enables you to appreciate and respect cultural diversity, fostering a more cohesive and harmonious society. It encourages you to step outside your comfort zones, challenge your assumptions, and develop a deeper understanding of the world around you. By engaging with different cultures, you can gain valuable insights, learn new ways of thinking, and build meaningful connections.

As businesses and consumer bases expand internationally, the ability to communicate effectively across cultures becomes a critical skill. Misunderstandings or misinterpretations due to cultural differences can lead to conflicts, lost business opportunities, and damaged relationships.

Communicating more effectively across cultures begins with understanding the complexities and nuances of different cultures, which is the subject of this section.

Recognizing the differences that make a true difference

Understanding cultural differences is vital for effective business communication. And, although not all differences are significant, many are. Being aware of the following nuances and communicating respect in light of them can make a real difference:

>> **Nonverbal gestures do *not* convey the same meaning everywhere.** You may have heard the cliche "Everyone smiles in the same language," but various smiles in different cultures, and even within a culture, can mean different things! Smiles can be friendly, smug, flirtatious, contemptuous, fake, and so on. Misreading gestures, facial expressions, or body language that have different meanings across cultures can lead to unintended offense or confusion. For example, if someone smiles and nods and shakes your hand in Japan during a business negotiation, that doesn't indicate that the two of you have reached an agreement — it means only that you were heard and understood.

>> **Using an inappropriate level of formality or tone in communication can appear disrespectful or overly familiar.** For example, some cultures frown on the practice of acting like a friend to a subordinate. Failing to recognize or respect cultural norms regarding authority and hierarchy can result in perceived insubordination or disrespect, which can harm business relationships.

>> **Literal translations that don't account for cultural context can lead to misinterpretations, especially when idioms or colloquialisms are involved (in either the source or the translation).** Language barriers exist — even among people speaking the same language from the same culture! Make a conscious attempt to avoid using acronyms, jargon, or cliches that don't translate literally. Applying your own cultural communication style in every situation — regardless of audience composition — can lead to misunderstandings. For example, being too direct in cultures that value indirect communication may come across as confrontational. (Knowing your audience, as explained in Chapter 12, holds true in intercultural communication, too.)

>> **Attitudes about punctuality, deadlines, work-life balance, business practices, and more vary across cultures.** Overlooking or misunderstanding cultural norms in business can result in failed deals or strained relationships. For example, in some countries, bribes are considered illegal in business negotiations. In others, they're expected as part of the process. This difference definitely matters.

>> **What's funny in one culture may be offensive in another.** Using humor or references that aren't culturally relevant or acceptable can offend or alienate colleagues or clients from different backgrounds.

>> **Decision-making processes vary across cultures.** Certain cultures prefer individual over collective decision-making or vice versa. Not understanding a negotiator's preference can lead to frustration and inefficiency. How decisions are made in different cultures (heck, even in different companies and teams within companies) is important to understand.

WARNING

Assuming that everyone communicates in the same way and that words and nonverbal cues convey the same meaning across cultures can cause conflicts and inefficiencies. Increasing your awareness of the challenges of intercultural communication, as you're doing if you're reading this chapter, can help you become less susceptible to making dangerous assumptions — but it doesn't totally eliminate the risk. If you're ever unsure or you feel frustrated (which is a good sign you're unsure), ask. A simple inquiry can open the doors to improved understanding. For example, start by saying something like, "I'm not sure I fully understand what you're saying . . ." and then summarize what you heard and ask the person whether your interpretation is correct.

Understanding culture as a dimension

Hofstede's cultural dimensions theory, developed by the Dutch social psychologist Geert Hofstede, offers a framework for understanding how values in the workplace are influenced by culture. Based on extensive research, Hofstede identified six dimensions (see Figure 20-1) that highlight key differences in national cultures: power distance, individualism versus collectivism, masculinity versus femininity, uncertainty avoidance, long-term versus short-term orientation, and indulgence versus restraint. Each dimension represents a spectrum along which cultures can be placed, providing insight into how cultural values shape behavior, communication, and management practices in various groups.

Low power distance	versus	High power distance
Individualism	versus	Collectivism
Masculinity	versus	Femininity
Low uncertainty avoidance	versus	High uncertainty avoidance
Long-term orientation	versus	Short-term orientation
Indulgence	versus	Restraint

FIGURE 20-1: Hofstede's cultural dimensions.

People who have a grasp of these cultural differences can tailor their communication strategies to align with the values and expectations of their coworkers and teammates, enhancing collaboration and effectiveness across diverse cultural contexts.

WARNING

Like any framework or theory, Hofstede's cultural dimensions theory is based on what's "most likely" as discerned from substantive research. This doesn't mean that it applies perfectly to every situation. And, although the framework is based on nationality, variations are common within nationalities. Knowing the tendencies is a good starting point toward becoming cross-culturally savvy. So use your sleuthing powers (see Chapter 6) and your communication skills to evaluate each person and each situation. Think of these frameworks and dimensions as tendencies, not absolutes.

High versus low power distance

Power distance measures the extent to which less powerful members of a society accept and expect power to be distributed unequally. In high power distance cultures, such as Malaysia and Mexico, hierarchical structures are prominent and authority is seldom questioned. Subordinates are unlikely to approach or contradict their superiors directly. Conversely, low power distance cultures, like Denmark and New Zealand, promote equality and encourage more participative decision-making processes. In these cultures, superiors and subordinates often interact as equals, and they place greater emphasis on minimizing inequalities.

When is this difference significant? Communicating for decision-making is a significant area. In high power distance cultures, higher-level executives typically make most of the important decisions (not always consulting those below). Communication flows downward, and subordinates are expected to follow instructions without much questioning. This approach can lead to slower decision-making because approvals from higher-ups are required at each step. In low power distance cultures, decision-making is more decentralized. Employees at all levels are encouraged to contribute ideas and participate in discussions. This approach can lead to faster decision-making and a greater sense of ownership among employees because their input is valued and considered. If you're part of a lower power distance culture and trying to get decisions approved through management from a higher power distance culture, using upward communication strategies (see Chapter 12) and making sure management from the higher power culture is involved in the decision-making process early on is essential.

Power distance also makes a difference in giving and receiving feedback. In high power distance cultures, giving direct feedback or criticism to superiors is unthinkable. Subordinates may use indirect language or avoid raising issues altogether, which can lead to unresolved problems and misunderstandings. In low power distance cultures, open and direct communication tends to be more encouraged, and employees typically feel more comfortable providing feedback and constructive criticism to their superiors.

In the context of working in teams, stricter hierarchical structures can impact team dynamics, with team members deferring to the authority of the leader — even if the leader is less qualified than other members of the team. This situation can result in less open communication and collaboration among team members because they may be hesitant to share their ideas or challenge the leader's views.

Individualism versus collectivism

This dimension explores the degree to which individuals are integrated into groups. Individualistic societies, such as the United States and the United Kingdom, tend to prioritize personal achievements and individual rights. People are expected to take care of themselves and their immediate families. In contrast, collectivist cultures, such as China and Colombia, emphasize group cohesion and loyalty. Individuals in these societies see themselves primarily as members of a group, such as a family, a clan, or an organization, and often prioritize group goals over personal ambitions.

In individualist cultures, communication around motivation and rewards often focuses on personal achievements and individual performance. Recognition, promotions, and bonuses are often awarded (in part or full) based on individual accomplishments. Praise and feedback to motivate employees is generally given to the individual. In collectivist cultures, communication regarding motivation and rewards is more likely to emphasize group achievements and collective success. Recognition may be given to teams rather than individuals, and rewards may be distributed equally among group members.

This dimension also impacts how people resolve conflict. In individualistic societies, conflict resolution is often handled through direct and open communication. Employees are encouraged to express their opinions and confront issues head-on. This approach aims to resolve conflicts quickly and assert individual viewpoints, with the expectation that honesty and transparency will lead to effective solutions. In collectivist societies, conflict resolution tends to be more indirect and subtle, prioritizing group harmony and relationships — also known as saving face. People in collectivist societies often avoid open confrontation.

Masculinity versus femininity

Though I'm hesitant to include this potentially gender-polarizing dimension, these are Hofstede's named categories and not mine. This dimension examines the distribution of emotions, values, and actions based on gender-stereotyped dynamics. Again, these are tendencies and do not apply to every member of a population; they're also *fluid* — they evolve over time.

More masculine cultures, such as Japan and Italy, value competitiveness, assertiveness, and material success. They draw a clear distinction between gender roles, with men expected to be ambitious and women more nurturing. Feminine cultures, such as Sweden and the Netherlands, see all citizens placing a higher value on caring for others, quality of life, and consensus. In these societies, gender roles are more fluid, and both men and women are encouraged to be modest and empathetic.

In more masculine societies (which doesn't necessarily mean that only males play these roles), leadership communication tends to be more directive and authoritative. Leaders are expected to be assertive, decisive, and focused on achieving results. Communication often emphasizes competition, achievement, and performance. This approach can create a high-pressure environment in which success and material rewards are highly valued. In contrast, in more feminine cultures, communication is more likely to be collaborative and participatory. Leaders focus on consensus-building, quality of life, and the well-being of employees. Communication is characterized by empathy, inclusiveness, and a focus on work-life balance.

In masculine societies, conflict resolution often involves direct confrontation and assertiveness. Individuals are expected to defend their positions and strive for a clear resolution. The emphasis is on winning and demonstrating strength, which can sometimes lead to competitive and adversarial interactions. In feminine societies, conflict resolution is more likely to involve negotiation and compromise. Communication aims to preserve relationships and achieve mutually beneficial outcomes. The focus is on understanding different perspectives and finding solutions that maintain harmony and consensus within the group.

High versus low uncertainty avoidance

How comfortable a culture is with uncertainty and ambiguity impacts many business communication situations. High uncertainty-avoidance cultures, such as Greece and Portugal, have a low tolerance for unpredictability and ambiguity, leading to a preference for strict rules, regulations, and structure. These societies tend to resist change and are more hesitant to foster innovation. On the other hand, cultures with low uncertainty avoidance, such as Singapore and Denmark, are more accepting of ambiguity and risk. They tend to be more entrepreneurial, adaptable, and open to new ideas and experiences.

Cultures that avoid uncertainty often emphasize the need for thorough analysis and careful planning before making decisions. Employees and managers prefer clear guidelines and detailed instructions to minimize ambiguity and risk. As a result, communication tends to be more formal, with extensive documentation and approval processes. Extending the approval process can lead to slower decision-making and resistance to innovative ideas that lack a clear precedent or guaranteed outcomes. Communication around decision-making is more flexible and open to experimentation in cultures that accept and even embrace uncertainty. These cultures encourage taking calculated risks and embracing new ideas, leading to a more informal and adaptable communication style. Discussions may focus on exploring possibilities and potential benefits rather than on strictly adhering to established protocols. This approach fosters a dynamic and entrepreneurial environment, in which change is viewed as an opportunity rather than a threat.

High uncertainty-avoidance cultures approach conflict resolution and problem-solving with a focus on minimizing uncertainty and restoring order. Communication tends to be structured and formal, with an emphasis on finding definitive solutions and avoiding ambiguity. They may have a preference for established procedures and protocols to handle conflicts and problems, which can sometimes limit creative problem-solving and flexibility. In low uncertainty-avoidance cultures, you find more open-ended and exploratory communication. These cultures value diverse perspectives and encourage innovative approaches to addressing issues. Communication is often informal and collaborative, with a willingness to experiment with different solutions and adapt as needed. This approach can lead to more creative and effective resolutions but may require a higher tolerance for ongoing ambiguity and uncertainty.

Long-term versus short-term orientation

This dimension reflects the extent to which a culture prioritizes future rewards over immediate benefits. Long-term-oriented cultures, such as China and South Korea, value perseverance and thrift and adapting to changing circumstances. They emphasize long-term planning and success; they're often willing to sacrifice current benefits to meet future goals. In contrast, short-term-oriented cultures, such as the United States and Canada, prioritize immediate results. These societies tend to focus more on short-term gains and quick outcomes.

If your culture is more long-term oriented, business communication often emphasizes long-term goals and strategic planning. Managers and leaders focus on future success, discussing visions and plans that may span several years or even decades. Communication tends to highlight the importance of perseverance, sustained effort, and continuous improvement. This long-term perspective encourages patience and a strategic approach to business development, valuing long-term achievements over immediate results. By contrast, cultures that tend to be more short-term-oriented have business communication that is more likely to focus on short-term objectives and quick wins. Discussions often center around immediate results, quarterly performance, and rapid return on investment. Communication emphasizes agility, quick decision-making, and the ability to seize short-term opportunities. Although this approach can foster a dynamic and responsive business environment, it may sometimes overlook the benefits of long-term planning and investment.

Communication in long-term-oriented cultures often involves detailed discussions about investments and resource allocation aimed at future growth and sustainability. Companies prioritize investments in research and development, infrastructure, and employee training, viewing these as essential for long-term success. The language used in business communication reflects a commitment to building a solid foundation for the future, with an emphasis on prudence and careful planning. In comparison, in short-term-oriented cultures, communication centers around investment and resource allocation that tends to prioritize projects and initiatives that yield immediate benefits. Companies focus on maximizing short-term profitability and shareholder value. Business communication often highlights quick returns, cost-cutting measures, and short-term performance metrics. This approach can lead to rapid growth and adaptability but may sometimes sacrifice long-term stability and innovation.

This dimension also reflects differences in how businesses evaluate and reward employee performance. In long-term-oriented cultures, performance evaluations and rewards are tied to sustained contributions and future potential. Performance reviews emphasize employee development, long-term career growth, and contributions to strategic goals. Rewards and recognition programs are designed to encourage loyalty, perseverance, and ongoing improvement, aligning with the culture's focus on long-term success. In short-term-oriented cultures, performance evaluation and rewards are typically tied to immediate achievements and short-term results. Performance reviews are direct and focus on recent accomplishments, sales targets, and productivity. Bonuses, promotions, and other rewards are used to incentivize quick performance improvements and short-term gains — an approach that can drive high levels of motivation and competition, but at what cost?

Indulgence versus restraint

This dimension measures the degree to which a culture values the satisfaction of human needs and desires versus withholding pleasures to align with societal norms. Indulgent cultures, such as Australia and Nigeria, encourage the pursuit of happiness, leisure, and personal fulfillment. They tend to have a more positive outlook on life and place a higher value on well-being. In contrast, restrained cultures, such as Poland and Hungary, suppress gratification of needs and regulate it through strict social norms. These societies often have a more pessimistic outlook and emphasize duty, discipline, and control over personal desires.

In indulgent cultures, business communication often emphasizes the importance of work-life balance, employee well-being, and personal fulfillment. Managers may encourage taking frequent breaks and vacations and participating in social activities. Internal communications may include messages about wellness programs, flexible working hours, and opportunities for leisure and relaxation. In restrained cultures, communication around work-life balance tends to be more focused on duty and discipline. Emphasis is placed on obligations and productivity and on maintaining a serious work ethic. Messages from management are likely to stress the importance of hard work, dedication, and adherence to strict schedules.

Similar to individualistic cultures, indulgent cultures use motivational communication strategies that often highlight personal achievements, rewards, and enjoyment of work. Business communication may include recognition of individual contributions, celebrations of success, and encouragement of creative expression. Managers use positive reinforcement and create opportunities for employees to find joy and satisfaction in their work. In restrained cultures, much like collectivist cultures, motivational strategies are more likely to focus on collective goals, responsibility, and long-term benefits. Communication from leaders is likely to emphasize the importance of perseverance, self-control, and adherence to company standards. Rewards and recognition are often tied to fulfilling duties and contributing to the organization's overall success.

WARNING

Don't judge a culture or create a communication strategy based on one dimension only! Although the individualistic and indulgent dimensions may align in some ways, they don't necessarily align in all characteristics.

Business communication in indulgent cultures tends to support innovation, creativity, and risk-taking. Companies in these cultures encourage employees to think outside the box, experiment with new ideas, and pursue opportunities for growth and improvement. Communication channels are often open and informal, fostering a dynamic and flexible work environment in which employees feel free to express their ideas and take calculated risks. In restrained cultures, communication around innovation and risk-taking is more cautious and controlled. Companies emphasize the importance of careful planning, adherence to established protocols, and minimizing risks. Innovation is approached methodically, with thorough evaluation and approval processes. Communication tends to be more formal and structured, focusing on maintaining order and control. This tendency can lead to a more stable and predictable work environment but may also limit spontaneous creativity and rapid innovation.

TIP

To see how various countries and cultures compare with respect to their dimensions, use The Culture Factor Group's country comparison tool at www.hofstede-insights.com/country-comparison-tool. Using this tool, which was created by the originator of the six dimensions, is a helpful way to understand cultural norms and communication tendencies across cultures.

Creating an Environment Conducive to Open Communication

A large part of communicating successfully across cultures involves creating an environment where everyone feels safe to ask questions, share their ideas and opinions, and contribute to discussions. In this section, I offer two practical techniques to encourage open, honest communication in your organization.

Making sure each voice is heard

Whether you're a leader (especially if you're a leader) or a member of a team, fostering an inclusive culture is essential for facilitating and promoting open communication within and across cultures. Promote diversity and inclusion by encouraging open dialogue and demonstrating that you and your organization value diverse perspectives. Regular training on cultural competency and unconscious bias (see the nearby sidebar) can help create an environment in which everyone feels respected and heard.

DEFINING "UNCONSCIOUS BIAS"

Unconscious bias refers to the automatic, implicit attitudes or stereotypes that often influence a person's understanding, actions, and decisions without the person's conscious awareness. In business communication, unconscious bias can significantly impact interactions and decision-making processes by perpetuating stereotypes and permitting or even promoting unequal treatment. It can lead to favoritism, exclusion, and miscommunication, affecting everything from hiring practices to team dynamics. For instance, a manager may unintentionally favor employees who share similar backgrounds or communication styles, thereby marginalizing diverse voices and perspectives. Addressing unconscious bias is crucial for fostering an inclusive, equitable work environment in which all employees feel valued and understood.

So how do you make everyone feel respected and heard? Here are a few strategies:

» **Implement structured communication methods, such as round robin discussions.** This approach ensures that all participants have an opportunity to contribute, and it prevents dominant voices from overshadowing quieter individuals.

» **Use anonymous feedback tools.** An assurance of anonymity contributes toward creating an environment in which everyone can feel safer expressing their opinions and offering suggestions. It's especially helpful for empowering those who feel uncomfortable speaking up in group settings.

» **Create diverse teams with balanced representation from different cultural backgrounds and personality types.** Build diversity into teams at both the leadership and lower levels to ensure that varied perspectives are considered in the decision-making processes. If someone feels as though they have no peer or representation on their team, they're less likely to speak up.

» **Practice active listening, showing genuine interest in team members' ideas and concerns.** Encouraging mentorship and allyship within the organization can further support underrepresented voices in a way that helps to bring all ideas to the table.

» **Review and adjust policies and practices as needed to address any disparities or barriers.** Implementing policies and practices that promote diversity and inclusion can help your organization maintain an equitable environment in which every voice is valued equally. However, before reviewing and adjusting policies, make sure you have a system in place that collects and considers feedback from everyone!

Providing multiple pathways to contribute

In diverse cultural environments, providing multiple communication pathways for people to contribute is essential for fostering inclusivity, maximizing engagement, and leveraging the full potential of a diverse workforce. Different cultural backgrounds often come with varying communication styles, preferences, and comfort levels for speaking up in a one-on-one meeting or a group setting. By offering various avenues for expression, businesses can ensure that every individual has an opportunity to share their ideas and perspectives in a manner that suits them best.

For instance, some employees may thrive in face-to-face meetings, in which verbal communication and immediate feedback are possible. Others may feel more comfortable expressing their thoughts in written form, such as in emails, online forums, or anonymous surveys, especially if they come from cultures that value indirect communication. Providing digital platforms for collaboration, such as chat tools or project management software, can also accommodate those who prefer asynchronous communication or want time to formulate their responses.

Offering multiple pathways not only respects these cultural differences but also encourages broader participation. It helps to capture a wider range of insights and ideas, leading to more innovative solutions and better decision-making. Furthermore, it empowers employees by validating their preferred communication methods, enhancing their sense of belonging and engagement within the organization. Ultimately, this approach fosters a more inclusive, dynamic, and productive work environment.

Embracing the Growing Field of DEI and Respectful Communication

Initiatives promoting diversity, equity, and inclusion (DEI) are growing in the workplace — and rightfully so! These DEI initiatives heavily involve business communication because it's the primary means by which organizations can create an environment that makes their employees feel valued, respected, and empowered to contribute their best. I don't intend to minimize the importance of having DEI policies and procedures but to stress that business communication plays a key role as well. DEI initiatives promote a diverse workforce, bringing together individuals from various backgrounds, cultures, and perspectives. This diversity enriches the workplace with a broader range of ideas and solutions, enhancing creativity and innovation.

Equity in communication means providing equal opportunities for all employees to participate and be heard, regardless of their background or position. It involves recognizing and addressing any barriers that may prevent certain groups from fully engaging. Inclusion encourages open dialogue and the sharing of diverse viewpoints. It creates a safe space for employees to express their ideas and concerns without fear of discrimination or bias. Here are a few suggestions for promoting DEI in the workplace:

>> **Encourage open, honest dialogue.** Make the workplace a safe space where everyone feels comfortable discussing their experiences and perspectives and calling attention to areas that can be improved.

>> **Use inclusive language.** Be mindful of the language you use in all forms of communication. Avoid jargon, idioms, or terms that may exclude or alienate certain groups.

>> **Provide DEI training and highlight initiatives.** Offer regular training on cultural competence, unconscious bias, and inclusive communication practices. Ensure that everyone understands the importance of DEI. Share information openly about the company's DEI efforts and challenges. Transparency builds trust and demonstrates a genuine commitment to improvement.

>> **Celebrate diversity out loud.** Recognize and celebrate diverse cultures, holidays, and traditions. Being vocal and visible about the organization's support for DEI creates a sense of belonging and respect for different backgrounds. (And if your organization isn't doing this, you can make sure that your team does!)

>> **Actively seek input from a diverse range of people.** Take the initiative to solicit input. Some may not feel comfortable sharing their ideas or asking questions. They may need encouragement.

>> **Use a variety of channels to reach everyone.** It's common to have a group of people who prefer (and thrive by using) different communication methods. Use multiple channels, including meetings, email and text messages, live chat, videoconferencing platforms, and online collaboration platforms.

>> **Use surveys, suggestion boxes, and anonymous feedback tools to gather diverse perspectives.** Regularly review and act on this feedback.

In the context of business communication, DEI ensures that messages are inclusive and resonate with a diverse audience. It helps to prevent misunderstandings and cultural insensitivity that can arise from homogeneous perspectives. Inclusive communication practices ensure that all voices are heard and considered, leading to more effective and collaborative decision-making processes.

TIP

For more about DEI, check out *Diversity, Equity, and Inclusion For Dummies*, by Dr. Shirley Davis (Wiley Publishing). Though I barely scratch the surface in this section, Dr. Davis offers much deeper and broader coverage, providing practical steps you and your organization can take to create a more diverse and inclusive workplace capable of increasing productivity and innovation.

Avoiding the Assumption Trap

Assumption. There it is — that word again, "making an ass out of you and me" (ass-u-me). Making and acting on assumptions regarding culture and diversity in business situations is dangerous because it can lead to misunderstandings, miscommunications, and biased decisions. Assumptions often stem from stereotypes or limited knowledge, which can distort our perceptions of individuals and groups. When these assumptions are incorrect, they can result in actions that are disrespectful, exclusionary, or even discriminatory in the following ways:

>> **Misunderstandings arising from cultural assumptions can disrupt business interactions.** Different communication styles, attitudes toward hierarchy, or approaches to conflict resolution may be misinterpreted if those involved don't understand cultural nuances.

>> **Biases based on assumptions can lead to unequal treatment in the workplace.** Decisions about hiring, promotions, and assignments may be influenced by unfounded beliefs about a person's capabilities or fit rather than their actual skills and potential. Remember: This also includes unconscious bias!

>> **Actions based on cultural assumptions undermine the value of diversity and prevent the organization from fully leveraging the unique perspectives and talents of its workforce.** Embracing diversity requires recognizing and challenging assumptions, ensuring that every individual is valued and respected for their true contributions.

People rarely make assumptions consciously, so assumptions often fly below the radar — you may not be aware that a deeply rooted belief or an error in your understanding is causing you to think a certain way. You need to put forth a conscious effort in battling assumptions. In the following sections, I share two techniques for avoiding the assumption trap.

Seeking clarification from others on how they want to be treated

Although I encourage you to develop an overall understanding of cultural differences, any generalizations can lead to false assumptions or beliefs about an individual. Everyone is different. Even people who share a common ethnicity and who were born and raised in the same community can have vastly different communication styles. All you need to do is look at members of the same family to realize how different individuals can be despite the environment in which they were raised. So the best way to figure out the most effective way to communicate with an individual is to interact with them. And, when you're first getting to know them, don't hesitate to ask about their preferred communication style and ask them to speak up if what you're trying to communicate isn't clear.

Understanding those you work with on a personal level helps build trust and rapport, which are essential for effective teamwork and collaboration. It demonstrates that you value them as unique individuals, not just as teammates or employees, which helps foster a sense of belonging and engagement. When people feel respected and understood, they're more likely to be motivated, loyal, and committed to their roles, teams, and organizations.

By taking the time to find out about your coworkers' and team members' preferred working styles, communication methods, and career goals, you can create a more supportive and accommodating work environment. And, as a major bonus, you'll be identifying and leveraging the diverse strengths and talents within your team. A sincere desire to understand others can lead to better problem-solving, innovation, and overall performance. Plus, with a clearer understanding of your colleagues, you have a better chance of ensuring that management practices are fair and equitable, promoting a positive workplace culture in which everyone feels valued and empowered to contribute their best. That helps position you as part of the solution!

Collaborating to make adjustments and meet in the middle

Communication is a two-way street, requiring mutual understanding and flexibility. Adapting your communication to others, and vice versa, is an effective way to have valuable interactions and strong relationships in business. When both parties adapt because they've taken the time to understand the nuances of each other, it ensures that messages are clearly understood, reduces the likelihood of misunderstandings, and fosters a collaborative environment.

When both parties make an effort to adapt, it creates a balanced dynamic in which neither party feels misunderstood or marginalized. This reciprocity builds trust and strengthens professional relationships. In a diverse workplace, being adaptable in communication can lead to better engagement, higher job satisfaction, and improved performance. Here are a few practical tips to facilitate a collaboration toward a mutual understanding:

>> **Practice active listening.** You *know* I can't end a chapter without mentioning the importance of listening (see Chapter 5). Pay close attention to what the other person is saying and ask clarifying questions to ensure understanding. You must listen actively in order to formulate relevant questions and avoid making assumptions.

>> **Engage your communication partner in a discussion about cultural norms and communication styles.** Talking about differences in your cultures can give both of you greater insight into one another's values, beliefs, communication tendencies, and preferred communication channels. And remember: You can ask people how they prefer to communicate. We all have preferences for communication channels (for example, who still wants to bother with voicemail — just send a text!), and it's good to communicate those preferences and to ask for and understand the preferences of others.

>> **Identify what I like to refer to as common communication denominators.** Look for anything you may have in common, such as a shared interest, value, or belief. See the nearby sidebar "Common communication denominators" for more info.

>> **Actively seek feedback!** Ask coworkers questions to gather feedback on your communication style, and be open to making adjustments based on the input you receive. You'll be surprised by how much more effective, efficient, and energizing a fluid, smooth, productive communication collaboration can be!

REMEMBER

I wrote this book focusing on you, the reader. But that doesn't mean that your communication partner is the only "other." In fact, you're the "other" to them! It's equally as important that you focus on letting people get to know you and your culture as it is for you to understand them and theirs. Successful communication is a two-way street.

COMMON COMMUNICATION DENOMINATORS

Allow me to delve into a concept I call "common communication denominators." Think back to elementary school math class when you learned to add and subtract fractions. To do so, you had to ensure the fractions had the same *denominator* — the bottom number (like the 2 in ½). When that bottom number is the same in two or more fractions, it's called the *common denominator* — the lowest possible number that both denominators can divide into. For example, to add ½ and ⅓, you find a common denominator (6, in this case), converting the fractions to ³⁄₆ and ²⁄₆, which then add up to ⅚.

If math isn't your thing, think of a common communication denominator as a feature shared by all members of a group. It may be the fact that you all work on the same team or for the same organization, that you all have MBAs, or that you all love Thai food. Anything you have in common can serve as a starting point for a conversation that leads to a deeper understanding of one another. Similarly, you'll want to use language that's common to everyone in the room. If not every person in the audience will understand the meaning of an acronym, you must use the common communication denominator and spell it out.

Yeah, it's math that has nothing to do with math. How cool is that?! My point is that in order to be an effective, dynamic, and adaptable communicator, you need to identify the common communication denominators in any audience you address. Understanding these shared features enables you to tailor your message and how you convey it in a way that resonates with everyone in your audience.

7

The Part of Tens

Glimpse the future of business communication by exploring ten key changes that are on the horizon.

Discover ten tips for conveying technical data and information effectively to nontechnical audience members.

Explore ten ways to improve your virtual presentations without having to invest a great deal of extra time or effort.

IN THIS CHAPTER

» Automating messaging and interactions with the latest technologies

» Addressing the heightened expectations for personalized responses

» Recognizing the challenges of communicating and collaborating on virtual teams

» Adapting to trends toward more informal and more inclusive language

» Addressing the increasing need for transparency and consistency in communication

Chapter **21**

Ten Business Communication Trends That Are Here to Stay

Since the dawn of humanity, people have found ways to communicate. These means of communication, or *channels*, have evolved significantly over time — from cave painting and petroglyphs to print media, radio, and television to modern digital communications. Those at the forefront of understanding and using new channels of communication often have a significant advantage over those who lag behind.

This chapter provides insight into ten developing trends in the evolution of business communication that you need to be aware of, adjust to, or take advantage of to maintain or improve your ability to communicate effectively and efficiently in business.

Generative AI

The rapid advance of generative AI technology is reshaping the landscape of business communication, providing those who harness its capabilities with a significant competitive edge. *Generative AI* is artificial intelligence capable of producing new content consisting of text, images, audio, video, and other media personalized to an audience and/or in response to a prompt. It automates routine tasks such as drafting emails, creating reports, and generating content, freeing up valuable time for you to focus on more strategic, high-value activities.

This efficiency gain not only accelerates daily operations but also enables businesses to scale their communication efforts without proportional increases in resources. For example, AI can personalize mass customer communications in a fraction of the time it would take a human team, ensuring that messages are both relevant and timely. The ability to produce high-quality content quickly can enhance your responsiveness, making your communication more agile and better positioned to capitalize on emerging opportunities or address client needs quickly.

REMEMBER

The field of *prompt engineering* — the process of refining questions and instructions to elicit quality outputs from generative AI solutions — has become a major part of using generative AI tools. Think of AI as a separate audience! You have to be clear and precise in your questions and instructions to get it to generate content that meets your expectations.

TIP

See the "Anatomy of a Prompt" section of the online Cheat Sheet at www.dummies.com for information about the most effective way to construct your AI prompt.

Integrating generative AI into business communication extends beyond efficiency; it also drives innovation. By leveraging AI to analyze data and generate insights, businesses can uncover new patterns and trends that inform decision-making and strategy. AI-powered tools can suggest optimizations for marketing campaigns and highlight communication bottlenecks that could be streamlined. Companies adept at using these technologies are likely to outpace their competitors, who may struggle with slower, more traditional methods of communication management. As generative AI continues to evolve, its strategic importance grows, making the early adoption and mastery of these tools crucial for maintaining a competitive advantage in an increasingly digital business environment.

Humanizing Automation

Humanizing automation means creating a work environment in which automation complements and amplifies human capabilities and creates better outcomes and experiences for customers. In the context of business communication, it involves combining generative AI with automated audience analysis to personalize messaging and interactions. AI can segment audiences based on their behavior, preferences, and previous interactions, allowing for tailored messages that are more likely to engage each segment. For example, intelligent systems can customize email marketing campaigns to address the recipient by name, recommend products based on past purchases, or remind them of items left in their shopping cart. These systems are transforming how companies interact with all their stakeholders — both internal (employees, leadership) and external (customers, investors).

You can also deploy automated customer support systems that are powered by your company's data. Chatbots are growing in utility and power, based on the model they're trained on and the data used to build the experience for customers. These chatbots — and now video chatbots — can handle basic and intermediate inquiries, provide instant responses 24/7, and escalate more complex issues to human representatives. They not only improve customer service efficiency but also enhance the user experience by providing immediate assistance.

Synthetic Media

The term *synthetic media* describes text, images, voice, video, and other content fully or partially generated or combined in unique ways through the use of AI. From images generated from a desired description to creations of digital twin facilities to the essential cloning of the digital likeness of a person to create a hyperrealistic avatar, these media are already having, and will continue to have, a large impact in business communication. Here's a small sample of how you'll be able to use synthetic media to your advantage:

>> **Create compelling presentations using generated content paired with existing content.** Produce a complete PowerPoint presentation from existing content, combining synthetic imagery and video with generative AI text.

>> **Communicate and interact with synthetic stock avatars that represent human characters.** You'll be able to type scripts and create applications that combine audio and video in a way that creates an intelligent and interactive human presence. Synthetic avatars have been used as teachers in virtual classrooms.

>> **Capture your physical likeness and vocal qualities and process them into a hyperrealistic custom avatar that looks, acts, and talks like you, engaging in personalized interactions with others at scale in minutes.** It's possible, and it's already happening in companies like Render (www.rendermedia.ai), a business that provides digital likeness solutions. They've built batch rendering capability with data integration so that with a single script and a data import, you can create individual synthetic media videos for every member of your audience, ensuring a completely personalized experience.

REMEMBER

Personalization and customization will be the rule, not the exception. Now, companies can get away with using avatars to deliver generic messaging. In the not-so-distant future, customers will expect a far more personalized interaction.

Predictive Analytics

You can leverage AI-driven predictive analytics to anticipate customer needs and market trends and, as a result, be more proactive in adjusting your messaging and interactions. For instance, if data predicts a rise in demand for a particular service or product, generative AI equipped with predictive analytics can adjust your communications strategy to highlight these offerings, prepare informative content, and align the business's inventory or services accordingly.

You can also employ AI tools to optimize the content of your communications for different platforms. AI can suggest the best times to post on social media, the most effective keywords for SEO, and even adjust the style and tone of the content based on the target audience's preferences. These automated adjustments ensure not only that your communications are well-timed but also that they resonate with the intended audience.

Predictive analytics can also facilitate the integration of multimedia with other content, which is critical to communication success. Businesses are increasingly using videos, podcasts, and infographics in their communications to better engage audiences and simplify complex information.

By integrating these AI and automation strategies, businesses can significantly enhance the effectiveness, efficiency, and personalization of their communications, leading to improved customer satisfaction and operational productivity.

Heightened Expectations

With the increasing availability and sophistication of technologies that allow for the simplified implementation of personalized messaging and interactions, people will no longer settle for generic messages and scripted responses. They will expect systems to adapt to their needs and communication preferences seamlessly. Generative AI content, responses, and interactions will need to be accessible to anyone, anywhere, all the time.

REMEMBER

With built-in or low-cost speech accessibility, captioning, and other translative services, organizations no longer have an excuse for not personalizing their automated messaging and responses and ensuring universal accessibility. AI can be particularly useful for creating transcriptions of meetings and presentations that are accessible to individuals with hearing impairments. Additionally, speech recognition can facilitate voice-controlled interfaces, allowing users to interact with your systems hands-free, which is especially useful for accessibility and multitasking.

Increased Prevalence of Virtual Teams

As businesses recognize the benefits of remote work, such as reduced overhead, increased productivity, and access to a broader range of talent, more organizations are adopting flexible work arrangements. Enhanced communication tools, cloud-based collaboration platforms, and improved cybersecurity measures support this shift, enabling seamless remote operations. And, they introduce new communication challenges.

Since the COVID pandemic, organizations are trending toward having smaller offices and more decentralized locations (instead of a single headquarters). This trend is impacting workplace communication significantly. Businesses are increasingly digitizing communication channels to improve efficiency and reach. This change includes the adoption of communication platforms like Slack, Microsoft Teams, and Zoom, which facilitate instant messaging and videoconferencing and enable connectivity and productivity on any device.

The growing popularity of flexible work arrangements has also increased the value that workers place on maintaining a healthy work-life balance. As a result, expectations regarding when and how communication takes place have changed. Be sure to set clear expectations about when and how you will communicate with other members of your virtual teams. And stick to those boundaries to protect your own work-life balance.

Increased Expectations for Timely Communication

The expectation for real-time responses is growing. Businesses are expected to respond quickly, particularly in customer service interactions, leveraging instant communication tools to meet this demand. AI tools are revolutionizing real-time communication in business, particularly in enhancing customer service and engagement. By integrating AI-driven chatbots and virtual assistants, organizations can deliver instant responses to customer inquiries, ensuring that customers receive timely, often immediate, feedback. These AI systems are capable of handling a vast array of queries, from simple FAQs to more complex transactional interactions, thereby increasing efficiency and customer satisfaction. Moreover, AI can analyze customer data to personalize interactions, making communication more relevant and impactful.

For internal communications, AI tools help streamline collaboration by suggesting responses, automating routine tasks, and managing workflows, thus facilitating faster and more efficient team interactions. This immediate and automated response capability is crucial in maintaining the pace required, where quick decision-making and responsiveness are highly valued. These changes reflect a broader transformation in how companies approach communication internally and externally, driven by technological advancements and changing societal expectations. If you're not serving your customer well, another company will be there and be able to do it better.

Increasing Popularity of Informal Communication

The divisions between work life, home life, and digital life are becoming increasingly blurred. As these two areas merge more and more, organizations — even those in traditionally formal industries — are adopting more casual, conversational tones in their corporate communications, to appear to be more relatable and accessible. Adopting a more informal communication style in corporate settings can make interactions feel more personal, fostering a stronger connection between employees, leadership, and customers.

Your organization can start to make its communications more casual by revising communication guidelines to allow for a more conversational tone, especially in less formal communications such as internal emails, social media posts, and team updates. Training sessions can help employees understand the boundaries of this style, ensuring professionalism is maintained while putting relationships first. Using first-person narratives and active voice can also make communications feel more direct and engaging. Additionally, encouraging senior leaders to share personal anecdotes or lessons learned in communications can humanize them and make leadership more approachable.

Diversity, Equity, and Inclusion (DEI)

In recent years, a growing emphasis on inclusive communication has become prevalent — communication that respects and acknowledges diverse cultural, gender, and racial backgrounds, reflecting broader societal shifts. Emphasizing inclusivity and diversity in corporate communication not only enriches the workplace culture but also resonates more deeply with a global audience. Here are a few ways to make DEI a more integral part of your business communication (for details, check out *Inclusive Leadership For Dummies*, by Shirley Davis):

>> **Become more aware of using language that's gender-neutral and culturally sensitive.** Use terms like "they/them" rather than gender-specific pronouns in situations where a gender isn't assigned, and avoid idioms or colloquialisms that might not translate well across different cultures. (For example, in this book, I focused on alternating genders and also on assigning they/them in many examples. In one example, a boss may have been male, and in another, female, and in another, gender-neutral. Be conscious of not assigning a single gender to all instances.)

>> **Represent a diverse range of voices and perspectives in company materials.** For example, feature stories, testimonials, and case studies from employees of varying backgrounds, or showcase how products and services meet the needs of diverse populations.

>> **Provide cultural competence training for employees.** This training can help them understand and respect different perspectives and backgrounds, which in turn informs how they communicate internally and externally.

By actively fostering an environment that values and reflects diversity, organizations can enhance their communication strategies and build stronger, more inclusive relationships with all stakeholders. See Chapter 20 for additional guidance on how to communicate more effectively across cultures.

Increased Emphasis on Transparency

To address the increasing value consumers are placing on sustainability and social governance, businesses are focusing on effectively communicating their efforts and commitments to sustainability practices. These efforts extend beyond environmental issues to social impact — how a business is integrated into a community and how the organization is conscious of its impact, in everything from day-to-day operations to sourcing vendors. Effective communication of sustainability initiatives requires transparency and consistency.

Your organization can start by clearly defining its sustainability goals and the steps it's taking to achieve them, ensuring that these initiatives are deeply integrated into its corporate strategy and culture. Then communicate this information regularly via multiple channels — including social media, company websites, annual reports, and internal newsletters — to reach diverse audiences. Storytelling can be particularly powerful, highlighting real-world impacts and personal experiences that resonate with audiences and illustrate the tangible benefits of the organization's initiatives. Additionally, inviting feedback and engaging in dialogues with key stakeholders can help maintain accountability and demonstrate genuine commitment, fostering a positive corporate image and reinforcing the organization's dedication to sustainable practices.

Chapter **22**

Ten Tips for Conveying Complex Concepts to the Average Person

When you're explaining complex concepts or sharing insights based on data and analytics, you may need more than words. Fortunately, additional tools and techniques are available to clarify a message — literary devices such as similes and metaphors, visual elements such as charts and illustrations, and stories. In this chapter, I explain how to use these tools and techniques to clarify complex information and unfamiliar concepts, and I point out a few ineffective practices you should avoid.

Use Similes to Compare Unlike Objects

Similes are comparisons that use *like* or *as*. For example, "Life is like a box of chocolates" (the famous quote from the 1994 movie *Forrest Gump*). In the movie, Forrest Gump goes on to explain its meaning — ". . . you never know what you're going to get." Now, he could have simply said, "Life is unpredictable," but then nobody would remember what he said or the movie's main theme. Comparing life to a box of chocolates drives the point home.

When you're sharing complex data or concepts that are unfamiliar to anyone in your audience, a simile can be a powerful tool for conveying your point and reaching a mutual understanding faster. It works because it frames something your audience hasn't thought of or doesn't clearly know or understand in the context of something they do clearly know and understand.

Leverage the Emotive Power of Metaphors

Like similes, *metaphors* use comparison to clarify or convey an idea, but without using *like* or *as*, and they often evoke more emotion than similes. Metaphors can be simple, such as calling someone a couch potato — comparing a sentient being to a sedentary object and creating a stark mental image of a massive potato resting on a couch. Metaphors can also be much more evocative, such as drowning in an ocean of debt, which conveys the severity of a financial situation. In both of these examples, a word or phrase is applied to a situation or action to which it is not literally applicable.

Create a Contextual Understanding

Facts and figures often fall short of conveying the relevance or importance of the information you're delivering. They can make your audience think, "So what?" or lose interest or draw conclusions that don't align with the point you're trying to make.

When presenting facts and figures, look for ways to create contextual comparisons. For example, telling your audience that your net promoter score (NPS) is 32 out of 100 may lead people to believe that your company is failing its customers. However, when you first explain the context of an NPS, realizing that anything over 0 is good, anything over 20 is favorable, and anything over 50 is excellent — that puts the number 32 in a very different context. The contextual understanding here is essential.

Contextual comparisons may be to last year's data, a competitor's data, an industry standard, a goal, or another relevant data point. What's important is to present the data in a context that clarifies its relevance and importance.

Combine Similes, Metaphors, and Contextual Comparisons

Similes, metaphors, and contextual comparisons are not mutually exclusive. If you want to be super powerful, you can combine them, often in ways that make them exponentially more effective.

EXAMPLE

Suppose that you work in manufacturing and your team is responsible for producing a specific widget — shipping one million per year. Your organization is experiencing a return rate of 2 percent linked to issues with product quality, which is below the industry average of 4 percent. However, as team leader, you want to do better because you're concerned that having 20,000 returns translates to having 20,000 disgruntled customers, and that could be the reason your company is losing market share. If you can cut that number in half, that could drive a significant improvement in customer retention.

To achieve your goal, you want to create an automated feedback loop between manufacturing and quality control at a total cost of $200,000, and you must petition the executive team to approve the funding. You realize that a defect rate of 2 percent or 20,000 parts out of a million may seem insignificant, so you need to present that data in a way that shows its potential impact on the company's bottom line.

You decide to use a metaphor along with a contextual comparison to convince the leadership team to invest in the technology you're proposing, and you know that your plant operates in a town with a population of approximately 20,000 people. So, you say, "Though our team is proud to be below the industry standard for returns, we can do better. Currently, we ship 20,000 widgets a year that customers return due to quality issues. As a result, every year we risk losing 20,000 customers. Imagine what would happen to our town if every one of its 20,000 residents moved out. We're suffering a mass migration of customers, and losing market share as a result, when a one-time investment would enable us to retain 50 percent of those customers."

Go Visual with Charts, Illustrations, and Infographics

Humans are visual creatures. Nearly 90 percent of the data most people process daily is visual, and according to research from MIT, the human brain processes visual data nearly 60,000 times faster than it does text. People also tend to trust visuals more than they trust text. So, when you're trying to communicate complex concepts or information, consider using visuals, either alone or, more commonly, combined with text. Visuals include the following:

>> **Charts/graphs:** Bar charts, pie charts, line graphs, scatter plots, and histograms, for example

>> **Illustrations/diagrams:** Flowcharts, organizational charts, decision trees, Venn diagrams, journey maps, and more

>> **Infographics:** A blend of text and various visuals that typically tell a story, make a point, or present an overview

>> **Maps:** Geographical/location maps or heat maps (which use different color intensities to represent data density or distribution across an area)

>> **Tables:** Information presented in rows and columns for easy comparison and reference

>> **Photos and videos:** Camera images and video that convey narratives, show examples, or demonstrate concepts or processes

>> **Timelines:** Visual road maps that illustrate progression through various stages or milestones or show change over time

Find a Common Communication Denominator

When I tell you to find a common denominator, I'm not asking you to solve a math problem involving fractions. I'm using the term *common denominator* in reference to a trait, a characteristic, an experience, or a belief shared by everyone in your audience — or what I like to call a *common communication denominator*. In organizations, a unifying common communication denominator can be something that everyone in the company has experienced, such as a unique and memorable orientation day or a rite of passage required of all new employees or a goal that everyone in the company shares. If you can tie your data and information back to this shared concept, people will be more likely to understand and retain your message.

Avoid Acronyms and Jargon

Making sure that everyone is on the same page is hugely important when you're trying to communicate data, so avoid using acronyms or jargon that might alienate or confuse anyone in your audience. Unless you're sure — and I mean 100 percent certain — that everyone in the room is familiar with the term or acronym you're using, spell out the acronym the first time you use it and define any specialized terminology at first usage or follow up with a simpler term your audience will understand.

WARNING

Even when you're delivering a presentation within your organization or professional group, don't assume that everyone in the audience is familiar with the acronyms and technical language you're accustomed to. If you assume incorrectly, you divide your audience into the In Group and the Out Group — you'll connect with some people in the audience and alienate the others. If you're trying to reach a consensus, this is not the way to go!

Avoid Being Sesquipedalian

Did you just pause for a second trying to pronounce that word in your head? Did you search online for its definition? Good. I already made my point! It's actually one of my favorites, and also quite ironic. Someone who is communicating in a *sesquipedalian* way is using long words unnecessarily. For clear examples of sesquipedalian communication, read an article in any scientific or academic journal. They're full of sesquipedalian prose. Often in organizations, to appear smart, someone will use a much larger word than is necessary to convey a point. Not gonna lie — I'm guilty of this in many situations when my academic world and my practitioner world collide. However, I've become quite good at recognizing when I'm proverbially puffing my semantic chest, and immediately follow up with a synonym or comparison to make sure everyone in the room is on the same page.

Even worse than being sesquipedalian, and I'm sure you've experienced this yourself, is someone trying to appear smart and tossing out a complicated word and either mispronouncing it or using it in the wrong context. Wow, did that attempt to appear smart backfire!

REMEMBER

Keep it simple. Use language your audience understands. You wouldn't speak Mandarin to an audience of English speakers, so don't use highly technical or academic language to communicate with an audience that uses a more common vocabulary. If you can't come up with a simpler way of saying something, define the term the first time you use it so that everyone can be on the same page.

Suppose that you're delivering a presentation on defect rates and you need to discuss the topic of *escapement* — a mechanism that controls the motion of a device to keep it operating within specified tolerances. Though those in the room who are mechanically inclined know what an escapement is, those who aren't won't. So, when introducing the concept, you could define the term and use a simile to clarify by comparing an escapement to the bumpers that are often put up for children at bowling alleys to prevent the balls from rolling into the gutter. You explain that an escapement functions in a similar way by providing guardrails that limit the movement of components. You further explain that without a properly functioning escapement, serious consequences are likely to occur, much like a child constantly bowling gutter balls and throwing a tantrum.

Tell a Story

Stories can be quite effective at getting a point across, expressing the urgency or importance of an issue, or showing the impact an event has had on an individual, an organization, or a community. In a previous section, I relate a story of a child throwing a tantrum after having constantly bowled gutter balls. That story demonstrates the power of a brief narrative.

For maximum impact, try to tell the story about a hero, never you. That hero may be your team, a customer, or a member of the audience. Build up a full narrative that follows the hero's journey through a specific situation — for example, a customer's journey in navigating your organization's automated customer service system or a customer's experience with a defective product your company produces, detailing the cascading impacts that your defective product had in their life. That will make more of an impact than merely saying "our 2 percent defect rate causes issues for our customers."

Effective presentations often begin with the first part of a story, stopping short of telling the audience the outcome until the very end of the presentation. In the middle is everything else — data, explanations, insights, and so on.

Perform or Lead the Audience in a Physical Demonstration

A physical demonstration of a product or process can be quite an effective way to convey a message and leave a lasting impression, especially if it includes audience participation. For example, you may try to impress upon your production team the importance of producing high-quality products. You pass out defective products to several team members and instruct them to use the product as a customer would to perform a specific task. While they're struggling with the product to perform the task, you can see the frustration on their faces. After a certain amount of time, you tell them to stop trying, and then you ask them how they're feeling and whether they would ever again buy a product from this company.

Then you can transition to your data and insights on quality control, stress the importance of quality control on customer satisfaction, and deliver your call to action — urging team members to make a commitment to your zero-defects initiative (or whatever your call to action happens to be).

IN THIS CHAPTER

» Setting the stage for a successful session

» Boosting energy and engagement with live chat, polls, and surveys

» Collaborating in real time with virtual whiteboards

» Incorporating fun activities to foster bonding

» Delegating the session's logistics so that you can focus on engagement and content

Chapter **23**

Ten Tips for Outstanding Virtual Presentations

When I first started talking about virtual presentations in 2008, people looked at me like I was crazy. "Nobody is going to want to do this," people said. Fast-forward to 2018, when I was trying to persuade my clients to train their sales teams on how to conduct virtual meetings, and more of the same came back at me: "We are a people business. We don't conduct business meetings online. That will never stick."

Next up, 2020: COVID-19 changed everything. Overnight, my on-stage business disappeared, and requests poured in from clients to help their teams with what I had proposed years earlier.

Now, everyone knows how effective virtual presentations and meetings can be — when done well. After reading this chapter, you'll have ten strategies to employ to avoid common mistakes and make your next virtual meeting a step above the rest.

Provide Platform Orientation

Though most businesspeople have used at least one virtual meeting platform, don't assume that everyone in your virtual meeting has the same level of experience on the platform you're using. To ensure that all participants can attend and participate, follow these steps:

1. **Email clear instructions to all participants on how to join the meeting, including login credentials and a link to the meeting, and instructions for downloading any necessary software.**

2. **Advise attendees to test their audio, video, and Internet connection before the meeting begins, and provide guidance on how to find technical help if they need it.**

3. **Spell out the ground rules, such as whether attendees need to have their camera and audio enabled or disabled.**

4. **If you plan to use specific tools during the meeting, tell attendees where the tools are located and how to use them.**

   For example, if you're going to use the chat feature, say something like, "Throughout today's meeting, we will be using the chat feature. If it's not already open for you, go to the lower-right corner of your screen and click the icon that looks like a message bubble. A small chat window will appear, allowing you to follow along. To participate in the chat, type your message in the small text box at the bottom and click Send."

Communicate Expectations for Interaction

If you want people to engage and interact during the presentation/meeting, let them know what you expect and how to use the platform's tools to participate. Here's a sample script you can flesh out with your own details:

Welcome to the XYZ meeting! We want it to be as interactive and engaging as possible. To facilitate participation, we will use the chat area extensively. To make sure we all know how to do this, click on the [insert instructions for accessing chat on your meeting platform] and type in [insert a question that has a one-or-two word response, such as, "Where are you logging in from today?" or "Who is your favorite childhood cartoon character?"].

Now, as the responses start to come in, repeat the instructions for where and how to find the chat, and then repeat your question. Comment on a handful of responses that come in. I always like to give out the "fastest on the keyboard" award to the first person to respond.

TIP

Call out a few attendees by name — not everyone, just a few — to build a sense of community and let everyone know that the meeting is live and it's a shared experience in which they can be recognized at any time.

Lead Your Audience Through Quick-Chat Exercises

From my first virtual presentation in 2008 (see the nearby sidebar "Lessons learned from my first virtual presentation"), I discovered that it took three people (of a total 44 on the line) a full minute to find the chat feature and enter their responses to my question. It was a question that required a full-sentence response.

Don't make my mistake.

From there, I quickly pivoted to what I call *quick-chat* questions — these are one-word or two-word, or one-letter or two-letter, responses that people can type in quickly. Responses instantly boost the energy in the room. And, as a speaker, you're eliciting immediate feedback from your audience (which *really* helps because speaking to a virtual void is an energy challenge for some). My favorite quick-chat technique is the Y/N chat, which I start by saying:

All right, everyone. Get ready to type in the chat area. I just mentioned that the majority of our communication is nonverbal. Please type Y for yes or N for no to this question: Do you have an excellent poker face?

Note in this example that I've set the stage, telling attendees what to get ready to do, and then I instruct them to type a one-character answer, which is quick and easy. To increase engagement, repeat:

Again, type Y for yes or N for no into the chat box: Do you have a serious poker face? Are you able to stay stoic in any situation and hide your expression from other people easily?

Then repeat the question at least once more so that everyone has a chance to respond. After a few seconds, comment on what you're seeing:

I see the majority of you are saying that, yes, you have serious poker faces. Remind me not to challenge any of you to five-card draw!

The quick-chat and Y/N chat strategies have changed my entire virtual presentation experience. After using them for over 15 years, I can promise you that if you start integrating them into your virtual meetings, you'll see a positive difference, too.

LESSONS LEARNED FROM MY FIRST VIRTUAL PRESENTATION

I'll never forget delivering my first virtual presentation in 2008. I was so excited — I had prepared an appealing PowerPoint deck and written some engaging questions to get people talking in the chat area (because I knew engagement was important), and I was (of course) camera-ready.

Then it happened. Early in the presentation, I asked the first question and told people to type in their response in the chat area.

Crickets.

Crickets.

Then one person's response came in.

More crickets.

Then one more response.

And another.

A full minute of awkward silence later, that was it — three responses.

I learned two insanely useful virtual meeting and presentation tips from this experience:

- Don't assume that people know how to use the technology you're using.
- If you're going to ask people to participate, make it simple.

By following the advice I share in this chapter, you can ensure that people know how to use the technology and have simple ways to interact.

Encourage Virtual Applause

Many virtual conferencing platforms have applause icons, which (to me) seem cheesy, disappear quickly, and often go unnoticed by the speaker, depending on their presentation mode and platform permissions. So I created my own means of applauding in virtual environments, and now you can start using it, too. Here's how I encourage attendees to applaud:

> Now, before I bring the first speaker onto the virtual stage, I know that, if we were in person, we'd all be giving rousing applause right now. And we can't all unmute at the same moment to applaud, because that would be a disaster! So let me give you all a way to express your approval now or at any point in our conference experience: Go into chat right now and give me rousing applause by entering a series of exclamation points — that's right — exclamation points in chat will signify applause in our virtual setting.

Do this and watch the magic unfold. Seriously. In seconds, you'll see hundreds of excited "!!!!!!" messages populating the chat window, along with the names of attendees — all driving energy, engagement, and collective camaraderie.

Conduct Quick Polls or Surveys

Most virtual conferencing platforms come with a survey or polling tool. These tools are useful for engaging an audience and getting them involved in the meeting at a different level. Polls are especially useful if you're able to share the results or if everyone can watch the results as votes come in. This real-time engagement creates a sense of immediacy and energy in a virtual meeting environment because attendees can observe each other engaging in the activity together. Live polls and surveys subtly apply peer pressure; when attendees see others engaging, they feel compelled to engage. You can use polls and surveys in a number of creative ways, including the following:

>> **Break the ice and check engagement.** Start the meeting with a fun, non-work-related poll to break the ice and warm up the participants. This can be about preferences or fun facts. "If you could have any superpower, what would it be?" Then list answers and have an Other option with a box in which they can type their answer. This light-hearted question can kick-start interactions and lighten the mood. (If the platform has no polling feature, you can do this as a chat activity.)

>> **Assess premeeting knowledge or opinions.** Conduct a poll to assess participants' baseline knowledge or opinions on the meeting's topic before diving into the agenda. The feedback generated helps you tailor the discussion to the audience's level or perspective. For example, "How familiar are you with our new product line (Not familiar, Somewhat familiar, Very familiar)?" This information can guide how deeply you dig into the topic.

>> **Elicit real-time feedback on discussion points.** After presenting a segment of your meeting, use a poll to garner immediate feedback or gauge understanding. For example, "Do you feel the proposed strategy will meet our Q4 objectives (Yes, No, Need more information)?" Poll results can guide whether to move on or revisit key points.

>> **Prioritize discussion topics.** Let participants vote on which topics they want to discuss first or delve deeper into during the meeting. For example, "Which topic should we tackle first today (Project X, budget review, team expansion plans)?" This approach gives attendees an opportunity to provide input on how you structure your presentation.

>> **Gather input for making a collective decision.** Use polls to make collective decisions on specific questions or issues or to choose between options. Polls and surveys make the decision process transparent and democratic and enable you to reach consensus quickly. For example, "Which vendor should we select for our next project (Vendor A, Vendor B, Vendor C)?"

>> **Facilitate interactive learning.** During training sessions or workshops, use polls to make the learning process interactive and to test knowledge retention — for example: "Which of the following is a key benefit of our new software (Option A, Option B, Option C)?" A poll like this helps reinforce learning and lets you immediately see what the audience has absorbed.

>> **Check the audience's mood and energy level.** In longer meetings, use polls to check the mood and energy levels of participants, which can help you adjust the pace and tone of the meeting. For example, "How's the energy right now (High and energetic, A bit sluggish, Need a break)?" You may decide, based on responses, to take a quick break or engage everyone in a physical activity.

>> **Solicit post-meeting feedback.** End the meeting with a poll asking for feedback on the meeting's effectiveness and suggestions for improvement. Example: "How effective was today's meeting (Very effective, Somewhat effective, Not effective, Additional comments)?" The feedback you receive can help improve future presentations/meetings.

Engage and Collaborate via the Whiteboard

A virtual whiteboard is an excellent tool for brainstorming and team collaboration. Whether you present a blank slate or use it to mark up an existing document, a virtual whiteboard is a great tool for engagement. It's especially useful for an idea-mapping session, an editing session, or collaborative design. What's helpful about most whiteboard applications in virtual conferencing platforms is that you can save the output for future reference.

TIP

Explore advanced whiteboard features, such as templates and breakout frames, which are available in some whiteboard apps. With templates, you can create reusable whiteboard spaces for specific collaborative exercises, such as conducting risk analysis, mapping a sales strategy, or brainstorming marketing ideas. With breakout frames, you can have individual teams work on separate whiteboards so that they're not drawing over one another.

Increase Participation via "Voluntelling"

One of my favorite terms is a portmanteau of *volunteer* and *telling*: voluntelling. In the context of virtual conferencing, *voluntelling* involves the presenter volunteering an attendee to share information or respond to a question. In virtual meetings, and in traditional meetings, when you ask the audience a question, you often hear crickets — no one responds. In person, these situations are easier to navigate. When you're running a virtual meeting, that silence can be deadly. Voluntelling is a helpful strategy to get people engaged without having to suffer through an awkward silence.

When I use this strategy, I like to call it out, and I like to use the word *voluntelling* because it gives people a laugh. Often, I set the expectation that I will be doing this throughout the meeting, but that anyone is of course encouraged to speak up whenever they have something to contribute. I may say something like, "Okay, everyone! We're going to take some time to get feedback from everyone on the team. Juan, I'll let you go first, and then Terry will follow you." Then, when Juan wraps up, I jump in as the moderator again and say, "Thanks, Juan! After Terry, we'll have Ramsey and then Amit." This keeps things flowing and keeps the energy level high.

Leverage Synchronicity

Virtual conferencing offers one feature totally absent from traditional, in-person conferencing: *synchronicity,* or the ability for multiple people to communicate at the same time without disrupting the conversation or presentation. Synchronicity facilitates and encourages interaction and is a fantastic way to obtain real-time feedback that enables you to adjust your presentation on the fly.

TIP

Use the visual power of having all attendees on camera simultaneously to get people physically involved in the meeting. One way to use synchronicity to drive engagement is to have everyone gesture at the same time. For example, you may say something like, "Okay everyone, I'm going to ask a question and, on a scale from 1 to 5, where 1 is the lowest and 5 is the highest, show your fingers in response to the following question. (And Branlyn, I know you're the cheeky one in the group — not *that* finger!) How clear was the communication that management sent out about your new benefits and policies?" Now you'll see everyone making gestures and holding up their fingers simultaneously to answer the question. Then, as the presenter, calling out (or voluntelling) a couple of people to comment on their rating can continue the engagement and provide you with more insights. You can conduct similar polls with thumbs up or down and other nonverbal gestures.

Gamify Your Meetings

To make meetings more fun and engaging and encourage people to loosen up, consider incorporating interactive group activities, such as the following:

» **Challenge people to grab, within 30 seconds, an object that reminds them of their most recent day off from work.** Watch people scramble around to find the object and then hold it up on the screen. Everyone will be amused at seeing others' objects. Then you can voluntell a few people to share. This activity not only breaks the ice but can also be an amazing team-bonding experience. A manager I consulted with during 2020 continues this tradition at every monthly meeting, giving alternating team members a chance to share so that everyone gets to know each other better.

» **Instruct participants to build something related to your meeting or organization.** I once led a challenge for a cruise line that provided supplies for completing the challenge to team members ahead of time in a surprise box. During the meeting, everyone opened their boxes to find miniature marshmallows and toothpicks. The challenge was to build a model of one of the cruise line's ships in ten minutes, as uplifting music played through the speakers. The quality of these creations wasn't high, but the fun level certainly was. Even better, you can follow up with a poll for people to vote on the best (for example, the funniest or most original) creation and award a prize.

Be creative! Gamifying your meetings is a fun way to inject energy and enhance engagement.

Recruit a Producer

When running larger meetings, having a designated "producer" on hand enables you to focus on engaging the audience and rocking your content as your producer handles other essential tasks, such as the following:

>> Setting expectations and ground rules before the meeting.

>> Providing technical support to attendees who are having trouble connecting or using the platform's features; for example, that one person who can't seem to figure out how to mute themselves when they aren't talking.

>> Creating polls on the fly.

>> Recording the meeting.

>> Calling your attention to questions and concerns you need to be aware of during the meeting, such as an important point someone posted via chat that needs to be addressed right away.

Index

body language
  eye contact, 43
  facial expression, 42
  in feedback conversations, 231
  gesturing with hands, 40–41
  gesturing with head, 39
  overview, 38–39
bouncing questions back to
  audience, 123
bragging, issues with, 140–141
brand advocates, 300
brand messages, confirming
  key, 275–276
breakout rooms, 172
breaks, during conflict
  management, 257
bullet points, in slideshows, 168
Bush, George W., 47
business communication
  common mistakes,
    avoiding, 14–16
  communication audit,
    conducting, 33–35
  communication models, 23–26
  definitions of
    communication, 22–23
  elements of, 26–27
  fundamental skills,
    sharpening, 13–14
  history and
    environment in, 31–33
  importance of, 10–11
  making simple changes
    for impact
    focusing on pertinent
      details, 120–123
    getting to yes faster,
      117–120
    making people less
      defensive, 113–117
    overview, 14, 113
    purging "sorry" and "just" from
      vocabulary, 123–125
  noise, 28–31
  overview, 1–5, 9
  personal communication
    versus, 11–12

putting theory into
  practice, 18–19
self-assessment, 12–13
setting stage for
  challenging the status
    quo, 128–131
  overview, 14, 127–128
  prepping audience's
    brain, 132–135
  putting it all together, 136–137
  virtual conversations, 137
in specific contexts, 16–17
trends in
  diversity, equity, and
    inclusion, 355
  generative AI, 350
  heightened expectations
    related to, 353
  humanizing automation, 351
  informal
    communication, 354–355
  overview, 349–350
  predictive analytics, 352
  real-time responses, 354
  synthetic media, 351–352
  transparency,
    emphasis on, 356
  virtual teams, 353
buyer's remorse, 130

C

call to action (CTA), 163–164, 201,
  206–207, 209
candidates, attracting and
  interviewing, 305–309
Carnegie, Dale, 120
cause-effect presentation
  structure, 160
challenges, discussing in
  performance review, 243–245
challenging status quo, 128–131
channels of communication. See
  communication channels
character, feedback focused
  on, 232–233
chatbots, 351

ChatGPT, 296–299
checking for confirmation, 108
checking in with
  audience, 134–135
cheesy sales talk,
  avoiding, 120–122
choices, providing, 118–119
chronic complaints,
  187–188, 264, 265
chronological presentation
  structure, 159
Cialdini, Robert, 98, 117–118
clarifying questions, 78
closed-ended questions, 87
coaches, expanding reach
  with, 152–153
cognitive process,
  listening as, 73–76
collaboration. See also teams
  as benefit of conflict, 249
  as conflict management
    style, 260
  and lateral communication, 190
  overview, 17
  reducing hierarchical noise
    through, 30
colleagues, asking for help
  from, 144–146
collectivism, 334
color, in slideshows, 168–169
commitments, getting
  upfront, 134
common communication
  denominators, 345, 360
common ground, in conflict
  management, 254–255
communication, business. See
  business communication
communication audit, 33–35
communication channels
  asynchronous, 55–56, 63–65
  choosing wisely, 66–67
  communication audit, 34
  comparing by richness,
    55–57
  conveyance and
    convergence, 58–59

open-ended questions, 87, 102, 307

openings, presentation, 202–204

organization

  researching before interview, 293–294

  tailoring cover letter to, 295–296

organizational structures for presentations, 159–161

others, featuring in self-promotion, 142–143

outcomes

  of conflict, 250–253

  in conflict management, 255

  in definition of communication, 23

  desired, knowing before negotiation, 212–213

  role in self-promotion, 143–144

overloading audience, 15

oversight, on teams, 324

ownership

  of feedback message, 231

  giving stakeholders sense of, 197–198

P

pace of conversation, tuning in to, 105–106

paralanguage, 49–51

parallelism, 59

paraphrasing, 80, 108

parroting, 80, 81

Pascal, Blaise, 65

passion, "vomiting", 207–208

passive-aggressive communication style, 263

passive/submissive communication style, 261–262

pathos, 161

pausing, 52, 79

peers, asking for help from, 144–146

performance reviews

  cultural differences in, 337

managing yourself during, 243–246

negotiating, 224–225

overview, 235–237

performing stage of group development, 317–318

personal communication, 11–12

personal space, 45

personalization

  in media richness, 56

  of resume, 294–295

persuasion. See also audience

  clarifying goal and aligning with audience, 198–200

  mistakes affecting, 207–209

  modes of, 161–162

  Monroe's Motivated Sequence, 201–207

  overview, 17, 195–196

  stakeholders, sizing up, 196–198

persuasive presentations, 156

Phelps, Michael, 172

physical demonstrations, 362–363

physical noise, 28

physical presence, jobs requiring, 57

pitch, 50

pivoting to someone else, 122–123

plan, crisis communication. See crisis communication

planning response while listening, 78–79

platform orientation, providing, 366

pointing, 40

policies

  crisis communication, 274

  promoting diversity and inclusion, 340

polls, in virtual environments, 369–370

possible, rethinking, 103

post mortems, 318

posture, 38

power distance, 333–334

practice, theory as informing, 18–19

practicing

  for interviews, 305

  presentations, 174–175

  workplace negotiations, 222

predictive analytics, 352

premature asks, 117

presentations. See also persuasion

  clarifying goal and aligning with audience, 198–200

  informative versus persuasive, 156

  mistakes affecting, 207–209

  and Monroe's Motivated Sequence, 201–207

  overview, 155

  practicing, 174–175

  preparing for successful

    environmental considerations, 164–167

    overview, 164

    slideshow presentations, 168–169

    virtual presentations, 170–172

    visuals and other media, 169–170

  structuring

    body, 159–162

    conclusion, 162–164

    introduction, 157–158, 202–204

    overview, 157

  visualization, power of, 172–173

pretend listening, 76

principled negotiation, 218

problem-solution presentation structure, 160

problem-solving

  as benefit of conflict, 249

  curiosity as facilitating, 84

  turning complaints into, 265

procedures, crisis communication, 274

producer, in virtual environments, 373

professional correspondence, 306

project assignments, negotiating, 223

promoting yourself. *See* self-promotion

pronunciation, 48–49

proxemics, 43–47

psychographic audience analysis, 181–182

psychological noise, 28–29

public commitments, in call to action, 207

public distance, 45–46

purpose

  matching communication channel to, 60–67

  and media synchronicity theory, 58–59

  stating in presentation introduction, 158

Q

questions

  bouncing back to audience, 123

  clarifying, 78

  closed-ended, 87

  curiosity, nurturing, 84–88

  to extract information and clarify understanding, 88–93

  to initiate and guide conversations, 93–95

  on interviews, 302, 304–305, 307

  open-ended, 87, 102, 307

  overview, 14, 83

  in virtual communication, 31

  as way of checking in with audience, 134–135

quick-chat exercises, 367–368

R

rate, 49

reach, expanding, 148–149, 152–153

reacting, understanding before, 77–78

realistic goals, 109, 199–200

real-time responses, expectation for, 354

receivers, 24, 25, 27, 33

receptiveness, enhancing, 113–117, 230–231

reciprocity

  building through self-disclosure, 99

  on first dates, 100

  overview, 98–99

  putting into practice, 102–104

  subtly framing requests to create, 117

recognize, empathize, and respond (RER) framework, 285–288

recommendations, asking clients for, 153–154

recruitment process. *See* hiring process

redirecting conversations, 106

referrals

  asking clients for, 153–154

  for job positions, 293, 300–301

rehearsability, 59

remote presentation applications, 171–172. *See also* virtual environments

remote work, 57

reporting, post-crisis, 277

reprocessability, 59

requests

  for performance review, 245–246

  subtly framing, 117–118

  for time off, 224

RER (recognize, empathize, and respond) framework, 285–288

researching organization and position, 293–294, 300

resources, negotiating, 223

respect, in upward communication, 184–185

response team, crisis communication, 273–274

responses

  to interview questions, crafting, 303–304

  to objections, preparing, 192–193

  in RER framework, 287–288

  understanding before giving, 77–78

responsibilities, negotiating, 220–222

responsibility, taking in crisis communication, 283–285

restraint, 337–339

results

  role in self-promotion, 141–142

  in STAR method, 303

resume, 294–299, 301

rethinking what's possible, 103

returning serve, 123

rewards

  cultural differences in, 334, 337

  and workplace equity, 239–240

rhetorical strategies, in presentations, 161–162

rhythm of conversation, tuning in to, 105–106

richness, of communication channels, 55–57

risk analysis, 272

risk management, 84–85

risk-taking, cultural differences in, 338

roles, in teams, 319–323

roller coaster moments, creating, 50–51

routines, 131–132

S

salary, negotiating, 220–222

sales talk, 120–122, 135

scarcity, creating sense of, 118

Schiefelbein, Jill

  coaches, mistakes by, 153

  contacting, 4

symbol sets, 58
synchronicity
  gauging, 58–59
  leveraging, 372
synchronous chat, 62–63
synchronous communication channels, 54, 55–56, 60–63
synthetic media, 351–352

T

tabling topics for later, 123
taking responsibility, in crisis communication, 283–285
tasks
  matching communication channel to, 60–67
  prioritizing, and willpower, 131
  in STAR method, 303
  team, 313–314
teams
  acknowledging contributions and achievements, 325–327
  building diversity into, 340
  communication with, 324
  featuring in self-promotion, 142–143
  goals, objectives, and tasks, 313–314
  group dynamics, 314–318
  versus groups, 312–313
  overview, 311–312
  and power distance, 334
  roles in, 319–323
  virtual, 353
technical issues, 30–31, 169
technologies. See also communication channels; digital communication; virtual environments
  embracing latest, 4
  in recruiting process, 306
  testing before presentations, 167, 170
testimonials, getting, 150–154

text-based communication, asynchronous, 64–65
theory, as informing practice, 18–19
thesis, stating in presentation introduction, 158
time off, requesting, 224
timely communication, expectation for, 354
timely goals, 109
timing, in slideshows, 169
title, negotiating, 220–222
too much information (TMI), 15
topical presentation structure, 159–160
topics
  tabling for later, 123
  transitioning to new, 94–95
touch, study of, 47
transactional models of communication, 26, 27
transitioning to new topic, 94–95
transmission velocity, 59
transparency, emphasis on, 356
transparent communication on teams, 324
trust
  building through self-disclosure, 99
  lost, due to ignoring crisis, 268
  and taking responsibility for crisis, 283
Tuckman, Bruce, 314
tuning out, when networking, 150
two-way interaction, cultivating, 101–102. See also conversations
Tylenol crisis of 1982, 270

U

uncertainty avoidance, 335–336
unconscious bias, 339
underlying cause, seeking in feedback conversations, 233

understanding
  asking questions to clarify, 88–93
  as benefit of conflict, 249
  colleagues, 343–344
  confirming at end of performance review, 246
  curiosity as leading to, 84
  mutual
    checking for, 106
    in downward communication, 188
    role in communicating with confidence, 114
  processing thoughts to develop, 74–76
  before responding or reacting, 77–78
  summarizing to check, 78, 81–82, 108
undivided attention, giving, 77
upward communication, 183, 184–185
urgency
  in call to action, 163, 207
  creating sense of, 118

V

Valacich, Joseph, 58, 59
venue, for presentation, 165
video, asynchronous, 63–64
videoconferencing, 61–62
virtual environments
  applause, encouraging, 369
  environmental considerations for, 33
  expectations for interaction, 366–367
  gamifying meetings, 372–373
  overview, 365
  paralanguage in, 49
  platform orientation, providing, 366
  polls or surveys, conducting, 369–370

Dedication

To my nieces and nephews — by blood and by choice — Chance, Ella, Gibson, Jolie, Avery, and Andrea:

While the world you're growing up in looks different than the one I grew up in, the one constant is our need to form meaningful connections with each other. Communication is what builds relationships, and working on improving yours is an effort that will never be wasted.

About the Author

Dr. Jill Schiefelbein thrives at the intersections of communication, education, and technology. She's an award-winning business owner, professor, and author. She taught business communication at Arizona State University for 11 years, analyzed terrorist documents to provide counterterrorism messaging strategies to the military, and was a pioneer in the digital education space. Now Dr. Jill is a leading researcher and keynote speaker in the space of generative AI and synthetic media, particularly around humanizing automation and using hyperrealistic avatars to communicate. Her business, The Dynamic Communicator, Inc., serves clients ranging from brick-and-mortar businesses to Fortune 500 brands, helping them find dynamic communication strategies to serve their audiences. She's the Chief Experience Officer and a partner at Render, a start-up specializing in digital likeness solutions and providing integrated synthetic media and generative AI services. Dr. Jill also teaches as an adjunct professor in the doctoral program at the Muma College of Business at the University of South Florida. Though she's quite proud of her degrees, research, and business titles, the name she's most fond of is unquestionably "Aunt Jill."

Acknowledgments

Publishing a book involves a symphony of effort, and this book is no exception. Thanks to Wiley senior acquisitions editor Tracy Boggier, for serving as the conductor and choosing me to write the book (and, even more, for trusting my previous editor Jen Dorsey's recommendation when she passed my name to you — thanks, Jen!). Life threw us a lot of curveballs during this process, but we were able to manage all of them.

Charlotte Kughen, my development editor, is another example of patience and understanding. Thank you, Charlotte, for realizing what I needed before I did. To the managing editor, Kristie Pyles, and copy editor Rebecca Whitney, thank you for sticking the process out with me and for putting your expertise to work for all those who will read this book.

Writing this book taught me new lessons as a businessperson and reinforced lessons that I've known to be true throughout my life: It's definitely easier to write a longer story than a shorter story. It's undeniably easier to give a 30-minute presentation than a 5-minute presentation. Being able to communicate succinctly is a skill and also a muscle that takes work to flex properly. Writing succinctly, however, is not the same as trying to put your words into a book style that isn't natively yours. The *Dummies* brand is successful for a reason, and I needed a translator to help me make this book stylistically solid. That's where Joe Kraynak came in. Thank you, Joe, for collaborating with me and for putting the "*Dummies* lipstick" on my writing so that it can better reach the audience it's intended to reach.

My friends don't always understand why I take on certain projects, but they always support me, and I'm so fortunate to have the random assortment of crazy, loving people I do in my life. There are too many of you to name, but thank you for listening to me prattle on about this book for way too long. And even more gratitude to all of you for understanding when I needed to hibernate at home during that rare time between trips to get those last pages written.

The biggest thanks, though, goes to my parents, who somehow managed not to say, "I told you so," even once during this process. And who, despite the number of wacky ideas I bring up, oddball opportunities I present, demanding contracts I sign, and crazy adventures I embark on, continue to not only smile and nod but also give me their unrelenting love and support. Mom. Dad. I love you and appreciate you more than words can ever communicate.

Publisher's Acknowledgments

Acquisitions Editor: Tracy Boggier
Project Editor: Charlotte Kughen
Copy Editor: Becky Whitney
Technical Editor: Rebecca Bollwitt
Sr. Editorial Assistant: Cheri Case

Production Editor: Saikarthick Kumarasamy
Cover Image: © simarik/E+Getty Images